THE PUBLIC WEALTH OF CITIES

THE PUBLIC WEALTH OF CITIES

How to Unlock Hidden Assets to
Boost Growth and Prosperity

DAG DETTER
STEFAN FÖLSTER

BROOKINGS INSTITUTION PRESS
WASHINGTON, D.C.

Library of Congress Cataloging-in-Publication data

Names: Detter, Dag, 1959– author. | Fölster, Stefan, author.
Title: The public wealth of cities : how to unlock hidden assets to boost
   growth and prosperity / Dag Detter, Stefan Fölster.
Description: Washington, D.C.: Brookings Institution Press, [2017]
   | Includes bibliographical references and index.
Identifiers: LCCN 2017000423 (print) | LCCN 2017016266 (ebook)
   | ISBN 9780815729990 (ebook) | ISBN 9780815729983 (hardcover:
   alk.paper)
Subjects: LCSH: Municipal finance. | Strategic planning. | Urban economics.
Classification: LCC HJ9105 (ebook) | LCC HJ9105 .D47 2017 (print)
   | DDC 352.4/216—dc23
LC record available at https://lccn.loc.gov/2017000423

9 8 7 6 5 4 3 2 1

Typeset in Adobe Caslon

Composition by Westchester Publishing Services

Contents

Foreword

DAN DOCTOROFF
Founder and CEO
Sidewalk Labs

THERE IS MUCH RUMBLING ABOUT FEDERAL cutbacks to cash-strapped cities. Overlay that with a clarion call to invest in crumbling infrastructure before the underpinnings of our great urban centers give way. *The Public Wealth of Cities* offers a solution for city leaders to amass the capital they need to balance municipal budgets, fill every pothole, and reinforce wobbly overpasses and tunnels. Our cities *can* continue to be great places to live, work, and play.

Cities have the assets to fill their coffers, to capitalize social development and human capital, and to avoid unnecessary poverty, unemployment, and crime. Cities in the twenty-first century should not have to face shrinking populations or falling life expectancy.

Having been deputy mayor for economic development and rebuilding for the city of New York in the aftermath of 9/11, I know how innovation and smart thinking can rescue a city. We completely rethought the way New York used its assets, especially land, to dramatically strengthen the city's physical *and* fiscal base.

This book calls for all cities, not just a city like New York, to unlock the value of public assets as a core urban strategy. Doing so can uncover hidden social, human, and economic wealth.

Dag Detter and Stefan Fölster make a powerful argument that cities can finance their future and emerge stronger by placing public assets under more professional guidance. Every city owns swathes of poorly utilized real estate or controls underperforming utilities. Smarter choices could meaningfully enhance the value of investments.

The urban strategy called for here is not geared for only big cities, those with a robust technology sector, or the ones featured regularly on urban innovation blogs. All cities throughout the United States and globally are sitting on real wealth. Their assets just need to be realized through better management, and as with any portfolio, officials need to know what to sell and what to hold. Shifting attention and resources from short-term spending to investments that can improve quality of life has already led to remarkable success in some cities.

At Sidewalk Labs, the urban innovation company that I founded in partnership with Alphabet, we work at the intersection of the physical and digital worlds to help make cities more efficient. I see every day the remarkable things that cities can accomplish, as well as how public sector commercial assets are often not tapped to the city's best advantage. Cities need clearer goals. They need to track results and accelerate what works.

This is a book I urge people to read carefully and absorb. Whether a city manager, a devoted urban dweller, or simply someone who cares about the future of cities, the arguments developed throughout these pages will resonate. Public wealth is exactly that: something valuable to us all.

Preface

MANY CITIES IN THE UNITED STATES and around the world are in a state of disrepair, some of them to the extent that their inhabitants are actually fleeing. Others cities do exceptionally well in nearly all respects, attracting jobs, pressing back social ills, and developing more pleasing and greener surroundings.

What do blooming cities do that flailing ones don't? Despite decades of research there is very little actual evidence. Recipes for success are either anecdotal or trivial, pointing to vicissitudes beyond a city's control, such as deindustrialization or social change.

In this book we show that there is a simple reason why researchers find it hard to pin down what makes cities succeed. Successful cities may be doing nothing remarkable now, but may have built public wealth decades ago. This insight also leads to surprisingly clear recommendations on how to turn a flailing city's fortunes. Our claim originates with insights we arrived at in a previous book on how successful nations manage their wealth.

Our book *The Public Wealth of Nations: How Management of Public Assets Can Boost or Bust Economic Growth* appeared in 2015.[1] Our mapping showed that few nations have any understanding of the size of their public wealth. Reasonably better management would easily allow most countries to double their investment in all infrastructure.

Transparency and accountability are prerequisites for good governance of public assets, but professionalism and creativity are also necessary. For cities it is not just management of economic assets that matters. Equally important is canny investing in social and human assets. In this book we focus on best-practice techniques for turning distressed cities into cities that invest smartly in their social, human, and economic assets. This volume is a practical guide to increase a city's public wealth and put it to better use.

We thank all who have helped us and given valuable suggestions, among them Bruce Katz, Bob Traa, Willem Buiter, Marco Cangiano, Ian Ball, Fergus McCormick, William Glasgall, Jeremy Nowak, Anders Bäck, Staffan Ingvarsson, Jenna DeAngelo, Lourdes Germán, David M. Walker, Greg Langley, Carsten Kock, Jacob Soll, Natalie Boulas Nilsson, Andreas Hatzigeorgiou, Jens Kramer Mikkelsen, Göran Tidström, and Greg Langley.

CHAPTER 1

The Investment Trap

MANY CITIES IN THE UNITED STATES and other countries face an impending investment disaster. Promising plans for city development and infrastructure are put aside for lack of funds. Often even the most necessary maintenance lacks funding. Public resources for investments in infrastructure and services are deeply constrained for reasons originating at the national, state, and local level. The national government is adrift. Many states are hostile or encumbered with debt. Local municipal finances are often saddled with obligations.

The funding crisis is much wider than just physical investment. Many cities are unable to invest in promising social development and training for those among their citizens who are at risk of being left behind by globalization or automation. One stark warning sign is the decreasing life expectancy of lower-income white men in many U.S. cities.[1] Around the world, in much poorer cities, millions live in squalor, and public investment in utilities and basic services is dramatically underfunded.

This matters because the 1.5 billion people who already live in the world's four thousand cities with a population above 100,000 will be joined by additional billions in coming decades.[2] Countries stagnate when too many of their cities fail to build economic, social, and human wealth.

In spite of the many eyesores that meet strollers on city streets, urban agglomeration is often hailed as one of mankind's most important fulcrums for human development.[3] But such progress does not come automatically with population growth. While some cities spearhead human and economic advance, many others simply do not pull their weight or provide good quality of life for their citizens and their countries. Often cities find themselves administering the results of poverty and crumbling infrastructure. Instead, they could be investing in smart solutions that improve lives at an affordable cost—a lower cost than what is generally considered possible. They could become "smart cities."

Smart cities can become growth engines that boost both their inhabitants' quality of life and their country, even when national governments fail them. Smart cities provide ladders for their inhabitants where other cities leave them untended or even create chutes (trap doors). The difference between the ladder and the chute cities is so glaring—is so important for the children who grow up in them and therefore for human development—that understanding what successful cities do is critical. In fact, helping more cities to build social and economic wealth may be the most promising route to national success. After all, essentially all currently rich countries with high average incomes and living standards were initially pulled along by pioneering successful cities, and many still are. For example, London, New York, and Hamburg were locomotives for their countries and still are.

We start this book by taking a fresh look at what separates what we call wobbling "treadmill towns" from blooming "turbo cities." Cutting through the mountains of myths, hypotheses, excuses, and self-serving contentions, we find a robust dividing line between the flailing and the healthy conurbations. Treadmill towns cannot get off the fiscal treadmill of living from hand to mouth, budgeting from tax revenues directly to public consumption—not unlike hunter-gatherers. Often these cities have assets that are hidden or locked into inefficient uses. The lack of long-term perspective keeps cities from developing them and putting them to work.

In contrast, turbo cities, like turbo-charged engines, generate more power from the resources they have. These cities have, at least in periods, invested in their economic, social, and human assets, and they keep developing them. Like investors, they can often flourish on the yield from previous good investments. As turbo cities continue to unlock their assets and put them to good use, they become engines for growth and quality of life for their citizens.

A focus on asset governance makes all the difference for cities' success. In fact, we claim that putting city assets to better use could self-finance a remarkable boost in infrastructure investment, perhaps even double it. Furthermore, a canny asset strategy can increase household incomes by much more than, say, minimum wage laws ever can, and mitigate many of the social ills that plague too many cities.

The coming decades also offer cities an extraordinary menu of investment opportunities in digital technology. Some can generate enormous value, and not just in cutting administrative costs. According to some studies the wise use of digital technologies could provide people in need of care with much better-quality care and services at two-thirds of current cost.[4] As another example, local transport with self-driving cabs could reduce the number of private autos and free up 25 percent of road space, very valuable space often owned by cities and towns. Also, paving the way for thriving innovations hubs in cities can boost incomes and tax revenue.

But these opportunities are the gold nuggets in a menu that also contains many duds: technologies that don't work, do not spread, or are implemented poorly. Only cities with a professional approach to asset governance will be able to cherry-pick skillfully among investment proposals.

To some city leaders a focus on unlocking public wealth may come naturally. For most it does not. Yet city politics, administration, and institutions can be shaped to develop a knack for governing public wealth. We offer a practical guide to developing cities' social, human, and economic assets, and to designing institutions for professional caretakers of city assets. In fact, we argue that less political meddling in the governance of public wealth actually strengthens democracy.

RICH CITY, POOR CITY

Cities do many things. Each has its array of flagship programs, awards, showcase projects, and slogans whose purpose is to propound unique selling points. Alas, most cities also have a plethora of financial black holes, deadbeat programs, and political stalemates. This concoction is frustratingly difficult to interpret. Are all the good initiatives sufficient to compensate for the mishaps? How can one even tell?

While the net effects of a city's recent policies are hard to assess, it is easy to see that some cities are blooming and others are not. Some keep both their citizens and their finances healthy and wealthy, without closing doors to newcomers. In others, debts pile up, and some neighborhoods deteriorate while others become unaffordable to most. We argue in this book that there is a dividing line between winning cities and tottering ones that is rarely formulated explicitly. Yet it is intuitively quite obvious and is similar to the difference between success and stagnation for individuals or corporations.

For most people, born without a silver spoon in their mouths, the early adult years of life demand emphasis on gaining employment and a wage. Part of this income is set aside over time and accumulates into assets. Later in life, the importance of a person's savings—his or her balance sheet—grows. The quality of housing, ability to invest in children's education, and ability to handle shocks hinge more on accumulated assets and returns than on current income.

Some people are much better than others at building assets, and not just because they have higher incomes. In a widely read book, *Rich Dad, Poor Dad*, Robert Kiyosaki and Sharon Lechter argue entertainingly for how a focus on building assets early in life and managing them well to earn a return makes a big difference in peoples' ability to move from the "rat race to the fast track," that is, moving from consuming out of current wages to having more of one's consumption covered by asset yield.[5] Having been raised by two fathers, Kiyosaki compared their two different approaches to life. His educated dad advised him to work for a wage. His rich dad advised him to consume little and invest more and end up paying wages to employees. Both life paths required education, but the subjects of study were completely different. His educated dad encouraged Robert to be a knowledgeable person. His rich dad encouraged Robert to know how to invest wisely, hire smart people, and use the right tools.

A similar logic applies to companies. Many of today's multinational retailers such as Walmart, Tesco, and IKEA were able to build up a vast portfolio of real estate assets to serve their expansion of retail outlets. As the retail industry is shaken up by globalization and online retail, these legacy firms can fall back on their real estate cushion when necessary to revamp their business model and prosper again.

A similar logic also shapes the fate of cities. Even poor cities usually sit on a gold mine of assets that are not being used well or developed. These include real estate, municipal firms such as utilities and bus companies, and commercial ventures that cities often own. Cities that have a good understanding of the assets they own and that govern them well to help develop the city and earn a return, can spend and invest more without raising taxes. This would be comparable to Wall Street working for Main Street rather than the other way around. They will not be shaken by recessions or pension debt, which can push less well-organized cities to the brink of bankruptcy.

This may seem trivial. But in fact, cities rarely have a good understanding of the assets they own. And they rarely manage them with an eye to long-term value creation. Yet having this perspective makes all the difference.

The totality of a city's assets comprises not just money in the bank or real estate, but also social and human assets. A city that makes the right kind of long-term social investments can face lower costs twenty years down the line. For example, an intensive program to help school beginners at risk may reduce social costs resulting in unemployment, crime, or drug addiction decades later. Such a delay between social investment and social return will be easily accepted in a city that focuses on developing the long-term value of its assets, but risks being rejected in cities that are preoccupied with making ends meet during the coming budget year.

A focus on assets changes how cities think of education. Rather than counting years of schooling or the share in the population of the college-educated, the important question becomes, what value do citizens' knowledge and skills have? That shifts focus to the quality of education, specifically: how well does education and knowledge match employers' needs? And how can more employers be attracted that demand the skills that inhabitants have?

Some very successful cities around the world, such as Singapore, have built public economic, social, and human wealth out of seemingly nothing—without help from circumstances, such as natural resources or economic trends—while their surroundings remained poor. Although cities are certainly affected by their surroundings and circumstances, they are not slaves to them. Their fortunes are largely of their own making. Today, comparing Singapore with, say, Jamaica, or with Jamaica's capital of Kingston, appears completely unreasonable, even though both small countries became independent from Britain in the same year and were initially equally poor.

While some cities, like Kingston, never developed their assets well, others have stumbled more recently. A city like Detroit was not just the latest victim of deindustrialization but also very much of poor governance of its assets. We will show examples of cities around the world that lost as many industrial jobs as Detroit, but now are doing better than ever. The difference is that Detroit over long periods administered its affairs from hand to mouth. Much of its wealth, and its debts, remained hidden and did not show up in any accounts.

Detroit, like most local governments, sits on unexploited gold mines way beyond the obvious well-known official buildings in the city center, or operational assets such as the local airport, harbor, and railway station, or utilities such as water and electricity. Underneath this tip of the iceberg cities usually own less obvious real estate assets, often portfolios of buildings for now outdated needs, such as telephone exchanges, post offices, or administrations that nowadays should be automated and on the Internet. Undeveloped land and brownfield spaces, if professionally managed, can be transformed into attractive and valuable assets, as can the land around and above railway tracks and stations.

Cities are often much wealthier, in terms of public assets, than nation-states, but their holdings remain strangely opaque and largely ignored. U.S. cities are home to more than 90 percent of the country's GDP and own vast portfolios of commercial assets, greatly in excess of their debts (which can be quantified as the $3.7 trillion debt market in municipal bonds). Even poor cities own large swaths of poorly utilized real estate, utilities, and other commercial assets.

Since the early twentieth century, a polarized and polarizing debate has pitted privatization against nationalization. We don't propose sneaky ways to open the door to turning museums and libraries into amusement centers, or the City Hall into a bowling alley. It is time to stop focusing on this phony war about ownership, and instead focus on the quality of asset management.

Developing city real estate and other assets is also an indispensable tool for creating human and social value: innovation hubs instead of decaying city centers, a healthy mixture of high- and low-cost housing instead of segregated communities, proximity to workplaces instead of long-haul commutes. These are dimensions of city development that turn out to make a big difference to many city dwellers' life prospects.

Our calculations suggest that achieving a reasonable yield on publicly owned real estate and other commercial assets could free more resources than total current investments in infrastructure, including roads, railroads, bridges, water, electricity, and broadband put together. In other words, most cities could double their investments in infrastructure with smarter use of their commercial assets. Unlocking public assets should be a core urban renewal strategy.

CITIES ARE THE LOCOMOTIVES OF NATIONS

Dysfunctional national governments have become a cliché across the developed economies in Europe and the Americas. Often unemployment, inequality, and poor schooling, housing, or health care emanate from political failures at the national level. Even in rich countries such as the United States, faith in the political system and the social contract appears to crack in the face of actual social deterioration such as the remarkable decline in labor market participation among white men. In spite of a healthy recovery from the 2008 financial crisis the U.S. employment rate remains considerably lower than in the year 2000, in fact lower than that of France, and productivity growth is anemic. Many economists point out that the kind of national policies that are important to encourage growth and social progress have seen very little reform for decades.[6]

Cities are also hostage to national policy failures such as lagging infrastructure investments, regulatory deadlocks, and misdirected social policies. Therefore, much of economists' research has focused on the effect of nations and national policy on growth and development. For example, Daron Acemoglu and James Robinson recount vividly in their famous book *Why Nations Fail* how the town of Nogales is poor on the Mexican side of the border and relatively much better off on the U.S. side of the border.[7]

Yet such illustrative comparisons also miss an important point. In many respects the people who live in and run their cities form their own living and working conditions. Some cities can actually find creative ways to untangle themselves from the shackles of national policy that would otherwise hold them back. In some cases they manage to become more like city-states, which have always had to rely on their wit and economic acumen to survive and prosper in hostile environments, such as ancient Athens and Sparta, or medieval Florence and Venice.

Consequently, it should be no surprise to find fairly well-off and destitute towns close to each other within the same country. For example, Detroit is often described as a city that was hit by deindustrialization and therefore lost half its population. Yet many other cities that were hit by deindustrialization have adapted more successfully, such as Akron, Albany, Raleigh-Durham, Minneapolis–St. Paul, and Portland in the United States. In Europe, some cities, such as Munich, have lost as many manufacturing jobs as Detroit, but nevertheless are blooming.

A more accurate diagnosis of Detroit's ills is that it is an extreme example of a city that did not stop digging when it found itself in a ditch. Many of its inhabitants moved to more successful suburban cities that surround Detroit. The overall population of the larger urban area has changed little over the past decades.

If the United States had been dominated by cities that acted like Detroit, its overall growth might have turned out to be more like Italy's. There, GDP growth and incomes have flat-lined for the past two decades, as too many cities seem incapable of fixing even basic services such as garbage collection. In fact, recent studies that we will review later make a convincing case that cities that build their social and human assets experience significantly better employment and income growth by lifting their current inhabitants, not just by attracting high-income earners from elsewhere.

Surprisingly, some U.S. cities with impressive economic growth still do little to raise national U.S. growth, according to a recent thorough-going study.[8] The reason for their disappointing contribution is that these cities grew more by attracting already successful people and putting them to work in high-productivity industries. But these cities performed way below their potential in terms of lifting resident middle-income or poor people into jobs with higher productivity. National GDP would be nearly 10 percent higher, the study concludes, if New York, San Francisco, San Jose, and other cities like them had developed their assets in ways that made them more accessible to average earners to the same extent as the median U.S. city.[9]

Even booming cities could often do even more for national growth and balancing out weaker communities. For example, Stockholm, the capital of Sweden, does extraordinarily well by most measures, but it could compensate even better for smaller towns' faltering industrial growth. Smaller towns' traditional manufacturing firms are reeling from the world's most demanding environmental and labor regulations and highest marginal income tax, which has left Sweden's industrial output, mostly spread out in towns all over the country, trailing far behind that of its main trading partner, Germany. But this has been more than compensated for by a booming digital growth sector in Stockholm, which is happily unfettered by environmental and union demands. Stockholm, with just a fifth of the country's population, contributes half of the country's productivity gain and is the fastest-growing metropolitan area in Europe.[10]

This is not just a large-city effect. The other two larger Swedish cities, Malmö and Gothenburg, are doing noticeably less well. The main reason for Stockholm's leading edge appears to be that many of the municipalities that make up the Stockholm region also top the league in providing good schooling and a good business environment. Yet, Stockholm also has an Achilles heel, an unwillingness to open for enough building of new residential housing. Without that brake on growth, Stockholm might be Europe's answer to Silicon Valley, and would contribute even more to overall national growth.

The drag on national growth owing to cities that do not live up to their potential is much larger in, for example, Italy, where many cities impose a burdensome bureaucracy on top of national regulations. In another country, India, many cities seem willing to do what is needed to boost growth, but Indian democracy locates too much power at the state level rather than the city level. State governments are often dominated by the choices of rural voters, leaving cities less room to control their own destinies.

One reason that the role of cities' varying success for national growth has been ignored is that research on the role of cities has largely focused on so-called agglomeration effects. It has been easy for researchers to correlate the size of cities with subsequent growth. This has made it appear as though city growth is mainly a result of agglomeration—the role of agglomeration is viewed almost like a natural law. Studies in both developed and developing countries do find that wages and productivity rise faster in larger cities.[11] Causality of course goes both ways, and there is a chicken-and-egg aspect to the issue. Some cities grow larger because they are better organized and more innovative. These cities attract more workers—in particular, the most productive ones.

But size is hardly the most important factor. In fact, many large cities are by no means overachievers in economic vibrancy. A recent World Bank study finds that cities vary enormously when it comes to their economic performance.[12] Twenty-eight percent of cities grow more slowly than their countries, while the top 10 percent of cities increase their GDP at almost three times the rate of the remaining 90 percent. The report finds that this is no accident. Cities that drive national growth take a host of constructive initiatives that slow-growth cities do not. Silicon Valley, and the cities it spans, is an extreme example of a region that is a growth engine for the rest of the country—a turbo region—and is known the world over. But there are many other turbo cities that are not as well known. Some international examples are Kigali in Rwanda, Saltillo in Mexico, Meknes in Morocco, and Coimbatore in India. Conversely, some cities that have been drags on their country's growth would be Glasgow in Scotland (at least until recently) and Mt. Isa in Australia.

In sum, some cities can do much better than others, and in fact can pull their countries along toward better growth and social development. Successful cities seem to be able to compensate for many of the policy errors of their national and federal governments. National growth and quality of life, we argue, hinge on prospering cities.

So how do thriving cities do it?

THE TURBO CITY

Given the widely varying fortunes of cities, one might expect to be able to access a large body of research that provides clear evidence and recipes for turning cities around. Alas, this research is minuscule. Most narratives about the success of cities are based on anecdotal evidence, not actual research.[13]

Academic economists have often been guided by a presumption, perhaps a prejudice, that national policies determine growth and development with only a marginal role for local policies. We think this is a questionable stance, as we noted earlier.

More important, the connection between a city's policies and how well it is doing turns out to be unexpectedly difficult to prove statistically. One source of confusion in the attempt to understand true causes and effects is that as with a self-playing piano, the music continues to play once the mechanism has been cranked up. A city that has built its assets at one point in time can continue to enjoy the music for years or decades. When it comes to cities, "Nothing succeeds like success." Assets continue to generate a yield, even in periods when their management or city policies are less inspired.

Our term for this kind of city is a "turbo city." A turbo, or turbocharged, engine uses energy from its exhaust to help inject fuel into the cylinders, rendering the engine leaner and more powerful. Similarly, a turbo city has made canny investments that make its daily operation cheaper and more effective and sometimes even yield a direct return. This provides economic muscle for further investments.

For example, a town that has managed to attract some high-tech start-ups may see these grow for decades thereafter, attracting more tech wizards that start more firms. Similarly, a city that at one time fostered many local entrepreneurs finds that these provide good models, entrepreneurship know-how, and capital to young people starting new firms.

As another example, a city that has managed to establish social norms that are positive to education and respect for the law has "social assets" by which citizens influence each other. Parents emphasize law-abiding behavior to their kids. Neighbors keep an eye on each other. Crime rates remain under control.

All these things build up over long periods and take on a life of their own. Cities that succeed in this way have lower costs for social services and employment services. They may earn higher tax revenue. If the economic competence of their citizens spills over to city administration they may find it easier to maintain good programs and put the city firms, utilities, real estate, infrastructure, and other wealth to good use and manage pension funds well. Putting all this together, they can maintain better services with lower taxes.

Such a city is a humming engine with an unstoppable momentum. City politicians really have to kick and abuse it to make it stop running.

THE TREADMILL TOWN

Quite the opposite happens in a city on the brink of ruin. Debts have piled up and pension liabilities and budget costs skyrocket in relation to income from taxes and assets. Taxes need to be raised to pay bills, not to improve services. People with better options move out, further eroding the tax base and entrepreneurial talent. Higher unemployment and crime rates require high costs in social programs just to handle acute situations.

Such a city finds itself on a treadmill. It has to work hard just to stay in place and make ends meet. There are no resources to invest in big changes. A city on the treadmill is also a fragile city. When a treadmill town does try to mend its ways it finds that things may get worse before they get better. Closing the budget shortfall and paying down debts may require cuts in services that make the city less attractive in the short run. This may erode political support for reforms and push the city back onto the treadmill, even if current bills have been paid.

For example, when New York City narrowly escaped bankruptcy in 1975 with the aid of a federal loan and concessions by city unions on pension cutbacks, the first order of business was serious budget cuts: over the next three years, the number of police officers and teachers each dropped by about 6,000 and the number of firefighters by about 2,500, transit fares were raised, and tuition was imposed for the first time at the City University of New York. These cuts added an extra economic burden and political uphill battle for efficiency-oriented reforms. It took great effort and skill to implement some of these reforms, which laid the foundation for New York's much improved development in recent decades.

Today Rome finds itself in a similar bind as New York in 1975. After decades of mismanagement, a new leadership has to handle an acute economic crisis and cutbacks while trying to tackle long-term reforms at the same time.

These mechanisms also explain why researchers have found it so frustratingly difficult to show which policies actually lead to better outcomes. The actions that turned one city into a turbo city and forced another onto the treadmill may have been taken many years earlier. Even for voters the nexus between good policies and city success can remain muddled.

And it's not just the time lag. The key issue is that a city's success largely depends on whether it has accumulated assets that remain productive over time. One can think of a human settlement by a creek that provides drinking water. The dwellers can drink when there is water, but their existence is fragile. The creek can dry up and force them to move or fetch water from afar.

Now suppose the dwellers build an asset, a water reservoir, where they accumulate water. Now they are less dependent on what the creek provides in any particular month. Even more important, the reservoir provides additional yield in the form of fish and water management that allows fields to be irrigated as well.

This, in short, illustrates the secret of turbo cities. The assets they have and put to good use not only keep them in good financial shape, even in periods when they do not pursue any particularly enlightened policies, but the cities may also reap additional benefits through the improved health and social well-being of their residents.

So, what are these assets? The easiest to define are the economic assets. We identify two types of economic assets, commercial and policy assets, depending on how they are funded. Policy assets are tax funded to

Box 1-1. *Public Commercial Assets*

Commercial assets are economic assets or operations that generate non-tax revenue or could do so if properly structured and used.

Typical commercial assets include the following:

- Incorporated enterprises in various sectors, typically providing services such as energy, water, waste, and transportation

- Noncorporatized activities and services, such as utilities, parking, natural resources, air rights, and broadband spectra

- Real estate, developed and undeveloped, currently used by public entities or third parties

- Infrastructure that is toll-based (such as a highway or bridge) or related to a private-public partnership (such San Diego's Petco Park)

- Financial institutions such as banks, insurance companies, and mortgage institutes

Not included are assets that do not earn returns, such as parks, museums, and historic and legacy real estate and land. Public commercial assets do, however, include the real estate and land currently used by civic entities such as schools, hospitals, and fire and police stations, since the services offered are not especially tied to the real estate, but may actually benefit from being relocated, as well as the specific real estate may be worth more if used for other purposes.

provide a public service, and cannot easily generate revenue. In contrast, commercial assets are those that can conceivably render a revenue stream, if managed properly (see box 1-1).

Equally important are two types of noneconomic assets that have a crucial impact on finances of cities and the well-being of their citizens. These are social assets, which provide ladders rather than chutes for people's health, ambitions, and happiness, and thus minimize the social afflictions that often make life more difficult even for citizens and strain city budgets (see box 1-2). And there are human assets, the value of skills

Box 1-2. *Social Assets*

Social assets are social norms, attitudes, and functioning institutions along with a city structure that reduce the incidence of crime, homelessness, addiction, and other social ills. Social assets can have an impact on lowering a city's costs and making the city more attractive to employers.

Principal social assets are the following:

- A social environment favorable to education, work, and safety
- Functioning and successful schools (inadequately educated children are much more likely to become a social burden later)
- A high level of civic engagement in improving neighborhoods

These assets often characterize areas that have no large, geographically segregated, low-income demographic groups. We do not include equal income distribution as a social asset per se, since this mainly reflects values and is not a direct determinant of social assets, even though it may be an indirect factor.

or knowledge, which are crucial for individuals to achieve economic independence and for cities to elevate municipal tax revenue (see box 1-3).

In the course of this book we will show how municipalities have shaped up their investment in human and social asset management and have been richly rewarded. For now, just consider an instance of rare experimental evidence that arose in southern Sweden in the early 1990s. At the time tens of thousands of people were fleeing from the civil war in former Yugoslavia. Large numbers of Bosnian refugees arrived in Sweden in 1993 and 1994. During those years arriving refugees were more or less randomly assigned to different municipalities rather than being allowed to choose where they wanted to live. This created an unusual natural experiment that made it possible to measure how different municipal environments affect the integration and employment of refugees. It turned out that after a few years the employment rate for Bosnians differed sharply in different towns. Some 80 percent were employed in

Box 1-3. *Human Assets*

Human assets are not easily quantified: they cannot be measured simply in terms of residents' years of education or university degrees. Rather, they represent the value of knowledge and skills that citizens possess and apply in their work or through entrepreneurship. Human assets can be increased by a city administration that supports both its residents and business via the following:

- High-quality schooling

- Effective education that is geared toward developing skills that existing and potential employers value

- Entrepreneurial spirit

- A city administration that provides a good business climate, thus increasing demand for and increasing the value of citizens' skills

municipalities that score highly on the measures of social and human assets that we describe later in the book. This happened in spite of the fact that many of these were relatively small and isolated.

In municipalities that scored low on social and human assets, as few as 10 percent of Bosnians managed to enter employment, even in large and growing cities. As a result these towns faced much higher costs for welfare payments as well as lower tax revenue. That made it even harder for them to escape the treadmill.[14]

Towns and cities are not slaves to circumstance. They can change their own fortunes.

FROM TREADMILL TOWN TO TURBO CITY

Most cities can point to imaginative initiatives and impressive programs they have created to improve their town. Alas, not all of them work. And most cities also support an array of dysfunctional policies that undermine the good work. To succeed a city needs a sufficient amount of good policies to more than outweigh the less-inspired ones.

Anecdotal evidence lauds New York and Chicago, where competent mayors and their administrations have achieved significant improvements in important areas. But there is no consensus as to how much specific policies contributed to success. For example, exactly how New York's remarkable reduction in crime rates was brought about is still a matter of contention among researchers. And many young New Yorkers face huge challenges of poverty, finding work, and improving their general life prospects.

Many cities that turn out to be successful have a pattern of not limiting themselves to trying one thing at a time. Instead, they simultaneously do many things, one or more of which might work. Later in this book we will describe turnaround cities that succeed with this approach. Unfortunately, they are not that common. Few cities are blessed for long with a combination of leadership that bases its decisions rationally on evaluation and scientific evidence, and voters that give them carte blanche to do so. More commonly city politics plays out more like dancing the tango—two steps forward, one back, and one sideways.

One reason for such uncoordinated political movement is that many cities actually are complex organisms made up of interdependent entities that, however, function to a great extent independently. For example, Chicago Public School, the Chicago school district, is part of the city government, yet it has its own balance sheet and taxes and funding program. Chicago has an independent metropolitan sewerage district, a parks district, and so on. Yet the city is within Cook County, which encompasses other municipalities and provides another layer of administration. Such balkanization combined with redundant structures is common in cities around the world.

Given such messy structures for political decisionmaking, decisions for long-term investments are easily sidelined as decisions are made to solve acute immediate problems or to satisfy powerful interests or groups of swing voters. Yet it is precisely the long-term investments that can lift a city from a treadmill town to a turbo city. That is why we advocate a strategy in this book that is all about making the value of long-term invest-ments more transparent and visible to the public, and making better use of professionals who make decisions based on evidence while remaining at arm's length from day-to-day politics.

Our strategy is simple. It consists of three steps:

1. Know your assets, be they economic, human, or social.

2. Use more professional management for better yield and results.

3. Shift resources from consumption to long-term investments.

1. KNOW YOUR ASSETS

Few cities have a balance sheet, and of those that do, few of them reflect the true values of the cities' commercial assets. Therefore city leaders at best fumble in the dark when they make investment decisions, and at worst ignore the effects of short-term decisions on long-term city wealth. The first step in creating a reliable and transparent balance sheet can be the preparation of an annual review. Later chapters describe how this has been done by some national and city governments that want to demonstrate an overview of their portfolios, including market value and yield. This process creates awareness among the general population and thus increases politi-cal support to take the next step. Political support is important to counter potential protests from interest groups that might benefit from a status quo that is maintained by hiding a proper understanding of a city's commer-cial assets. The next step to improve transparency is a more comprehensive, audited consolidated annual report that pulls together data on all city property to clearly show the true wealth of the city. The quality of report-ing and transparency should ultimately be in line with the best of any listed company on the stock market, for a city's portfolio is truly a public asset.

Every penny generated through an increase in yield from the portfolio of commercial assets is a penny less that must be found from budgetary cuts or tax increases. Any review or audit of spending should, in parallel, determine the extent to which additional yield can be generated from the government's commercial portfolio.

One might think that a city's noneconomic assets are not easily measured. But our approach is to find simple measures that—even though they may not represent the best "true" measure of value—capture value changes well and work operationally. For example, in theory, social assets might be valued in terms of the net present value of expected social expenditure costs. One might, more correctly, call this "social debt," although, such forecasts are uncertain and require much expertise. In chapter 4 we present techniques that make it simple and easy for city administrators to assess the value of social assets, and to answer questions such as, What is a social investment in six-year-olds worth that results in a payoff in the form of lower crime rates by the time they are fifteen years old?

Similarly, we show tools for making investments that raise the value of human skill assets and make them transparent and useful in city politics. The wage income per person of working age captures reasonably well how employers value citizens' skills and knowledge. But these are greatly influenced by factors that can be measured separately such as school quality, educational matching, and business climate improvements.

2. USE MORE PROFESSIONAL MANAGEMENT FOR BETTER RESULTS

We claim that cities can achieve better results and do so more systematically, and without relying on the good luck of having exceptional politicians. The key is to rely more on professional managers so as to better separate day-to-day governance from politics.

Some municipal administrations have a natural knack for asset development. For example, the historic center of London and the location of much of the UK's financial sector is actually called the City of London Corporation. This urban corporation claims to be the world's oldest continuous elected local government body. Here both businesses and residents are entitled to vote in elections. The City of London Corporation is just one of the thirty-two boroughs that make up Greater London, but it has an unusual professionalism in its approach to its balance sheet. This approach is comparable to that of the much larger and better-known modern city-states in Asia, such as Hong Kong and Singapore.

A modern version of the City of London Corporation that we advocate for any city is to move its commercial assets into what we call an urban wealth fund, where these assets are governed by professionals with some independence from day-to-day politics. As the successful development projects in the City of London Corporation illustrate, this approach may also facilitate joint development with surrounding local governments of projects that otherwise all too often might fall victim to political haggling.[15] A professional negotiation between managers of urban wealth funds of neighboring municipalities to exploit a common interest is much more likely to succeed than an uncoordinated, patchy approach. In some cases, several municipalities or boroughs may even decide to become part owners in a common urban wealth fund, to help manage and fund assets that cross administrative boundaries, such as bridges and roads, or are shared for reasons of scale, such as airports and port facilities. One example is the Port Authority of New York and New Jersey, which we discuss further in later chapters.

Not only purely commercial and concrete but also social and human assets stand a much greater chance of flourishing if city politicians devolve governance responsibility to professional managers, rather than being involved in many details. That gives politicians much greater leeway to formulate citizens' requirements rather than becoming entangled in operational details. Democracy is actually improved.

3. SHIFT EXPENDITURE FROM CONSUMPTION TO INVESTMENT

Cities have been built to invest in the future of their citizens—in schooling and skills, in quality social interaction, and in enduring infrastructure to move people, goods, energy, and ideas. Cities do these things through a mix of investments by a broad range of public, private, and civic investors. The urban stakeholders are networks of institutions and individuals: homeowners, universities, hospitals, philanthropies, private businesses, utilities. For example, the rebirth of entire sections of Detroit is being led by an eclectic consortium of philanthropies such as the Kresge Foundation and corporations such as QuickenLoans.

Yet, despite this future orientation, short-termism is a constant threat. In order to help cities make wise choices on long-term investments it is important to embrace an intellectually formulated strategy that emphasizes the use of evidence to make informed investment choices. This will automatically tilt investments away from short-term fixes and help cities take account of the fact that their success is not just a function of their current spending but rather of the stock of social, human, and economic wealth that they have accumulated. Evidence-based decisionmaking also encourages experimentation with new instruments such as social impact bonds, which invite outside investors into innovative social programs, or regional venture funds that give city networks the market intelligence to make smart decisions.

In sum, cities can be nations' locomotives if they build their assets and make them pay off, or they can end up as millstones around a nation's neck if they fail to invest their way off the treadmill. In the next chapter we show common ways in which cities fail, before we turn to the success strategies of turbo cities.

CHAPTER 2

Why Some Cities Fail

CITIES IN DECLINE have let their assets go to waste for decades. True, Detroit, Michigan, and Athens, Greece, were both hit by external shocks, but this alone is not what felled them. Mostly cities in decline could not weather the shocks because of a history of poor asset management, often coupled with few social investments, a disregard for human assets, and mismanagement at many levels.[1]

Many social historians of the city hype urbanization as one of the great, and mostly positive, global revolutions. In many developed countries cities contribute more than 90 percent to a country's GDP, as ever more people move to cities. But fewer experts have taken note of the fact that not all cities succeed. In fact, quite a number are actually in decline, with shrinking populations or increasing social malaise. Why does this happen?

A useful exercise is to apply a technique advocated by the Toyota Corporation as part of its "lean" production, a manufacturing philosophy that spread all over the world in the 1990s and is still a mainstay in the corporate culture of many firms. This exercise asks that any failure be met with an attempt to fix the root causes—not a quick fix—by asking repeatedly "Why?" to get to the underlying causes of any failure. Let us try this for a few hapless cities.

TREADMILL TRIBULATIONS

In 2005, the city of New Orleans was hit by a severe shock, seemingly an act of God, beyond its control. Yet anyone who scratches beneath the surface of proximate causes of the calamity of the hurricane named Katrina finds in New Orleans a city that was especially negligent in its failure to build its assets, and through this failure it exposed itself to grave risk.

Hurricanes Katrina and Rita resulted in the flooding of over 80 percent of the city. The storms displaced 800,000 people, which is the greatest demographic displacement in the United States since the Dust Bowl of the 1930s. By 2010 New Orleans had lost a quarter of the population it had only five years earlier.

Natural disasters may seem to be irresistible forces. Yet worldwide, the annual number of deaths due to natural disasters has fallen by 95 percent over the last hundred years. Even many poor countries have built dams and defenses. So first, why was New Orleans so vulnerable?

The proximate cause is that New Orleans invested much less in flood protection than many experts deemed necessary. Over the years, the city's overall infrastructure aged and very little was done to handle the growing risk of flooding due to the gradual sinking of the city that left large portions below sea level.

Question number 2: Why didn't New Orleans ask for assistance to construct flood protection? Well, in fact, it did. But when Katrina hit on August 29, 2005, there were over fifty failures of the levees and flood barriers. These failures allowed tens of billions of gallons of water to spill into vast areas of New Orleans, flooding over 100,000 homes and businesses. Responsibility for the design and construction of the levee system belongs to the U.S. Army Corps of Engineers. After Katrina, four major investigations were conducted by civil engineers and other experts in an attempt to identify the underlying reasons for the failure of the federal flood protection system. All concluded that the primary cause of the flooding was inadequate design and construction by the Army Corps of Engineers.[2]

The U.S. Army Corps of Engineers is a federal agency made up of some 37,000 civilian and military personnel, making it one of the world's largest public engineering agencies. Although generally associated with dams, canals, and flood protection, it is actually involved in a wide range of public works in more than ninety countries around the world. It also manages such diverse assets as a quarter of U.S. hydropower capacity and 4,300 recreational areas, funds beach replenishment, and upgrades local water and sewer systems.

Congress has used the Army Corps of Engineers as a source of pork-barrel spending for decades. Funds are earmarked for low-value projects in the districts of important members of Congress, while higher-value and more critical projects go unfunded. A history of scandals surrounds the corps.[3] The failure of the levees is just one example of how mismanagement and even corruption leads to very real disasters for thousands of people. Thus, an important partial explanation for the disaster was poor governance of federal assets.

But this does not exculpate the city. When a project is completed, the Army Corps of Engineers hands components of the system over to the local levee boards, which then bear responsibility for maintenance. In addition, one might argue that a city would not normally rely for its vital safety solely on a problem-ridden federal agency. Poor city management also meant that preparation for a possible flood was negligible.

Third, why did New Orleans not do more itself to protect itself? The most obvious answer is that New Orleans is a poor city with a relatively poor population. This poverty is hardly a law of nature, but very much a consequence of poor asset management. New Orleans was the archetype of a treadmill city.

After the U.S. government purchased the area from the French in 1803, the city's population grew with a large influx of European immigrants whose population soon overtook the previously largest demographic group, slaves and former slaves. In the late 1800s New Orleans had grown to be the fifth-largest city in the United States. As in much of the South, there was some industrial growth, but it never quite matched that of large northern cities, in spite of the presence of good railway and water connections and harbors. Already New Orleans was an example of a city that failed to create assets of value that it could have used later.

Even this could have been turned to advantage: if New Orleans had built other nonindustrial assets, their existence might have left it less exposed to the kind of industrial decline that hit Chicago and Detroit over the past decades. But on the contrary, New Orleans began to see population loss after 1960—of about a fifth even before the hurricanes hit. Furthermore, many of those who remained were poor. By 2005, New Orleans had almost twice as many people living below the poverty level as the national average and an average income that was just 70 percent of the national average.

A direct reason for population flight was that many municipalities in the surrounding suburbs, such as Elmwood and Belle Chase, developed their assets, while New Orleans did not. The suburbs drained swamps, creating attractive suburban areas, and promoted infrastructure and transport. Many people with higher incomes moved to the suburbs.

This development was not unavoidable. Many cities around the world developed their assets to create attractive city centers and avoided the extremes of urban flight. In a later chapter we discuss in greater depth how Singapore has gone from poor to rich by developing its public assets. For the moment, consider how it has invested in flood control and created other values at the same time.

Singapore has been flooded a few times over the past hundred years, but it is not considered to be one of the Asian cities at greatest risk for flooding. Yet for a city with a long-term perspective, even small risks are worth taking seriously and worth finding ways to create value at the same time. In Singapore the outcome of such thinking was the Marina Barrage, which holds back ocean surges during storms while creating a freshwater reservoir and a protected waterfront for a new botanical garden and a growing financial district (see figure 2-1).

Three floors up, on the roof of a pump house next to Singapore's first urban reservoir, is an extensive lawn where children play right next to some of the most expensive real estate in Singapore—tall office towers, a conference center, a hotel and shopping complex, and the popular Gardens by the Bay botanic garden, all built after the barrage came online in 2008.

For a single piece of infrastructure, Marina Barrage does a remarkable number of things. It stores fresh water that flows into the city from a massive catchment zone, helping the city-state wean itself off water imports from Malaysia. It holds back the ocean, offering low-lying areas flood

Figure 2-1. *Singapore's Marina Barrage*

Vietnamese photographer/Shutterstock.com.

protection during storms and a hedge against sea-level rise. And on a crowded island of 6 million people, the lawn and the reservoir itself have created some much needed open space that is popular for all kinds of recreation.

The barrage's design is fairly simple. The principal costs were for cleaning up the banks and the water quality of rivers in a catchment area of approximately 40 square miles. Thousands of squatters living near the rivers were resettled into public housing and many farms and other enterprises were relocated or were bought out. As the reservoir water was slowly desalinated, the brackish and dirty water turned fresh. The function of the barrage as flood protection was really an added bonus.

Today, other cities have their eye on the barrage's multipurpose functionality. New York has taken note of Singapore's Marina Barrage, because it creates value through a mix of uses, not just coastal protection.

A shock like the one in New Orleans when Katrina struck naturally triggers activity, and some of the asset building that might have prevented the city's erosion in the first place if it had been undertaken on an ongoing basis. Post-Katrina, the federal government has poured billions into new flood defense bulwarks. A variety of commissions and initiatives have given rise to unprecedented levels of citizen engagement in New Orleans. In 2007, the city along with a group of private foundations funded the Office of Recovery Management, which was created to develop a strategy for recovery. It was headed by Edward Blakely, who promoted strategies such as "trigger projects" in seventeen target areas to drive development, and the creation of target areas whose residents were determined to renew, redevelop, or rebuild zones. These are good initiatives, yet so far New Orleans has not managed a turnaround in its social and economic development.

New Orleans remains infamous because its gradual decline ended with a bang. In other cities failure is more gradual, and may not stimulate the same kind of belated rejuvenation. One of these is Berlin, Germany, which has failed to hone the value of its human assets and business climate, and therefore remains relatively poor. In usually well-organized Germany, Berlin's new Berlin Brandenburg Airport—cofinanced by the city, the surrounding state of Brandenburg, and the federal government—has become a caricature of its mismanagement. Construction started in 2006 and was due to be completed in June 2012, but four years after it was due to open, delays were still preventing the opening. Construction problems have continued to crop up everywhere and costs continue to soar.

If Berlin had had an asset-oriented approach to its infrastructure and a small dose of realism about its administrative shortcomings, the city leaders would have concentrated on specifying what functionality an airport should have, and how much the city would be willing to pay every year for this functionality, and then delegate to an independent holding company to invest and deliver. Instead, the flamboyant mayor of Berlin, Klaus Wowereit, insisted on being chairman of the airport's supervisory board, a role for which he was unsuited (in fact, an underlying reason for many cities' management errors along the way is the use of politicians as financial and construction managers). In the fall of 2014 Wowereit was forced to resign as mayor.

Yet the over-budget airport is the least of Berlin's problems. Berlin is a city with formidable natural advantages: the capital of Europe's strongest economy, centrally located in Europe, with beautiful built structures and parks. It markets itself as a "city of glamour." Local politicians focus on fashion shows and movie production. In recent decades it has spent more money than other German cities on sports and culture, but less on stimulating economic growth.[4] It undoubtedly has a large creative class. Yet in economic terms it does poorly, worse than many smaller cities with few cultural attractions. Even though Berlin has a bubbling Internet start-up scene, many larger businesses shun the city because of its poor organization. As a result, Berlin is also called "the capital of poverty," since it houses more people on welfare and other social transfers than other parts of Germany.

First, one can ask, why is Berlin relatively poor? Berlin features relatively high local taxes, a poor business climate, and wretched finances in spite of receiving large subsidies from the EU and the federal government.

Second, why doesn't Berlin shape up its policies? Wowereit described Berlin as "poor but sexy." Apparently neither he nor many of his voters seemed to realize that Berlin's poverty had much to do with its failure to manage its assets well.

Many cities are like Berlin. That is, they grow and develop. Life for their inhabitants improves. But the cities are actually performing way under their potential. A surprising number of cities, in fact, are actually contracting, not growing. More than a hundred large urban areas in the world have decreasing populations, at a time when others are rapidly growing.[5] Among smaller cities and rural communities decline is even more prevalent. In some countries with demographic contraction this may be less surprising. A third of German cities were shrinking before the inflow of refugees that started in 2015, and Japan has similar problems. The two largest cities in South Korea, Busan and Seoul, are both contracting.

More remarkably, even countries with growing populations have some shrinking cities. Almost one in ten American cities is in decline. Eight of the ten largest U.S. cities in 1950 have lost at least a fifth of their population since then.

Often city decline is attributed to external causes, such as deindustri-alization or urban flight.[6] In our assessment, however, every shrinking city is characterized by a previous prolonged spell of asset neglect. Inter-preting such overall trends in terms of where people "want to live" may simply hide that some cities make themselves more attractive to inhabit-ants, while others let things go and find that many people move else-where if they can afford to do so.

Deteriorating cities easily end up in a vicious cycle. Buildings and in-frastructure are too expensive for a smaller population. It becomes harder to honor pension pledges. Fewer firms and skilled workers may want to move to city with disused buildings and a declining local market. As fac-tories and homes are abandoned, the local economy can spiral downward.

Perhaps the best-known declining city in the United States is Detroit, which has lost more than half its population since 1950. It has become plagued by violence and hopeless schools. The city filed for bankruptcy in 2013, having failed to raise enough taxes from its diminished workforce to pay its debts and support an army of retired teachers and policemen.[7]

Many experts lay the blame for the problems of Detroit and cities like it on deindustrialization, urban flight, and a host of external causes. But deindustrialization is not in itself a cause of a city's demise. Cities are in a process of creative destruction all the time and mostly manage just fine. Compare Detroit with Munich, Germany. In the year 2000 in Munich and Detroit the share of total employment that was industrial employment was similar: about 30 percent. Both cities were more reliant on industry than many other large American and German cities. By the year 2012 Munich's industrial employment had shrunk by a third, to 20 percent.[8] The Detroit metropolitan area had a similar decline in manufacturing jobs (although with a greater dip after 2008 and a greater rebound in recent years). But all similarity ends there. By 2014 the overall employment as a share of the working-age population in Munich surpassed 60 percent, higher than in decades, despite the fact that Munich also accommodates a large number of refugees. In Detroit, in spite of a recent rebound in the automotive and other industries, the employment share is only 51 percent, way below the 2000 figure, in spite of the fact that the population has shrunk as many of the unemployed have moved away.

Some of this difference between the two cities can perhaps be ascribed to national policies and the business cycle. Germany as a whole had momentum after tax- and labor-market reforms around the turn of the millennium. But Munich has also honed its assets in most respects.[9] It has established one of the best business climates in Germany. It has among the best schooling in Europe, including vocational training, apprenticeship and universities in close cooperation with the local business community (the city administration is not directly in charge of its schools, which are run by the state of Bavaria).[10] This is one reason why BMW has been able to remain one of the most profitable car companies in the world for decades.

Munich also engaged in an intensive dialogue with citizens and business during the 1990s which initiated the "Perspektive Munich" process. The focus was on reusing and restructuring former commercial and industrial sites, military barracks, and disused railway land. After scanning such assets it turned out that Munich had sufficient development areas available for many years to come, much of which could be used for housing or attractive mixed-use development. These areas offer the advantage that they have already been developed and that their infrastructures only needed to be augmented and brought up to current standards.

Munich also invests in geographic integration with an excellent urban transport system, and city planning that aims to create shorter commutes and mixed neighborhoods rather than segregation. When planning permission is granted for new housing projects, priority is given to inner-city developments and in particular for mixed development that blend commercial use, high- and low-price housing, and open space.

This is all quite different from how Detroit acted. The Detroit area typifies U.S. suburban and exurban sprawl, with some job holders in the area commuting regularly for as long as seventy-five minutes one way from Jackson and Lansing, Michigan. The lack of a coordinated regional transit network—with the exception of a (somewhat unreliable) bus system—makes it difficult for Detroit's job holders and residents, even more so than for citizens in most other major U.S. cities, to move from inside and outside the city to their places of employment.

One reason for Detroit's difficulties might be that its decisionmaking is split among a city government, an independent school system, and Wayne County, which includes the city and some other towns. But Munich also has split authorities: for example, the state of Bavaria is completely in charge of schools.

Munich has built its assets over decades. But even cities that have neglected their assets and have been hit by external shocks can manage a better turnaround than Detroit. We will show in the next chapter how Pittsburgh did it. In the 1980s Pittsburgh's administration and residents began to realize that a downward trend would take some time to turn around. Instead of having lots of dilapidated buildings as a showcase for the city's misery, they enthusiastically bulldozed houses and factories, particularly along its waterfront, and replaced them with parks. With this and many other measures it has orchestrated a turnaround and has started to grow again.

Some cities that have experienced the loss of jobs and a shrinking middle class have been even more successful at reinventing themselves economically as new centers of the "knowledge economy." Three examples are Raleigh, North Carolina; Austin, Texas; and Denver. The area around Denver has attracted more than 600,000 new people since the turn of the century, and almost 40 percent of the population have university degrees.

In sum, cities that fail to mobilize their assets are more vulnerable to catastrophes. Even in the absence of shocks they may drift, at the expense of quality of life and sometimes with shrinking populations. Admittedly, population growth is not an end in itself. A shrinking city may work just fine for the people who live there, as long as it maintains sustainable social structures and a good quality of life. Unfortunately, not all cities do.

SOCIAL AND HUMAN WEALTH LIE FALLOW

People are the fabric of cities. To some extent human and social capital can be won by attracting successful people to move in. But the litmus test for a city's capacity to help its inhabitants flourish is whether they provide chutes or ladders for the children who grow up in them. Some cities work wonders even for disadvantaged children, whereas others let their children slide to an adulthood way below their potential. Not surprisingly, these cities pay a high price later on.

It turns out that canny asset development is a major factor that separates the ladders from the chutes. If the average U.S. city lifted only 5 percent of its children from the prospect of potential unemployment and social problems to normal life prospects, it could improve long-term city finances, freeing in the order of 20 percent of their budgets partly through lower costs for handling social problems and partly through higher tax revenue.[11]

Have too many cities invested too little to reap these long-term gains? Several recent studies conclude that Americans enjoy less social mobility than people in other industrialized countries—in other words, American children are less likely than foreign kids to grow up to do better than their parents.[12] In particular, children who grow up in disadvantaged neighborhoods tend to have little chance of moving up. What role do cities play in these negative prospects?

One might think that this question would be very difficult to answer. It would probably require establishing causal connections between city environments and children's fortunes in life, then following millions of families, keeping track of how they moved between cities and how well the children do later in life.

In fact, that is exactly what an impressive team of economists at Harvard and the University of California, Berkeley has done in a new study.[13] The team followed up on 5 million families' moves around the country, and tied that to how their children fared when they had become young adults. In the end they could calculate how much any neighborhood that a child grew up in contributed as a chute or a ladder for children's income prospects as adults.[14]

Poor children are least likely to end up among high-income earners in the Southeast and the industrial Midwest. Upward mobility is particularly lacking in Memphis, Indianapolis, Atlanta, and Columbus, Ohio. In contrast, poor children are most likely to be able to work their way to an upper-income life in the Northeast, the Great Plains, and the West, including in cities: New York, Boston, Salt Lake City, Pittsburgh, and Seattle.

Children whose parents move to a better neighborhood—one where children of non-movers within the same income percentile have higher earnings in adulthood—earn more themselves. On average, spending an extra year in a neighborhood causes some convergence of the outcomes of children who move to that neighborhood with permanent residents of the destination. An increase in average income is statisticians' way of capturing life outcomes. Each percentage point of improvement actually signifies thousands of young people who escape a life of crime, addiction, or homelessness, all of which cost a city a lot of money, quite apart from the human suffering involved.

Every additional year that children spend growing up in DuPage County, Illinois, raises their household income later in life. Among the hundred largest counties in the United States, DuPage is the highest-ranking in terms of its causal effect on upward mobility for children who reside there. For children who spend their entire childhoods in DuPage, this amounts to later incomes 16 percent higher than the national average. Baltimore, in contrast, generated a total earnings penalty of approximately 14 percent for children who grow up there from birth. The difference between the best and the worst environments is thus 30 percent. Although the immediate cause of riots in Baltimore in 2015 was the death of a black man in police custody, the social context was the economic hardship that has emerged over decades. Money has poured into the spruced-up business and tourist district near the harbor, but in the poorer areas of the city, which are populated mainly by African Americans, a complete lack of investment has led to an unemployment rate for men of approximately 50 percent.

But here comes the main point: If one simply studies the average outcomes of children who grow up in a city one can easily get a completely misleading impression. For example, families who live in New York City tend to have unusually high rates of upward mobility. The reason for this is a selection effect, not a causal effect: New York City has a very large share of the kinds of immigrants who in the United States have higher rates of upward mobility than average, such as people from all around the world who are recruited to the financial industry.

The causal effect of growing up in New York City on upward mobility as the study revealed by analyzing children who move into and out of New York is negative relative to the national average. This negative effect of growing up in New York is masked by the selection of people who move there, often recruited into high-paying jobs.

This might explain why some cities that are perceived as successful also have an increasing divide. New York is considered successful, yet it has seen a big rise in homelessness. San Francisco and Washington, D.C., are perceived as innovative and successful, yet they have relatively high percentages of poverty when compared to other major urban centers—roughly 20 percent—once cost of living is figured in. In Chicago, community leaders talk of there being two cities—the resurgent downtown with its corporate headquarters, tech hub, and new MATTER medical technology startup center—and the poorer southern and western areas of the city.

Income inequality as such does not have to be a sign of city failure, as the urban economist Edward Glaeser argues in *Triumph of the City*.[15] The presence of city slums can be a sign of the attraction of the city rather than its failure: slum dwellers may have come to a city because it actually offers better opportunities than the poor countryside they have escaped. But in many places rising inequality is not a result of success drawing in poor migrants. On the contrary, many of those who grew up in the city are the ones being left behind.

So, what determines whether a city fails to create ladders for its children rather than chutes? Is it greater spending on transfers to poorer people? The child mobility study actually provides some answers. Surprisingly, perhaps, heftier tax breaks for the poor or a stronger safety net did not contribute much to increased mobility. Even tax credits for the poor combined with higher taxes on the affluent seemed to improve income mobility only slightly. The economists also found only modest or no correlation between mobility and the number of local colleges and their tuition rates or between mobility and the amount of extreme wealth in a region.[16]

Instead the difference between high-mobility and low-mobility communities had more to do with broader-based factors that hinge on how a city invests in and guards its assets—for example, the quality of investments in early education, and the geographical planning of metropolitan areas. The researchers identified several broad factors that affect whether cities provide ladders or chutes.

First, children's upward mobility was higher in metropolitan areas where poor families were more dispersed among mixed-income neighborhoods.[17] For example, in Atlanta, the most common lament seems to be precisely that concentrated poverty, long travel distances on roads and highways, and a weak public-transit system make it difficult for workers to get to the job opportunities. We will show in later chapters how these factors are a direct consequence of how a city develops its own real estate assets, and engages or does not engage in smart city development and planning.

A second factor for children's income mobility is better elementary schools and high schools, which is often easier to achieve in mixed-income neighborhoods. The right kind of investment in school quality can be a very effective way of investing in social and human assets. We will return to this issue also in a later chapter.

Third, children's income mobility was also higher in areas with stronger civic engagement, including membership in religious and community groups and in areas with more two-parent households. These factors may seem to lie outside the domain of a city administration, but a community can take active and balanced steps to help build the social fabric in neighborhoods on the mend.

More than four-fifths of metropolitan areas in the United States have seen household incomes decline this century.[18] Studies like the Harvard study indicate that in many places the loss of manufacturing jobs is not the main culprit in creating troubled cities, and not even remarkable compared to what happened in others that managed to thrive. Instead the greater problem for stumbling cities—and therefore even of stagnating and more uneven incomes at the national level—seems to be failure to develop the right kind of public assets.

But, actually, the story is more complicated, and illustrates that social investments can work. Many cities as well as private and federal initiatives have targeted the poorest, and apparently with success.[19] One of the most important social indicators, mortality, is, unsurprisingly, higher in poorer counties. But mortality has fallen for almost everyone, and the biggest gains have been among young men in the poorest places.

Among the explanations are that most cities have taken measures to lower crime rates. The number of homicides has nearly halved since 1990 for young men, even more in poor neighborhoods. In addition, health care is better for mothers, babies, and children. During the 1980s, for instance, Medicaid coverage for pregnant women was greatly expanded, with long-lasting benefits. Other public-health improvements, such as cleaner air—particularly important for childhood health—have also disproportionately benefited poor areas. As a result, the life expectancy of whites is now just three-and-a-half years higher than that of blacks, down from seven years in 1990. In short, income and race have an ever-weaker effect on mortality, despite rising income inequality.

While this is encouraging, and is evidence of many initiatives' success, another large group has gone under the radar. Nine out of ten metro areas experienced a decline in the share of their populations that are middle income.[20] This also shows up in well-being and health. Middle-aged whites were more likely to die in 2013 than they were in 1999.[21] This is unique among developed countries, and is largely a reflection of the deteriorating prospects of parts of the American middle class. Other countries have also seen job losses due to globalization and automation, but these forces have not had the same drastic effect on incomes and life expectancy.

While gentrification as well as poverty have been much discussed in the sociology literature, the gradual degradation of middle-class neighborhoods may be what should set the loudest alarm bells ringing in city halls. For example, West Allis and Cudahy were once well-off middle-class suburbs bordering Milwaukee. Now the majority of students in local schools qualify for reduced-price school lunch programs. As incomes are squeezed, relatives move in together. At the same time, the better-off move to suburbs in the north of the city. This is a common pattern. Urban core areas have seen some revival while the surrounding rings deteriorate.[22]

Many U.S. cities continue to experience an asset deterioration in close-in urban neighborhoods, while the fastest growth has continued to be located farther out, in the periphery.

The Germantown neighborhood in Philadelphia, once solidly middle class, is now mostly low income. Chelten Avenue, one of its main thoroughfares, is a hard-luck strip of check-cashing stores and takeout restaurants. The stone homes on side streets speak of a more affluent past.

In these and many other neighborhoods on a downward slide, early intervention could perhaps have made a big difference. The crucial questions for a city are the following: First, can city assets be deployed to make a neighborhood on the slide more varied? For example, opening up to hubs, transport, and islands of gentrification in declining neighborhoods will vastly improve inhabitants' possibilities of obtaining new jobs and maintaining school quality. Second, how can the value of human skill assets possessed by people in a declining neighborhood be raised? And third, what social assets are worthwhile investing in proactively to prevent a slide into poverty and crime later on?

We would argue that the fragility of the middle class in America has much to do with many cities' weak attention to such assets. There has been some focus, from both federal and local initiatives, on lifting the poorest groups. But many cities have let their middle-class neighborhoods deteriorate instead of investing to strengthen them and create less segregated neighborhoods.

This lack of attention to assets has left large stretches of many cities unnecessarily segregated, and they have become a chute for children growing up. Guess which is the most demographically segregated town of all: Detroit.[23] That is one reason why Detroit was less able to handle a shrinking industrial base than many others. Integrating segregated areas has much to do with how cities plan infrastructure.

INFRASTRUCTURE DELUSIONS

Treadmill cities have often made the wrong calls in their infrastructure choices. Smart infrastructure decisions are an important ingredient in city asset management, not just to enable people from poorer neighborhoods to get to where the jobs are. Infrastructure investments are a city's toolbox that largely determine how a city grows. The upshot of the previous section was that future social costs can be reined in by making a city more mixed-use and less segregated by income or demographics.

For decades, most countries have underinvested in sorely needed public infrastructure such as roads, railroads, and other public transport, as well as water, wastewater, and electricity networks. Especially in developed economies, this has happened because the political process often gives priority to short-term expenditure rather than long-term investments. In a thorough review of the evidence, the International Monetary Fund concluded that investments in public infrastructure have fallen over time and that more investment could stimulate growth.[24] But even more important than just more infrastructure is picking the genuinely valuable, rather than the showcase, projects.

Public infrastructure spending in America experienced two great booms, one during the Great Depression and another after World War II, in the 1950s and 1960s, when most of the interstate highway system was built. Since then, infrastructure spending as a share of GDP has declined to about half the European level. The United States is one of the most car-dependent nations on earth, yet it spends about as large a share of GDP on roads as Sweden, where public transport is pretty good.

Failure to address its infrastructure deficit can cost a country the size of the United States trillions of dollars in lost economic output in the coming decades, according to a study published by the American Society of Civil Engineers (ASCE), which reports on the shortcomings in the country's roads, bridges, waterways, and airports. They claim that gross domestic product will take a $4 trillion hit between 2016 and 2025 because of lost business sales, rising costs, and dented incomes if the country continues to underinvest in its infrastructure.[25]

That would mean 2.5 million fewer U.S. jobs in 2025 than otherwise, stated the report. The ASCE warns that "deteriorating infrastructure, long known to be a public safety issue, has a cascading impact on our nation's economy, impacting business productivity, gross domestic product, employment, personal income and international competitiveness."

The situation is similar in many other Western countries. In Germany, autobahns are crowded, causing commuters to waste eight working days per year in traffic jams. The Kiel Canal in The German state of Schleswig-Holstein—the world's busiest man-made waterway, which connects the North Sea and the Baltic Sea—had to be partially closed last year after two worn-out locks, built in 1914, broke down. Major bridges crossing the Rhine are so dilapidated that they have been put off-limits for heavy lorries. Public investment in infrastructure plummeted from 13 percent of German federal spending in 1998 to less than 10 percent in 2016. In many emerging-market countries the situation is much worse.

Some infrastructure investments can actually pay for themselves by making land attractive for investors. Other infrastructure investments differ widely in their social value and costs. Unfortunately, cities and nations often make very poor spending choices that cost them dearly in the longer run.

To a certain extent cities are also in the hands of others than the actual leaders of a city, owing to mixed ownership of assets and fragmented responsibility for investments, as is the case in New Orleans. Three-quarters of all spending on infrastructure occurs at the state level. States in the United States cut their budgets by nearly 10 percent when the financial crisis hit in 2008, and have not made up the lost ground. Meanwhile, bills for repairs and maintenance are coming due. Much of what was built after the war was designed to last for fifty years and now needs replacing. That includes almost half the country's bridges.

The Pulaski Skyway over the Hackensack and Passaic Rivers, which separates Newark from Jersey City, is badly in need of renovation.[26] New Jersey's governor, Chris Christie, found himself with no money to pay for maintenance of the skyway. So New Jersey reclassified the Pulaski as an entrance to the Holland Tunnel—which on the map lies miles to its north—so that the Port Authority of New York and New Jersey could be tapped for funds. For this maneuver Christie's administration is now under investigation by the Securities and Exchange Commission and New York's district attorney.

Even though treadmill cities do not have full control over their infrastructure funding, they often make own choices that exacerbate things.

In India, Mumbai (former Bombay), in 1964, fixed a maximum floor area ratio—the total floor area of buildings in relation to the size of the land on which it is built—of 1.33 in most of the city as a way of limiting urban growth. As a result, space is extraordinarily expensive in Mumbai, office blocks must be built outside the city, and people have to travel far distances from the center of the city to jobs in these peripheral blocks.

Alas, Mumbai has also grossly underinvested in transport infrastructure, leading to dreadful congestion. In recent years height restrictions on buildings have been eased, but only modestly. Still, new skyscrapers are required to be surrounded by open space, which means that you still need a car to get around. Contrast that to Singapore and Hong Kong, which at one point were just as poor as Mumbai. The story of how these two Asian cities came to embrace both high-rise buildings and good public transport is one reason they are now vastly richer than Mumbai.

Having failed to make wealth-generating investments, cities and countries too often lavish funds on white elephants, investments that cost much more than they are worth. Spain spent a bundle on motorways (that are often quite empty and therefore hardly motivate their cost), which contributed to the financial crisis that erupted there after 2009. China has produced a large number of world infrastructure records, such as the largest hydroelectric project, the Three Gorges Dam, and 4,000 miles of high-speed rail. Many of these are prestige projects that have a negative value to society.

A popular proposition in cities all over the world is to build streetcar systems, also called trolleys or tramways, even though rapid transit buses would be much cheaper, more efficient, and better for the environment. The preference for rail mass transit often is emotional: streetcars are viewed as a quaint draw for tourists and shoppers, not as serious improvements in the city's transportation infrastructure. Washington, D.C., spent at least $135 million to build streetcar rails on a route of 2.4 miles in the city's northeast.[27] At least sixteen American cities have built similar systems, with dozens more in the works. Even bankrupt Detroit has begun work on a three-mile line of streetcar rails that is expected to cost $137 million. Most research finds that streetcars often cost a multiple of what buses cost, without necessarily moving people more efficiently, quickly, or even more environmentally efficiently. Their slow speeds and frequent stops often cause more congestion.[28]

An important reason why streetcar routes are being built is that federal subsidies have encouraged them. Under Barack Obama, the Department of Transportation made grants of up to $75 million available to "small" projects that promise to revitalize urban areas and cut greenhouse gas emissions. They need not be cost-effective in the conventional sense if they claim to make a place more livable or offer other vague benefits. Not only is this wasteful, it also tends to favor better-off riders, such as tourists and shoppers who experience the streetcars as picturesque and "fun." Not even the savings in greenhouse gas emission is guaranteed, since such savings depend on how electricity is generated in that region. If the source of electricity is coal-fired plants, streetcars hardly help reduce emissions.

Overall, more spending on infrastructure may not even be necessary if funds were used circumspectly. Too often investments in spectacular projects pay no heed to what renders the highest social return. Roads, railroads, local transport, and other public infrastructure are assets that are not treated as assets because they do not render financial returns, and cannot easily be sold or transferred. They generate no revenue. Yet they can often be put to much better use than they currently are without compromising their primary function.

Apart from subsidizing streetcars, the U.S. federal government also lavishes resources on other white elephants, such as President Obama's ill-conceived high-speed rail project, in a way that is also illustrative of many city projects. Despite the administration's spending nearly $11 billion since 2009 to develop faster passenger trains, the projects have gone mostly nowhere.[29] Critics say that instead of putting the $11 billion directly into those projects, the administration made the mistake of parceling out the money to upgrade the existing Amtrak network, which will still limit trains' speed to 110 mph because higher speeds would require much more expensive new tracks. None of the money originally went to service in the Northeast Corridor, the most likely place for high-speed rail. On the crowded route from New York to Washington the Acela train averages only 80 mph, and a plan to bring it up to the speed of Japanese bullet trains, which can top 220 mph, will take $150 billion and twenty-six years, if it ever happens.

In his 2011 State of the Union address, President Obama said, "Within twenty-five years, our goal is to give eighty percent of Americans access to high-speed rail." The Acela, introduced by Amtrak in 2000, was America's first successful high-speed train, and most days its cars are full. The train has reduced the time it takes to travel between Washington, New York, and Boston some, but aging tracks and bridges, including Baltimore's hundred-year-old tunnel, where trains come to a crawl, slow it down. The lack of upgrades has caused serious crashes, resulting in injuries and deaths.[30] It takes 165 minutes to travel from New York to Washington on the Acela, instead of the 90 minutes it would take if new tracks had been planned and built.

One problem is that Amtrak's funding is tied to annual appropriations from Congress, leaving it without a long-term source of money. After Amtrak was created in 1970, subsidies were supposed to be temporary, but this has not been the case, and Amtrak has provided a second-rate rail service for more than thirty years while consuming more than $30 billion in federal subsidies. It has a poor on-time record, and its infrastructure is in bad shape. Reforms elsewhere show that private passenger rail can work, but also that a public railway company can shape up considerably if it is professionally governed and exposed to competition. Such reforms have been implemented in Australia, Britain, Germany, Japan, New Zealand, and other countries. One common and fairly successful model is to let several operators compete on tracks on which they buy time slots and that are owned by a separate entity.[31]

The most interesting comparison is perhaps with places where infrastructure investments turn out to be profitable and extremely well run without much government planning. Compare the U.S. government–owned system with the city of Tokyo's private railroads.

Tokyo is one of the world's largest megacities, with a population of 35 million. Instead of the expected traffic chaos, vast numbers of people move efficiently with few delays on public transport. The rail networks of Japan's three largest metropolitan areas—Tokyo, Nagoya, and Osaka—are perhaps the most efficient in the world. The country's flagship high-speed line, the Tokaido Shinkansen, has operated for nearly fifty years without a single derailment or collision. Its average departure delay is less than a minute. Even more impressive than the few high-speed tracks is the complex web of metro and commuter lines, the result of a vibrant free market in transportation, all achieved with roughly similar ticket prices as in subsidized systems in the United States or Europe. Singapore and Hong Kong also have private companies, but competition there is weak and subject to restrictive price and other regulation, compared to Japan's array of independent firms.

After World War II, while nearly all railways and intracity buses in Europe and North America were nationalized, Japan stayed its prewar course, with the railway industry retaining its few sizable private firms. Private railways proved to be more efficient than those run by the state, which were losing cash even in the dense Tokaido megalopolis, the corridor between Tokyo and Kyoto. So in 1987 the government privatized the Japanese National Railways, which operated every type of transit except trams and inner-city metros. JR East, JR Central, and JR West, the three spin-offs operating around Tokyo, Nagoya, and Osaka, respectively, emerged healthy and profitable and mostly financed their own infrastructure. Privatization was later applied to Tokyo Metro, the largest subway network in the city.

While privatization is one route, it may not work as well as in Japan if it is not executed well. And in many situations rails are not the best investment at all. Generally, poorer residents are better served by fast buses, and at a fraction of the cost. A positive example in this direction is Cleveland's rapid bus service that has attracted $5.8 billion in private investment along its 6.8-mile route. It was built in 2008 for around $50 million, a third of the cost of streetcars for a similar-length route.

Our examples have focused on railroads and buses. But the story is similar in other infrastructure areas. Nearly all U.S. seaports are owned by state and local governments. Many operate below world standards because of inflexible union work rules and administrative hang-ups. A report from the U.S. Maritime Administration noted that "American ports lag well behind other international transportation gateways such as Singapore and Rotterdam."[32] Inefficient ports are a definite hindrance to exports. Privatization of ports has often been fairly successful in a number of countries, such as Britain, where nineteen ports were privatized in 1983 to form Associated British Ports.

Yet our main point is not to focus on opportunities for privatization. For decades, a war has raged between those in favor of public ownership and those who see privatization as the only solution—essentially a phony war. We argue that this polarized debate is partly to blame for neglect of a more important issue: how well public assets are governed. This makes all the difference to how well public wealth delivers value to its owners, the citizens. Public assets that are privatized can achieve widely differing outcomes, depending on professionalism during the privatization process, the quality of government tendering and regulation, and the expertise and professionalism of the new private owner-operators.

Cities that run into trouble have often made costly infrastructure choices that failed to give a good return and help to build the cities' social and human assets. An essential foundation of high-quality public asset governance is the ability to discard the lure of false prophets.

LISTENING TO PIED PIPERS

Maria Börjesson, head of the Center for Transport Studies in Stockholm, recently surveyed the beliefs of local politicians about local transport, and found most of them to be completely at odds with the research literature.[33] Here is her list of some transport myths that pervaded city politics, but were contradicted by the research (at least for the city of Stockholm):

- Subways or trams are better than buses.

- Congestion is bad for the environment.

- More roads increase carbon emissions.

- "Peak car": Over time fewer people want to drive by car.

- More regional transport stimulates economic growth.

- Free local transport reduces congestion and promotes equality.

■ More bicycle lanes reduce congestion and are good for the environment.

Failed cities tend to be short on economic competence. That may be one reason they are prone to follow bad advice. In many cases this is coupled with a disdain for evidence or an inability to distinguish robust insights from pseudoscience. When it comes to infrastructure investments this appears to be the rule rather than the exception. In an excellent study of all major infrastructure investments in Norway and Sweden over the twenty years starting in the mid-nineties, it turned out that there was no correlation between politicians' likelihood of funding infrastructure projects and the conclusions from the official social cost-benefit calculations for these projects.[34] Decisionmaking is hardly on firmer footing in other countries.

Another convenient notion in city politics over the past decades has been that big spending on culture to court the intellectual and artistic would remake and revive cities. The idea was popularized by Richard Florida with a widely read book that made it easy to believe that the presence of the "creative class" of the skilled, educated, and hip would benefit everyone else, too.[35] Art museums and tram lines have been built in troubled American and European cities, on the assumption that if you build such amenities, creative people will come, and soon, general uplift of the whole community will follow. For the most part, they will not come and general uplift will not follow.

The iconic successful contemporary cities of San Francisco and Seattle did become hubs of highly educated migrants, technology-based businesses, and high-end business services. But it is important to remember that they did not start out that way. Seattle was essentially a logging town in a beautiful but rainy part of the country that managed to transform itself.

But a number of the old Rust Belt cities that have tried to attract the "creative class" have not succeeded very well. Money spent on Detroit's topnotch Detroit Institute of the Arts (DIA) and other cultural spending apparently did little to head off the crisis. Interestingly, governance of the DIA was a key to avoiding the worst consequences of bankruptcy, which left some creditors being paid back just 14 cents on the dollar as part of the settlement deal, while pension payments to its retired work-force will be sliced by 4.5 percent.

Also, the city was forced to think how the DIA could be a less costly, or more profitable, asset. The museum has been owned by the city since 1919, and its collection includes works by Rembrandt, Van Gogh, and Matisse, as well as Pieter Bruegel the Elder's masterpiece *The Wedding Dance*. To save the DIA, an unusual arrangement was struck. In April 2013, the city's governor-appointed emergency manager, Kevyn Orr, informed the DIA that it would have to contribute at least $500 million to paying off Detroit's debts, even if meant selling off paintings at auction. Instead of selling a work from its collection, the museum essentially went on an ambitious fundraising drive, in which it managed to raise more than $800 million. Detroit gets to keep its art collection. And the museum never has to worry about municipal finances ever again.

Richard Florida himself has since conceded that the benefits of appealing to the creative class accrue largely to its members and do little to make anyone else any better off.[36] The rewards of the "creative class" strategy, he notes, "flow disproportionately to more highly-skilled knowledge, professional and creative workers," since the wage increases that blue-collar and lower-skilled workers see "disappear when their higher housing costs are taken into account." The "higher housing costs" result from gentrification by the creative knowledge workers.

To be sure, some "creative class" cities have much to recommend them. But the cities that Richard Florida ranked high on creativity had 39 percent new job growth during the period from 1983 to 2003, whereas the cities that Florida ranked lowest on creativity had a job growth of 62 percent during the same period.[37] The latter cities were more affordable than the "creative class" cities. Similarly, since 2016 the populations of Charlotte (North Carolina), Houston, Atlanta, and Nashville grew by 20 percent or more, at least four times as rapidly as those of New York, Los Angeles, San Francisco, and Chicago. This trend toward higher growth in more affordable cities is as evident in the most recent census numbers as it was a decade earlier.

The pattern is similar in other countries. During the 1990s Manchester, UK, started off with a busy building program in which the city government worked with the private sector in so-called public-private partnership (PPP) schemes to create prestigious buildings. The focus was on sport, leisure, and culture and was meant to help Manchester get back on top, where it had been for most of the Victorian era as the booming capital of Britain's textile industry. With the Manchester United soccer team earning global fame, the city concentrated on big sports events and applied to host the Olympic Games in 1996 and 2000; in 2002 they finally held the Commonwealth Games. Therefore, a lot of big sports arenas were built.

But Manchester also came up with a cultural strategy that led to the construction or repurposing of additional prestigious buildings in the city center such as the Bridgewater Concert Hall in 1990; the MEN (Manchester Evening News) Arena in 1996, the largest indoor venue in the United Kingdom, and third largest in the EU, situated above Manchester Victoria Station; PrintWorks in 2000, an urban entertainment venue with a cinema, clubs, and eateries in the former nineteenth-century print and press house; and the extension of the Manchester Art Gallery in 2002. The Bridgewater Concert Hall was built by the Central Manchester Development Corporation, which essentially was an urban wealth fund active between 1988 and 1996, to develop parts of eastern Manchester. Its projects included 1.5 million square feet of nonresidential development; 2,583 housing units, which were built on around 350,000 square meters of reclaimed derelict land; and 2.1 kilometers of new road and footpaths.

Even though Manchester managed to get into global media with a new music and art scene and areas seemed to recover in the city center and the middle-class suburbs, the gap between rich and poor in the city is getting bigger. The social disparity in Manchester is bigger than anywhere else in England, according to the Index of Multiple Deprivation, a UK government statistical study of deprived areas in UK local authorities.

Although Manchester's overall cultural strategy did not lift it into the league of flourishing cities, some assets were developed along the way. On June 15, 1996, Manchester was the target of a terror attack by the IRA (Irish Republican Army). Luckily nobody died, but in the inner city buildings were destroyed. The city managed to get something positive out of a horrible incident and started up an inner-city revitalization program which not only concentrated on the rebuilding but also on resettlement of residents to the area. The building activity revitalized and revalued the area, and apartments were built in formerly rundown factories and industrial buildings. These new buildings also became a cross-fertilizing ground for an underground scene of band, bars, art galleries, and a relatively young, well-educated, and fairly wealthy group of people.

Yet this limited success is far from what can be achieved by canny turbo cities. Many successful cities can, in fact, seem downright boring in their methodology. But they weigh the evidence, follow the research and their economic acumen, and get the fundamentals right. Learn more about these boring turbo cities in the next chapter.

CHAPTER 3

Turbo Cities

HUNDREDS OF SCIENTISTS AND JOURNALISTS have written thousands of articles trying to identify what makes a successful city. Although it is easy to rank cities in different dimensions, the sad truth seems to be that how cities became successful has largely eluded researchers. We have already argued that the time lags involved, and the confusing effects that previous asset investments can cause, makes it fiendishly difficult to tie specific actions to success in cities.

In this chapter we begin with a critical view of cities that have been widely hailed as successes, yet that in our view punch below their weight because they continue to ride on the strength of bygone achievements. Then we examine turnaround cities that provide a much better picture of how a city can pull itself up by its bootstraps and get off the treadmill of short-range and ill-advised measures. Finally, we summarize how successful cities cannily develop their assets, thus setting the stage for a more detailed discussion in later chapters.

THE FALSE PROMISES OF EXCLUSIVE AND EXTENSIVE CITIES

The Columbia River separates two reasonably successful U.S. cities: Portland, Oregon, and Vancouver, Washington. Yet they succeed in different ways with radically different strategies. Vancouver has grown rapidly, and now has four times as many inhabitants as in 1990. Portland's population has only grown marginally. Here city politicians administer one of the most restrictive sets of building regulations in the entire country. Apart from detailed zoning restrictions, the city is not allowed to grow into neighboring agricultural land, leading to higher property urban prices. As a result, Portland attracts mainly people with higher incomes who can afford to move in.

Portland and Vancouver illustrate two polar opposite types of cities that are often acclaimed as successful: the exclusive and the extensive. This pattern is more extreme in the United States than in many other countries. We will return to problems of extensive cities in the next section.

Consider first how exclusive cities—San Francisco, Boston, and Greenwich, Connecticut—are successful by attracting bright people, in times of both better and mediocre city governance. Absurdly high real-estate prices in such cities have accelerated even more in recent years. In San Francisco, since 1950 real estate values have grown at twice the national rate for the fifty largest metropolitan areas.

Many exclusive cities with top rankings in quality of living are similar to expensive "brand name" universities. They attract the best and the brightest who want to go there to meet other bright and successful people drawn by the town's renown, which does not always reflect the current quality of life but instead reflects what it was when the reputation was built.

Exclusive cities do well for home owners, but they do less well for the those who are poor and renters. In terms of employment and income, exclusive cities boast far more high incomes in finance and other business services. But these sectors employ relatively few people.[1]

Worryingly, and perhaps counter-intuitively, exclusive cities put a stranglehold on national growth. A recent study concludes that tight land regulation in exclusive U.S. cities has reduced national GDP by more than 10 percent, a staggering amount.[2] Additional suggestive evidence on this relationship between land use constraints and the labor market can be found in studies which show that an increase in labor demand in high-regulation cities leads to a smaller increase in the housing stock, greater appreciation of the price of housing, and lower employment growth than in low-regulation cities.[3]

Table 3-1. *Quality of Life in Cities, 2016*

Rank	Mercer Quality-of-Life Rankings	Economist Intelligence Unit Liveability Index
1	Vienna	Melbourne
2	Zürich	Vienna
3	Auckland	Vancouver
4	Munich	Toronto
5	Vancouver	Calgary
6	Düsseldorf	Adelaide
7	Frankfurt	Perth
8	Geneva	Auckland
9	Copenhagen	Helsinki
10	Sydney	Hamburg

Sources: Mercer Quality-of-Living Rankings, 2016 (www.imercer.com/content /mobility/quality-of-living-city-rankings.html#list); Economist Intelligence Unit, "A Summary of the Liveability Ranking and Overview," report, August 2016 (http://pages.eiu.com/rs/783-XMC-194/images/Liveability_August2016.pdf).

This brake on growth also afflicts London and similar attractive cities that do grow, but it prevents them from growing more than they could absent restrictive regulation. Exclusive cities usually have an enviable capacity for creating high-productivity jobs, but don't allow many newcomers a place at the table. Land regulation simply makes it too expensive. Instead, middle-class people have been fleeing expensive cities for more affordable ones.

Exclusive cities tend to top the dozens of rankings that are compiled on the basis of quality-of-life indicators such as personal safety, economic opportunity, environmental values, transportation infrastructure, affordability, personal safety, and so on. Table 3-1 shows the top ten cities according to two such indexes, the Mercer Quality of Living Survey, and the Economist Intelligence Unit Liveability ranking. In the Mercer index the top U.S. city is San Francisco, in twenty-eighth place.

Vancouver, Canada, regularly ranks high. It is in many ways blessed by nature with a moderate climate in both summer and winter. As in Canada at large, taxes are higher than in the United States, the streets are clean, and the safety net is more generous. It has a distinct urban planning philosophy with good local transport, tall skyscrapers, and a lot of open spaces in between. The city has attracted many. Forty percent are foreign-born, many of whom possess a college degree and are upwardly mobile. Its population has increased rapidly, from about 400,000 in 1960 to just over 600,000 today—a smallish increase for a successful city, but typical for exclusive cities. (The population of the greater Vancouver metropolitan area has increased from about 800,000 to about 2.5 million over approximately the same period.)[4]

Zurich is an example of cities that do very well in quality-of-life indices and have built their assets at one point in time, and may continue to do so, or may decide to surf on the wave of previous investments by serving as enclaves for the successful. These cities do not use their full potential for the benefit of their own less successful inhabitants, let alone potential new arrivals. A study that examines this issue more carefully finds that cities that score high on various quality-of-life indices have reached a high level of development in terms of productivity, income, and other indicators, but actually do less well in terms of job growth and their contribution to national GDP (see figure 3-1).[5] Interestingly, the Mercer index and the Global Financial Centers index both buck this trend, indicating that highly livable cities can also be growth engines. This is mainly because these indexes give more points for affordability than the other indices, thus lifting the rankings of cities that are high on both quality of life and affordability.

In fact, cities that offer a high quality of life may be able to attract competent people even with lower wages, provided the newcomers can afford the housing.[6] For example, hospitals in urban centers have a higher ratio of doctors to nurses, the doctors are paid less, and the nurses are paid more than their counterparts in rural areas. Urban doctors are more likely to be specialists and graduates of more highly ranked medical schools than rural doctors.

Figure 3-1. *Index Value and Growth of GDP and Employment*

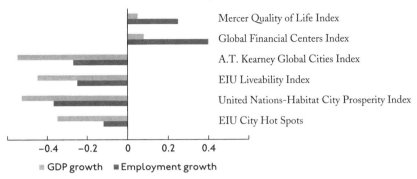

Mercer Quality of Life Index

Global Financial Centers Index

A.T. Kearney Global Cities Index

EIU Liveability Index

United Nations-Habitat City Prosperity Index

EIU City Hot Spots

GDP growth Employment growth

Source: Kenan Fikri and T. Juni Zhu, "City Analytics: Competitive Cities for Jobs and Growth, Companion Paper 1," Working Paper (Washington: World Bank, December 2015) (https://openknowledge.worldbank.org/handle/10986/23569).

Note: EIU = Economist Intelligence Unit. The EIU City Hot Spots is also an index, but focuses on long-term growth prospects. City livability indexes do not predict growth of jobs or incomes.

Even cities that are growth engines can suffer from exclusive-city syndrome and fail to pull their full weight toward national growth. For example, London has seen its population grow by 12 percent since the year 2000, compared to about 10 percent for Britain as a whole, and is full of high-income earners. Yet this motor of the British economy is producing below its potential. The fundamental problem is how land is used and regulated (an issue we return to in several of the following chapters).

Economists might welcome a shift from low- to high-value industries, but property prices threaten the necessary inflow of competence. For example, public services struggle when it is difficult to hire teachers and others for whom housing costs are too high. Those who hang on in the city do so at a cost: In inner London, the disposable income of private renters dropped by a quarter between 2001 and 2011.[7]

While many Londoners struggle, some are thriving, in particular homeowners, who see their property become more valuable. Income inequality has risen faster in London than in Britain as a whole over the past decade. This is bad for the city. Costly rents and mortgages transfer wealth from poorer people, who tend to spend what they have, to richer people with assets, who are able to save money. As a result, there is less demand to support the economy, and less diversity. The share of total employment that comes from start-ups is falling, and small firms are now closing at a faster rate than more established outfits.

Poor land-use regulation is the main reason for price escalation. One example of this is the much debated use of Green Belts. Over one-fifth of London's land is a Green Belt—open space encasing the city and largely off-limits to developers. There is enough Green Belt land in Greater London to build about 1.5 million houses, about thirty times the number of new houses London needs a year. But opposition from homeowners is strong—especially from those near the Green Belt, who do not much like the thought of development encroaching on green areas or bringing down property prices.[8]

Restrictive planning policies also inflate the price of office space in the West End by about 800 percent. A square foot there is twice as expensive as in Midtown Manhattan. This excess cost can be expressed as a "regulatory tax" that indicates the increase in the cost of buildings due to building restrictions (see table 3-2). For the City of London this "tax" is a factor of 4.49, which means that the market price is 4.49 times higher than the cost of building a new building.[9]

Stockholm, the capital of Sweden, is something of an exclusive city. In Stockholm the estimated regulatory "tax" amounted to 3.79 times the cost of building in 2005, and has probably become higher since then. Stockholm has long promoted the technology sector, and has pampered those who exploit it. Subsidies have helped to get personal computers and the Internet into almost every household, however poor. The city facilitated the construction of networks that connect 98 percent of homes and all commercial property with fiber-optic cables.

A string of successful digital firms has sprouted, exemplified by a large music-streaming business, Spotify. Programming is the single most common occupation in Stockholm. The tech sector employs 18 percent of workers, nearly twice as many as is typical in most European capitals. A digital boom is one reason why the Swedish capital region has one

Table 3-2. *Estimates of Average "Regulatory Tax" for Commercial Real Estate Markets in the UK and Selected European Cities*

City	"Regulatory tax" factor
London, West End	8.00
London, City of London	4.49
Frankfurt	4.37
Stockholm	3.79
Milan	3.09
Paris, City	3.05
Barcelona	2.69
Amsterdam	2.02
Paris, La Défense	1.67
Brussels	0.69

Source: Paul Cheshire and Christian A. L. Hilber, "Office Space Supply Restrictions in Britain: The Political Economy of Market Revenge," *Economic Journal* 118, no. 529 (2008): 185–221.

of Europe's fastest-growing populations—2.3 million as of 2017, up by 10 percent since 2010. One-fifth of all European investments in "fin tech" (financial technology) firms between 2010 and 2014 were made in Stockholm. One, Klarna, an online-payment firm, was valued at more than $2 billion in 2016 and is expanding in the United States. In 2015 Microsoft bought the Swedish tech company Mojang, the creator of the popular game Minecraft, for $2.5 billion. In 2011 Microsoft bought Skype, developed mainly by a Swede and a Dane, for $8.5 billion.

But housing prices in Stockholm doubled from 2011 to 2016. A large share of the housing market consists of long-term rentals with regulated artificially low rents. This has created a gray market for tenants, who at times resort to paying landlords premiums under the table. For years cumbersome building restrictions have limited a new supply of housing to about half the rate needed. Without this restriction Stockholm might have become Europe's answer to Silicon Valley.

There is another problem as well. As housing in many parts of metropolitan Stockholm become less and less affordable, new arrivals flock to the few suburbs that remain cheaper because of their poor reputation. Most refugees end up there. The segregation of these groups makes investment in social- and human-capital assets much more expensive and less likely to succeed.

THE FALSE PROMISE OF EXTENSIVE CITIES

The concentration of the poor is a problem also facing many extensive cities that, in contrast to exclusive cities, have provided generous building permits in sprawling suburbs. Low-income areas often end up far from jobs and opportunities in suburban sprawl.

But at least extensive cities pull their weight in terms of job growth and affordable housing. For example in the United States, more than a million people have moved to Houston since the turn of the millennium. Since 2000 opportunistic newcomer cities such as Houston, Charlotte (North Carolina), Las Vegas, Phoenix, Dallas, Riverside (California), Orlando (Florida), and Fort Worth have created the most new jobs and gained the most net inflow of people. Even rapidly growing hot spots such as Raleigh, North Carolina, and Austin, Texas, are not dense cities that one might think vibrate of city life. In fact, both are very low-density regions with compact urban pockets surrounded by vast suburban communities. West Atlanta has encouraged building, allowing office space to grow by 50 percent since 1990, and rents there are considerably below those of many other cities. Perhaps surprisingly, this urban configuration has also attracted the well educated. Central Atlanta has a larger share of college graduates than Boston. Charlotte has become the second-ranked banking center in the United States in terms of assets held by the banks headquartered there, surpassing San Francisco, Chicago, and Los Angeles—indeed, surpassing all exclusive cities except New York. There has been relatively little long-term net growth in jobs in exclusive cities such as New York, Los Angeles, Boston, and the San Francisco Bay Area.

Extensive cities can be quite pleasant for their middle-class suburban residents. Housing can cost half as much as in New York or Los Angeles, and most services are cheaper. The fact that many people move to these cities is evidence of these advantages. A main criticism of extensive cities has been that they invite low-density urban sprawl. As a result, urban transport is mostly by car, which forces inhabitants to burn much more fossil fuel than residents of cities who can rely more on other forms of local transport. In the end many inhabitants may also be forced to spend hours driving.

Another, much-debated, question is how exclusive and extensive cities provide conditions for their children that are conducive to social mobility. Advocates of regulation and planning claim that these instruments are useful tools to achieve integrated cities and neighborhoods that are supportive of children's development. Advocates of extensive cities claim instead that building and zoning regulation mostly has been used to exclude poorer groups, and that the dynamism and job growth in extensive cities help integrate poorer groups.

In our view this is another phony debate. Regulation is a double-edged sword that can cut both ways, depending on how it is used. One way to examine whether exclusive or extensive cities succeed better in terms of social mobility is to return to the Harvard-Berkeley study of children's income mobility that we described in chapter 2.[10] In table 3-3 we rank American metropolitan areas according to the income mobility they afford the children that grow up there according to the index based on Chetty and Hendren's data. An important reservation is that this mobility index covers the time period from 1996 to 2012. Some cities may have changed more recently.

As an indicator of whether a city is exclusive or extensive, we use the Wharton Residential Land Use Regulatory Index (WRLURI), one of the most ambitious attempts to measure how restrictive cities are in allowing new building.[11] Published in 2007, the index was created from a 2005 survey of local officials in 2,600 communities across the United States. Local officials answered questions about the land-use regulatory process, rules of local residential land use, and outcomes of the regulatory process. The data thus generated were used to create a summary measure of the stringency of the local regulatory environment in each community. The survey is ten years old, which is an advantage for our purpose because it

Table 3-3. *Social Mobility and Housing Regulation in Select U.S. Cities*

City	Mobility index value[a]	WRLURI regulation index value[b]	City	Mobility index value[a]	WRLURI regulation index value[b]
Seattle	11.6	1.01	Scranton	−0.5	0.03
Minneapolis	9.7	0.34	Grand Rapids	−1.4	−0.15
Salt Lake City	9.2	−0.1	Kansas City	−1.7	−0.8
Washington, D.C.	5.8	0.33	Philadelphia	−2	1.03
Portland, Oregon	5.2	0.29	Springfield	−2.2	−0.5
Harrisburg	4.6	0.55	Cincinnati	−2.3	−0.56
Fort Worth	3.7	−0.27	Dallas	−2.7	−0.35
San Diego	3.3	0.48	Houston	−2.8	−0.19
San Francisco	2.5	0.9	Dayton	−3.7	−0.5
Pittsburgh	2.1	0.06	St. Louis	−5	−0.72
Boston	2.1	1.54	Milwaukee	−5.4	0.25
Denver	1.3	0.85	Indianapolis	−6.6	−0.76
Allentown	1.3	0.1	Tampa	−7.4	−0.17
Oklahoma City	1	−0.41	Atlanta	−8.1	0.04
Phoenix	0.7	0.7	New York	−9	0.63
Cleveland	0.5	−0.16	Los Angeles	−9.2	0.51
Providence	−0.3	1.79	Detroit	−9.5	0.12
Newark	−0.3	0.6	Chicago	−11.1	0.06

Sources: Authors' compilation, based on Raj Chetty and Nathaniel Hendren, "The Impacts of Neighborhoods on Intergenerational Mobility: Childhood Exposure Effects and County-Level Estimates" (Cambridge, Mass.: Harvard University and National Bureau of Economic Research, 2015); Joseph Gyourko, Albert Saiz, and Anita Summers, "A New Measure of the Local Regulatory Environment for Housing Markets: The Wharton Residential Land Use Regulatory Index," *Urban Studies* 45, no. 3 (2008): 693–729, table 11.

a. The mobility index indicates the percent increase of income attributable to growing up in the city.

b. WRLURI = Wharton Residential Land Use Regulatory Index. High values indicate restrictive regulation, and negative values indicate less restrictive regulation. A low value in the Wharton index indicates less regulation of the local housing market. The index is standardized so that the sample mean is zero and the standard deviation equals 1.

captures the situation during the time period when the children whose experiences are captured in the mobility index were growing up.

Juxtaposing children's mobility and building restrictions in this way suggests that whether a city is exclusive or extensive is not very decisive for how well it succeeds in terms of social mobility (see table 3-3).[12] Instead, other factors seem to be stronger indicators. New York, Los Angeles, Detroit, and Chicago have mixed indices of land-use regulation. Yet they all stick out as metropolitan areas that have all let segregated areas arise, and have over time invested relatively little in creating mixed cities.

In some cases this may illustrate the long time lags between better governance and better outcomes. For example, Chicago lost nearly a fifth of its population between 1970 and 1990, and many of its governance mistakes date from that period. But since 1990 it is one of the few midwestern cities that has been growing, and it may be experiencing a turnaround that will become visible in future updates of the mobility index. Some observers claim that Chicago's former mayor Richard M. Daley (1989–2011) was one of America's most effective leaders. He focused on improving schools and creating a business-friendly environment, initiated a program to plant trees, and took initiatives to rebuild the city's Millennium Park. But most important, an openness to new construction has rendered Chicago much more affordable than, for example, New York or Boston, where land-use regulations are much more restrictive. Yet in Chicago these positive initiatives have not yet sufficed or have not been focused enough on what makes the most difference to children's social mobility.

Instead, as indicated in table 3-3, Seattle, Minneapolis, and Salt Lake City stick out as having the greatest upward mobility. All three have very different approaches to land-use regulation. But in quite different ways they proactively use their assets to invest in an inclusive city.

Since 1994 Seattle has pursued a comprehensive plan that aims to develop the city in ways that avoid large segregated areas. Infrastructure investments and use of city land pursues an urban village strategy, which is one that encourages job and housing growth in specific areas of the city. These are areas that in some sense are operating "below capacity" and therefore are best able to absorb and capitalize on new growth, while providing essential public services and making amenities available to residents. In Seattle's new urban village centers—Downtown, Uptown, South Lake Union, University Community, First Hill–Capitol Hill, and Northgate—the goal has been to create areas that successfully mix housing and workplaces. The urban villages have been evaluated in terms of quantified goals that are often met, such as accessibility with urban transport and proximity to jobs.[13]

Salt Lake City, Utah, was founded as a planned city in 1847. Both Salt Lake City and Minneapolis are enjoying the benefits of long-standing investments in social assets and civil engagement that were made decades ago and that continue to make a difference. Yet by now Salt Lake City may be less proactive in city planning than Seattle.

More cities are now attempting to do things in a way similar to Seattle. "Innovation districts" (a term coined by Bruce Katz and Julie Wagner) are emerging in dozens of cities' downtown and midtown areas, often near universities or science parks or other centers.[14] This is occurring in exclusive cities such as Boston, extensive cities such as Houston, and even in deindustrialized cities such as Detroit and Pittsburgh.[15] All of these cities understand the advent of a new preference for urbanized, vibrant environments and the long-run potential of expanding employment and educational opportunities for disadvantaged populations, which attractive hubs close to low- and moderate-income neighborhoods.

These examples point in a clear direction. Yet one could argue that they are not conclusive, because successful turbo cities have usually done well for a long time, and may have cultural, educational, or economic advantages that are difficult for treadmill towns to realize. Therefore, we need to look closer at cities that are actually managing a turnaround.

TURNAROUND CITIES

The connection between asset neglect and shrinking cities is often not recognized because of the time lags involved. For example, Pittsburgh, Pennsylvania, was once America's prime steel city, also called "hell with the lid off." The days when Pittsburgh was shrouded in haze and surrounded by towering steel mills are long gone. As steel lost its luster, Pittsburgh failed to invest in its assets sufficiently to spur alternative growth. Its population of 300,000 is less than half its peak back in the 1960s. In recent years it has been classified as a financially distressed municipality. Despite immense progress, the city still has a large pension shortfall.

But, it has managed something of a turnaround and seems well on its way to economic recovery. Pittsburgh has weathered the aftermath of the financial crisis far better than most cities. Today, robust nonprofit, biotech, and robotics sectors are part of a diversified economy. In fact, Pittsburgh has recently been branded the "miracle city," "America's smartest city," and "America's most livable city"—the latter by both *Forbes* magazine and *The Economist*. The accolades have come in droves, but the city's renaissance has not been a quick fix.

Already in the 1960s and 1970s, planning initiatives known as Renaissance I and Renaissance II included some urban renewal projects for the downtown area: the first real efforts at environmental remediation and the creation of new skyscrapers and underground parking garages. Renaissance II also formulated a vision of abandoning the gritty city's industrial past and creating a new economy and cultural identity. Industrial land was cleaned up. Dilapidated steel mills gave way to new residential and commercial uses. More than twenty-five miles of new trails were developed along the Monongahela River, as well as urban green space. Public-private partnerships were encouraged. Universities expanded. The University of Pittsburgh Medical Center, now one of the top ten hospital systems in the country, replaced U.S. Steel as the region's largest employer. An $8 billion health-care conglomerate with 50,000 employees, the medical center is now headquartered in the old U.S. Steel Tower, the city's tallest building.

Dozens of technology companies were born in the shadows of Pittsburgh's universities. For example, Fore Systems, a computer network switching equipment company, was founded by four Carnegie-Mellon professors in 1990. A few years after a very successful IPO in 1994, a London-based company acquired it for $6.4 billion (in 2016 dollars). More than thirty robotics companies make Pittsburgh one of America's major centers for robotic innovation. Google moved its regional headquarters into a converted cookie factory as part of $131 million redevelopment project in the neighborhood of East Liberty, which is wedged between some of Pittsburgh's wealthiest and poorest areas. Crumbling buildings have been converted into chic apartments for people working at the nearby hospitals and universities. With these asset-building initiatives, Pittsburgh has gradually bucked the trend of failing Rust Belt cities.

Yet challenges certainly remain. Aging infrastructure, large public pension liabilities, and underperforming public schools are among its ailments. But even here asset building is going on. Pittsburgh's high school graduation rates have risen from mediocre to among the better among metropolitan areas. The city has finally stopped shrinking, a sign that more people see an upside to being there. "The key is to understand your assets and build on them," Tim White of the area's Regional Industrial Development Corporation has stated.[16]

Can this success be duplicated? What can other Rust Belt cities learn from Pittsburgh? A new book by Antoine van Agtmael, who coined the phrase "emerging markets," and Fred Bakker, a Dutch journalist, in *The Smartest Places on Earth* argue enthusiastically that the rust belts of the rich world, especially in America, are becoming hot spots of innovation.[17]

There are certainly good examples, but they hardly amount to a flood yet. For example, Akron, Ohio, has capitalized on its heritage as home to America's four biggest tire makers by turning itself into America's capital city of polymers. Akron Polymer Systems and Akron Surface Technologies are inventing new ways to commercialize synthetic materials. North Carolina has done the same for textiles.

But these examples are patchy, and the same aims are also pursued by other cities. For example, North Carolina's Research Triangle Park in Durham, perhaps the twentieth century's most iconic research and development campus, is modeled on the idea of an "urbanized science park," where traditionally isolated, sprawling areas of innovation are "urbanizing" through increased density and an infusion of new activities such as retail outlets and restaurants.[18] The Raleigh, Durham, and Chapel Hill tri-city region, known as the Triangle, is luring nearly eighty new residents a day with strong job growth and a high quality of life.

Science parks are not the only way to create hot spots that break up knots of segregation and insert more racial and occupational diversity into the mix. Many cities have property that is misused and could have much greater value if repurposed. For example, the town of Vasterås, in Sweden, was using its prime waterfront property as a bus depot. Only after some economists showed clear calculations did it dawn on city politicians that there was a better use. The waterfront now houses some of the most attractive apartment buildings in the city, to the benefit of inhabitants who live there now, and the city made a pile of money. The bus depot is now on cheaper land outside of town.

Also in Sweden, the university city of Uppsala for many years lagged behind the much more successful capital, Stockholm, because local politicians were unwilling to let the city expand. Around the year 2000 they changed tack completely. They allowed building developments, removed regulation, and engaged in constructive city development. This has led to a radical makeover of the city, record levels of employment, and more successful firms and research institutions that now manage to recruit internationally on a scale not seen before.

Reimagined urban areas are often found near or along historic waterfronts: in the past, heavy industry required easy access to transportation, and water transport was a fraction of the cost of land transport. Many historical cities such as Rome, Paris, and London owe their origins to location by a river or the confluence of two or more rivers (Pittsburgh). New York benefited from being both at the mouth of the Hudson River and on the Atlantic coast. This model of reimagining and repurposing a waterfront or riverfront is best exemplified by the remarkable regeneration of New York's harbor districts surrounding Manhattan, Seattle's South Lake Union, and Boston's waterfront.

But many similar opportunities still lie fallow. For example, if Boston's Logan Airport were moved from prime waterfront land to cheaper land inland, it would stand to make a large windfall gain in real estate assets on the waterfront land that would probably well exceed the cost of building a new airport and infrastructure in the agricultural hinterland. Indirectly, GDP would also be affected due to ensuing investments and growth prospects. Living standards might rise since people appreciate waterfront views. But mainly it would represent a gain in wealth for state and city government, which could then be used, for example, for greatly needed infrastructure spending. As a bonus, the existing transport to Logan would continue to provide excellent local transport to what could become a spectacular part of Boston.

Some of our examples already illustrate that cities do not have to be big to take a turn for the better. Columbus, Indiana, is a blue-collar town, hit by deindustrialization, like many others. While other Indiana cities and towns often reduced the quality and quantity of services, or otherwise cut corners in a short-term quest to save money now, Columbus took a long-term approach instead. By national standards Columbus does not spend very much money at all. With some exceptions, like devoting funds to its performing arts center, it is actually quite frugal. It understands the concept of long-term total cost of ownership, and as a result has kept taxes low. A commitment to excellence, high quality, efficiently delivered public services, and an aggressive, pro-business attitude allowed them to buck the trend and have income and population growth in a state that has long lagged the nation in job and output growth.[19]

Other, initially small and extremely poor towns in other countries have also managed astounding turnarounds. As of 1950, the fishing village of Shenzhen in Guangdong Province in southeastern China had 3,148 inhabitants but grew to 30,000 by the late 1970s. In 1979 Shenzhen was designated China's first Special Economic Zone, and its population started to take off. Now it is part of the South Guangdong metropolitan area (it also includes Guangzhou and Dongguan), which saw its 5.5 million inhabitants in 1990 increase sixfold to reach almost 32 million in just two decades. Shenzhen did have a natural advantage, namely, its proximity to Hong Kong. This helped it to take lessons in successful public asset building from Hong Kong.

Other turnaround cities have an asset building strategy that focuses on creating a good business climate, and thereby increasing demand for its inhabitants' human assets. In 2015 the World Bank published a report on what makes cities succeed.[20] The authors identify what they call "competitive cities." One of these is Gaziantep, Turkey's sixth-largest city, located inland not far from the Syrian border. Gaziantep lacks natural resources, and its land is dry and ill suited for agriculture; it is not a port city; it is not a capital city; it does not have high-tech clusters; it is not a household name nor is it a large, primary city.

Yet Gaziantep is a center of light manufacturing and its firms sell products such as machines and electrical tools in 175 countries around the globe. Exports increased tenfold in just eleven years. It ranked ninth globally for economic growth in cities during the decade 1999 to 2009. As recently as the 1970s, it had a population of about 120,000 people. Now the city's population stands at 1.54 million, not counting approximately 300,000 Syrian refugees.

Gaziantep is competitive and, in fact, a turbo city in the making. City leaders have not let themselves be satisfied with a few measures, but have used a menu of initiatives to build assets, including institutions and regulations, infrastructure, skills and innovation, and enterprise support. In a later chapter we will show how building a favorable business climate is an important means for raising the value of local human capital, an important asset.

According to the World Bank, cities like Gaziantep used extensive dialogue and a solid fact base to minimize the ever-present risk of "capture" by special interests and market distortion (such as subsidies and protectionist measures) and eventually to show the necessary ability to let go when some sectors were recognized as not globally competitive.

Making use of competence in the community is also an important aspect of building assets. In Gaziantep, business leaders were consulted about their needs and the constraints they encountered in their operations; infrastructure investments were made in collaboration with the firms and industries they aimed to serve; skills initiatives were designed in partnership with firms, ensuring that school curricula addressed their practical needs; and industries were supported only when they had a real commercial potential, and through collective initiatives with the private sector rather than through the public sector alone.

The World Bank emphasized not only good ideas, but also quality in implementation and economic decisionmaking. This is a crucial insight, and a central theme in this book. In the next section we look more at how turbo cities often achieve this excellence in their execution of plans.

HOW TURBO CITIES BUILD ASSETS

Investments are forever—or close to it. Turbo cities have at some point cannily developed their assets. Often they find ways of letting their governments, elected for a few years at a time, make decisions as though they were accountable forever. Quality in economic decisionmaking favors long-term asset building rather than shortsightedness. Unfortunately, such quality is not just a question of acumen and knowledge. It is very much a function of decisionmaking processes that can withstand uninformed or self-interested political pressures. To succeed, three important principles are crucial:

1. Stick to facts and evidence.

2. Find added value.

3. Asset governance is independent.

1. STICK TO FACTS AND EVIDENCE

Key questions for a canny city are how robust the evidence for an investment or an innovation is; how to test and experiment in ways that provides insights and evidence; and whether testing innovations is an alibi for not implementing more boring but proven remedies.

Politicians and administrations in turbo cities nurture a culture that honors facts and evidence. A glaring example of a particularly deadly form of disregard for evidence in U.S. local politics is that a quarter of all road deaths take place at intersections. America's Federal Highway Administration, which helpfully supplies a "roundabouts outreach and education toolbox" to overcome public distrust, says that roundabouts eliminate four out of five deaths or serious injuries compared with stop signs or traffic lights. Yet few municipalities have been particularly interested in replacing intersections with roundabouts.

Interestingly, one of the towns that has been leading in the United States in replacing traffic lights with roundabouts, Carmel, Indiana, leads the way in many other respects as well. It has combined a rapid population growth with investment in a first-class business environment, high-quality public facilities, some of the best suburban transportation infrastructure in the nation, new "urban village" neighborhoods built from scratch, upgrading of utilities, and improving the environment. This has been well rewarded with a very attractive quality of life.

In canny turbo cities controlled experiments and other ways of evaluating what works are part of the toolbox. For example, housed in New York's Office of the Mayor, the Center for Economic Opportunity has hatched over fifty different antipoverty programs and initiatives since it was created in 2006, including initiatives that help low-income residents open savings accounts, advance in their jobs, find jobs after imprisonment, and graduate from community college while working or raising a family. The office coordinates the efforts of dozens of city agencies and creates goal-oriented programs whose effectiveness is rigorously tested through randomized trials.

Cities are not generally conservative when it comes to trying new things. Researchers at the Center for an Urban Future, located at New York University's Wagner School of Public Service and Policy, interviewed nearly two hundred policy experts in cities across the country and around the globe, looking for game-changing reforms that have proved effective in other cities, that are scalable in New York, and that the next mayor could implement.[21] This report, "Innovation and the City," presents fifteen of the most promising reforms—from San Francisco's bold plan to establish a $50 college savings account for every kindergartener in public school to Boston's pioneering approach to remaking the 311 system (for non-emergency municipal services) for today's smart-phone age and London's ambitious experiment with crowdfunding for public infrastructure projects. While many cities try new ideas, fewer evaluate systematically what works. In the end that evidence-based evaluation separates the failures from successful turbo cities.

2. FIND ADDED VALUE

Cities can often find ways of generating value and building assets in ways that at least partially finance their own way. The best-known way to build assets is through investment in public transportation, which increases private land values in surrounding neighborhoods. Governments can recoup a share of this real estate boom via "value capture" instruments such as the Community Infrastructure Levy, a tax on neighborhoods that stand to gain.[22] In London, the levy helped finance major infrastructure improvements, including the city's ambitious Crossrail, a major new commuter rail line connecting the suburbs to central London. To finance that project, neighborhoods surrounding the new route were assigned to one of three categories, depending on their proximity to the new line. In zone 1, the closest area, new development is taxed at £50 per square meter. In the next two closest zones, the levy falls to £35 and £20 per square meter, respectively. Due to be completed in 2018, the new rail line will increase the capacity of London Transport's network by 10 percent and cut commuter traveling time significantly. More than half the cost could be met from sources other than the taxpayer.

The story is similar in other infrastructure areas. Nearly all U.S. seaports are owned by state and local governments. Many operate below world standards because of inflexible union work rules and administrative bottlenecks. Inefficient ports are a definite hindrance to exports. But ports are also typical multi-use areas, where it is often possible to find other sources of revenue besides shipping, such as developing part of the land for other uses, or increasing revenue by creating the infrastructure for international deals. In Greece, Piraeus is one of the few successful privatizations in Greece, where Cosco, a Chinese state-owned enterprise, bought half of the port and tripled turnover and efficiency in less than two years.[23] Singapore's national wealth fund, Temasek, owns a successful operator of ports, often by finding ways of wringing more value out of existing assets.

Highways are another example where imaginative planning can create opportunities. A number of U.S. states have built, or are building, privately financed and operated highways. The Dulles Greenway in Northern Virginia is a fourteen-mile private highway that opened in 1995 and was financed by private bond and equity issues. In the same region, Fluor-Transurban is building and mainly funding toll lanes on a fourteen-mile stretch of the Capital Beltway. Drivers will use electronic tolling to pay for driving in the lanes, which will recoup the $1 billion investment. Fluor-Transurban is also financing and building toll lanes running south from Washington along Interstate 95. Similar private highway projects have been completed, or are being pursued, in California, Maryland, Minnesota, North Carolina, South Carolina, and Texas.

Yet, the main opportunity represented by highways does not lie in charging tolls for individual roads. Rather, it lies in overall value creation in connection with highways. Unlike most other physical assets, land can be a vehicle for managed capital appreciation, particularly when governments themselves are the primary source of allocating development rights and constructing the public infrastructure required to add value. When public authorities open up new land by building roads, providing infrastructure services, or relocating public offices, they create incremental land values, sometimes of great magnitude. When public authorities own the land in question, a shrewd infrastructure investment strategy, coupled with changes in the land-use designation, can recapture large portions of the costs of capital investment, and in some cases the entirety of costs, from land-value appreciation and subsequent land sales. For example, in Changsha, the capital of Hunan Province in China, more than half the financing for an eight-lane ring road came from the sale of publicly owned adjacent land, as well as interim borrowing against the value of the land parcels.

Another type of value creation lies in creating a toll system to relieve congestion. The Nobel Prize–winning economist William Vickrey was one of the first to write about congestion charges in transportation (alas, he himself died of a heart attack while driving in his car). Instead of charging for access to individual highways or bridges, a well-managed transportation system would introduce higher tolls during rush hour in order to reduce congestion. This has been unexpectedly successful in Stockholm, where the system was introduced in 2007. The city government introduced a charge for cars driving during peak traffic hours that led to a reduction in rush-hour traffic by about one fifth. A surprisingly large number of commuters were able to shift their trips to less congested times, while fewer chose not to travel at all or switched to public transport. Most of the city's residents were initially opposed to the fee, but now more than two-thirds of the population support the extra charge and the reductions in congestion.

A number of other cities, including London (2003) and Singapore (1975), have introduced congestion charges for motorists.[24] In Singapore, Prime Minister Lee Kwan Yew first introduced a simple version, but the city now has an electronic technology that smoothly registers cars and charges tolls. Traffic is fluid. The streets are often tree-lined, safe, and clean.

Congestion charges also appear to work for local public transport. The London Transport introduced a congestion charge in 2003 as part of its "Oyster" card. This makes a ride on the London Underground more expensive during peak hours. Several studies show that these charges help to reduce congestion, mainly by inducing some travelers to avoid rush hour. In the first ten years of the scheme in London, gross revenue was £2.6 billion, and around 46 percent of net revenue (£1.2 billion) was invested in public transport and walking and cycling schemes.

In many countries, such changes to fee structures for consumers, or fees that transport operators pay for the use of rails and other infrastructure, are subject to intense political haggling. A shortsighted political process will almost always oppose smarter fee systems. In many cases, these kinds of decisions could probably be made more rationally if they were spearheaded by public infrastructure consortia with some political independence. We will return to a discussion of such institutional reforms later.

Apart from infrastructure, cities can find opportunities to create value in many different parts of its administration. The City of Chicago developed a special fund instrument for this: a modern-day suggestion box. After Rahm Emanuel became mayor in 2011, he tasked the city's budget office with developing a $20 million pooled loan fund to support promising ideas proposed by agencies. There are few prerequisites for idea submissions, except that the proposed project has to pay for itself, substantively improve services, and under no circumstances lead to the hiring of additional staff. If the idea doesn't pay for itself within five years, the sponsoring agency will see the costs carved out of its budget.

The early results of the project are encouraging. In the first budget cycle, a dozen ideas bubbled up, and four received funding. One was a $900,000 loan to the Public Health, Consumer Protection, and Business

Affairs Departments to support a new effort to reduce the black-market sale of cigarettes. The program provides cash rewards to citizens who report illegal tobacco sales and is expected to pay for itself within three years through increased cigarette tax revenue. A quarter of a million dollars has been assigned to the Department of Buildings to ease the city's notorious inspection delays. The loan fund also provides an effective vehicle for encouraging cross-agency collaboration. The fund also strives for transparency, issuing press releases and recognizing and celebrating successes.

Value creation can also be achieved with the help of external finance. A limited but very interesting example is being tested in Chicago. Because so many cities are being crushed by pension costs and federal budget cuts, finding billions of dollars to pay for even critical infrastructure is increasingly challenging. But an innovative new vehicle called an infrastructure trust is actually allowing cities to raise large amounts of capital locally. The trust allows government to raise private funding and investment for infrastructure projects that have revenue-generating or cost-saving opportunities that can be used to pay back investors. The model is still a relatively new idea, and the Chicago Infrastructure Trust is the one being watched most closely because of its scale. The trust was able to raise initial funding of $1.7 billion, which included investments from Citi and JPMorgan Chase to fund retrofits that reduce energy consumption in residential buildings.

Some U.K. cities are even using crowdfunding to pay for infrastructure projects, modeled on what Kickstarter is doing for the venture tech industry (see box 3-1), even though crowdfunded infrastructure projects do not usually pay a financial return to the investors.

One way of using outside sources of financing for social investments is the so-called "social impact bonds" that are used to address some of the riskiest and most intractable issues facing government such as lowering crime rates and curbing chronic homelessness. These issues present complex challenges that often require bold approaches. A typical setup for social impact bonds is that private investments fund the efforts of a nonprofit contractor, whose niche is to reduce or eradicate specific social ills. The government then pays the contractor only if it met or

Box 3-1. *Spacehive*

Several cities in the United Kingdom have begun to transform their capital allocation processes. Rather than allowing projects to be determined chiefly by city and regional agencies, these cities are turning to their local communities for ideas. And rather than relying solely on government, they are opening the way to receiving private, individual, and philanthropic dollars to match public sector allocations. This radically different approach is being propelled by a London-based start-up called Spacehive. Launched in 2012 as the world's first "funding platform for public space projects," Spacehive is modeled on the pioneering crowdfunding site Kickstarter. The difference is that Spacehive is focused on the civic sector, building close relationships and full-on partnerships with local governments in the United Kingdom.

Using the Spacehive website (www.spacehive.com), any organization or individual can propose a new capital investment project or new use for a public space, and raise funds to launch it. To ensure its viability and success, a project only gets a green light when its funding target is met.

Project risk management, contract frameworks, and funding verification are all built in to the platform, and no project advances without required planning and regulatory permissions. In light of the project idea's popularity on Spacehive, both the national and local government authority pledged one-third of the needed funding.

exceeded the predetermined goals—for example, to lower homeless rates by 15 percent in two years.

Social impact bonds were first tested in London, starting in 2010, to finance a prisoner rehabilitation program. New York was the first U.S. city to launch a project. In 2012, as part of the Young Men's Initiative, the Bloomberg administration coordinated an arrangement in which the nonprofit Manpower Demonstration Research Corporation (MDRC) will receive a nearly $10 million loan from Goldman Sachs to finance a program to reduce the reincarceration of young people on Riker's Island. If the effort reduces recidivism by 10 percent, Goldman Sachs breaks even and the loan will be repaid by the city government. If the recidivism rate drops even further, Goldman could make as much as $2.1 million. However, if the MDRC fails to decrease recidivism by at least 10 percent, Goldman Sachs will lose up to $2.4 million and New York City will pay nothing. The loan is partially guaranteed by a grant from Bloomberg Philanthropies, and if the program is successful, the Bloomberg Philanthropies grant will facilitate future social impact investments in New York City. Since 2012 a number of cities around the world have followed suit.[25]

These are just a few examples of how canny cities creatively find ways to generate value, and achieve a better yield on their assets. Alas, too often these opportunities are lost in political maneuvering, or undermined by other, economically obtuse, initiatives.

3. ASSET GOVERNANCE IS INDEPENDENT

Therefore, an important part of a wealth-building strategy is to delegate wealth governance to somewhat politically independent professionals. At the national level this has worked well in a number of countries. Paradoxically, political independence can actually strengthen democracy.

When public wealth is within easy reach of governments it creates incentives for abuse, all too often in the form of outright corruption where government officials use public funds for their own purposes. But other forms of corruption by public officials include using lucrative contracts or positions in state-owned firms to buy political favors and support; offering organized interests free access to land or water from public water companies in exchange for political support; and buying support of unions by allowing higher wage increases in state-owned companies. In all these ways democracy for the common good degenerates into clientelism. Politicians can be rewarded who deftly buy support of various groups rather than enact reforms in the wider public interest. That is the essence of a "soft state" or "soft city."

In a clientelist soft city or state, governments have little interest in making state assets transparent. It is hardly an accident that Greece had virtually no accounts of its considerable state assets. As long as state ownership remains murky it is easier for governments to distribute favors without being scrutinized. This turned into a big disadvantage as the financial crisis hit in 2008. International investors quickly understood that it would take Greece many years at best to assess its state assets and reorganize them so that they could earn a return and represent a value on Greece's balance sheet. In fact, even after civil servants to the Greek government produced a balance sheet for state enterprises during the financial crisis, the government halted its publication. In a similar vein Detroit had little asset transparency when the financial crisis hit.

Even in cities with less outright corruption or clientelism, city-owned enterprises often force politicians toward a producer perspective. In countries as different as Sweden and India leading politicians have rarely been interested in formulating consumer demands for more reliable railroads. Why? Simply because the largest railroad companies are state owned. Any criticism of these raises the question of why the government is not managing these companies better. As it happens, both countries have grossly underinvested in railroad maintenance. Similarly, many cities that run their own local transport, or water services, directly under the charge of local government often show little interest in following up on expressions of consumer dissatisfaction.

Thus, a subtle effect of direct political control of city-owned enterprises is that politicians or politically appointed officials are held responsible for the production and service that is expected from the enterprise, which creates a clear conflict of interest. How decisively can mayors or city administrators take the side of the consumer and formulate consumer demands or the common interest vis-à-vis a city-owned enterprise, knowing that they themselves will be held accountable if the enterprise fails to deliver?

A natural, but misguided, choice by politicians is to react to voter demands by attempting to govern city-owned enterprises through directives, board representation, or appointing party members to managerial posts with the aim of forcing city-owned enterprises toward managerial decisions that voters demand. This is simply a way of exerting political power, and being able to show voters that local politicians are actually doing something.

Paradoxically, this strategy may often have the opposite effect. Political leaders who clearly put themselves in charge of a city-owned enterprise also assume responsibility in the eyes of the voters and are blamed if they fail. As a result, such politicians tend not to be terribly interested in transparent improvement targets, measuring efficiency, and criticism of city-owned enterprises, since the blame then falls back on to themselves.

For these reasons we claim that democracy is strengthened rather than weakened when a city removes its wealth from direct disposal of political decisionmakers and delegates governance to more independent professionals. A truly strong city is one where politicians have to compete with agendas for the common interest, instead of competing by dishing out favors in the form of access to the public purse.

For these reasons some city-states such as Singapore have placed much of their state-owned enterprises under the auspices of a national wealth fund by the name of Temasek (described in more detail in a later chapter). But similar principles can be applied more broadly. For example, a more independent body in charge of city development might replace cumbersome building regulations with a fee-based system that internalizes some of the negative external effects. This would allow more rational growth, simplify administration, and generate revenue. Such a fee-based system might meet much opposition if there is mistrust that it will be applied with a political bias, and may be easier to accept under the auspices of a more independent administrator.

In sum, there is great scope for unlocking hidden value. An urban wealth fund, which we will describe in much more detail in later chapters, provides a politically feasible vehicle for such a shift. In addition, such a politically independent fund can introduce an element of economic rationality into infrastructure investments. The arguments for a commonly owned urban wealth fund become even stronger when local government is split into different levels or covers adjacent municipalities.

SUMMING UP THE SECRET OF TURBO CITIES

Cities that appear successful may have been adroit or made lucky right turns decades ago, helping them to build their assets. Some of them are exclusive cities, and some are extensive. Both types are successful in their own ways, but many of them also perform below their potential. Exclusive cities can create a drag on national growth by not allowing more residents to participate in high-productivity economic hubs. Extensive cities easily sprawl into segregated areas in ways that generate social costs further down the line. Thus, many exclusive and extensive cities, to all appearances successful, still tend to miss big opportunities to live up to their potential.

We showed how turnaround cities around the world have worked to build assets. Pittsburgh and Gaziantep have come some way, and Singapore and Hong Kong even further. These cities have often shown foresight in a way that mirrors our recipe to govern cities to maximize city wealth rather than stay mired down on a hand-to-mouth treadmill. Some cities that succeed especially well with this approach have also delegated wealth governance to a more professional and independent body, as Hong Kong has done with its Mass Transit Railway.

Other cities are just beginning their turnaround, sometimes making astounding progress. In Medellín, Colombia, a succession of courageous mayors managed to bring about big changes by devoting more attention to tackling conditions in the poorest and most dangerous neighborhoods. The slums were deliberately connected with middle-class areas by a network of cable cars, bus transport systems, and first-class infrastructure. Together with smarter policing this reduced the murder rate by 80 percent, removing a major obstacle to growth and employment.

Even in rich countries, creating a good supply of affordable housing and a mosaic of interspersed high- and low-income neighborhoods are central elements for canny cities. These aims can be achieved in various ways that prominent economists and researchers have proposed. For example, Edward Glaeser and Joseph Gyourko have articulated an appeal for radical changes in federal incentives to stimulate building in highly regulated areas.[26]

Other urban economists, such as Roderick Hills and David Schleicher, argue that replacing zoning with better city planning may be a good way of raising intergenerational mobility.[27] Zoning restrictions are most common in high-income areas. The limited mobility brought about by zoning can contribute to putting high-opportunity areas outside the reach of the families whose children would benefit most.

Sometimes regional or central governments can take matters into their own hands. The government of Washington State is more involved in planning than that of California, which may have been a factor in the fact that in the 2000s Seattle's housing stock grew at twice the rate of that in the San Francisco Bay area. House prices correspondingly came down.

One approach is simply to neutralize local opposition to development by compensating neighbors for the costs they bear when new construction is approved—to bribe, them, in effect. David Schleicher, a professor of land-use law at Yale Law School, has proposed the use of "tax increment local transfers," or TILTs. New buildings normally generate some extra property tax revenue for the city once they have been completed.[28] Some portion of the expected rise in the tax take associated with a proposed new development (the tax increment) could be promised to nearby residents in the form of a temporary property-tax rebate, scheduled to last ten years, say, if the development went ahead.

We certainly encourage all these ideas, but fear formidable political barriers. For example, land-use regulation is usually promoted by inhabitants in high-income areas, who would then be the main beneficiaries of TILTs. That may be hard to swallow for many politicians running on a ticket of lowering the income divide.

Therefore, we argue that the most effective toolbox for cities is how they use and invest in their own assets. Infrastructure and local transport investments are crucial for how a city develops. City-owned land, real estate, and assets of municipal enterprises can be used in many different ways that increase yield and at the same time shape a more inclusive city.

Asset building is also a good venue for federal or state encouragement. For example, Stockholm and its surrounding suburban municipalities have allowed far too little building during the past twenty years. A recent upturn has been orchestrated by partial state financing of new subway lines from the city center to suburban municipalities, which commit to allowing new urban development around the subway stations.

All our examples of cities working their way up from treadmill towns to turbo cities may look like a pile of anecdotal fragments. In the following chapter we aim to present a more detailed toolbox for systematically building social, human, and economic assets.

CHAPTER 4

Taking Control of a City's Balance Sheet

DETROIT MIGHT HAVE BEEN able to avoid bankruptcy if it had been better at managing its balance sheet.[1] The Detroit bankruptcy alerted U.S. municipalities to the liability side of the balance sheet in its entirety, including pensions. Yet, many cities (and states) still do not have a complete handle on their liabilities, owing to fragmented balance sheet management, including multiple issuers of bonds within a city administration, lack of coordination, and inadequate fiscal risk management. More important, local governments are mostly ignorant of the market value of their assets and have yet to appreciate the usefulness of a proper balance sheet. Which leads to the question, Why have governments not adopted well-known, effective accounting techniques such as those required by law in the private sector?

Later chapters will show in more detail how social and human assets can be developed. Here the focus is on public commercial assets that could conceivably generate a return if managed professionally. Most cities have public assets that are several times the value of their public debt. While managing the liability side has become a matter of great concern during the financial crisis, the asset side remains opaque and largely underused. A polarized debate between privatizers and nationalizers has deflected attention from the most important point: the quality of asset management.

In the following three chapters we will describe in some detail how a city can take control of its asset management. In this chapter we start out with a brief account of the importance of balance sheet management and how crucial it is for a city to further develop an understanding of its assets and their potential. The following chapters present institutional arrangements for balance sheet management, illustrated with good (and bad) examples.

After the Asian financial crisis in the late 1990s, national governments around the world almost unanimously consolidated their debt issuing capacity under a single institution, a national debt office, in order to gain better transparency and improve fiscal risk management. With the latest financial crisis, in 2007–08, even cities were forced to acquire a much better understanding of their debt structure and contingent liabilities.

Taxpayers and other stakeholders—the "shareholders" of the public sector balance sheet—deserve to understand the true state of public wealth at all levels of government. This may also help governments to explain and garner support for politically unpopular but needed fiscal adjustments.

A private sector corporation would not be able to avoid sharing its financial statements, including a balance sheet audited by a certified registered accountant, with its stakeholders each year. The need of such financial disclosure, legislated by politicians, is self-evident in the private sector. Why should the same high standards not apply to the substantial share of the economy for which politicians are directly responsible, the public sector?

A proper understanding of a government's balance sheet is a necessary first step for anyone aiming to put public wealth to more efficient use. This way, taxpayers, politicians, and investors can better understand the consequences of long-term political decisions, and local government administrations are better able to mobilize returns and improve the well-being of citizens without imposing more taxes, debt, or austerity.

Unfortunately, high transparency in the public sector is an exception. More commonly, an incomplete understanding of the public sector balance sheet is an obstacle to accountability and proper management of public wealth. Consider what a big difference this may make for the common perception of a city's wealth.

THE HIDDEN VALUE OF PUBLIC WEALTH
IN CLEVELAND

Cities generally do not assess the market value of their economic assets, but even a rough calculation illustrates the magnitudes involved in the United States alone.

Consider a city like Cleveland, which does not appear to be particularly wealthy. It reports assets of $6 billion in 2014, an amount that while larger than its liabilities is still only a fraction of its true value.[2] Cleveland reports its assets at book value, valued at historic costs. Furthermore, due to a legal quirk, many assets acquired before 1980 are not accounted for at all. If reported using the International Financial Reporting Standards (IFRS), which require the use of market value for assets, the value of the assets would be many times what the city is currently reporting in its accounts.[3]

Suppose, conservatively calculated, that the price-to-book ratio (the multiple of the market value over the book value in the accounts) is about 5, then Cleveland's assets would be worth $30 billion, not including the many assets that are unaccounted for. We want to emphasize that we are not claiming that the price-to-book ratio is 5—it might be 3 or 7. But the point is that the Cleveland city administration and political leadership do not know which it is, and therefore are hardly in a position to develop its assets shrewdly and cannot understand the opportunity costs of failure to do so.

Accounting for the market value is the first step toward quality asset management. Next we want to understand the yield, the return that the city earns from revenue and rising market values on its assets. This is important not only to be able to compare it with other alternative investments, but also to understand whether the performance has been satisfactory, so that stakeholders can see that their wealth is well cared for.

By design or by default, Cleveland does not report any return on its assets. Assume, again very conservatively, that the city could earn a

3 percent yield on its commercial assets with more professional and politically independent asset governance. A modest yield of 3 percent on a portfolio worth $30 billion would amount to an income of $900 million a year, which is more than Cleveland's current annual net investments of about $700 million. In other words, even with a modest yield, Cleveland could double its investments.

If Cleveland is representative of the United States as a whole, then the total market value of municipal assets in the entire country would be at least $25 trillion.

A 3 percent yield would allow extra investments of $750 billion a year. This is more than the total annual infrastructure investments made by local, state, and federal governments, which today total about $450 billion.

Cleveland is by no means exceptional. To give an idea of how public assets measure up compared to debt, figure 4-1 shows an attempt to measure total assets, the sum of financial and nonfinancial assets, in twenty-seven countries.[4]

Nonfinancial assets are conservatively valued, and according to the IMF, many assets held by local governments are not included due to the lack of transparency at this level of government.[5] For what it is worth, the overall picture is that nearly all countries have current assets that exceed their debt. This is not an invitation to relax the fiscal stance, however. Rather it shows how important it is to unlock public wealth and achieve a reasonable yield. Using this approach, U.S. public assets are valued at about equal to GDP, that is, about $17 trillion in the year 2015.

Another commonly used ratio is net debt as a percentage of GDP (defined as government gross debt minus its financial assets). In 2014 in the euro area net debt was on average 70 percent and in the United States, 78 percent. Figure 4-2 shows how net debt compares to the conservative measure of nonfinancial public assets. This is another way of showing how important professional management of nonfinancial government assets actually is.

Public commercial assets—all assets able to generate an income if managed properly—are not a trivial wealth segment globally. Their value globally, excluding roads but including toll roads, national forests, and

Figure 4-1. *Value of Public Assets and Gross Debt, 2011–13, as Percentage of GDP*[a]

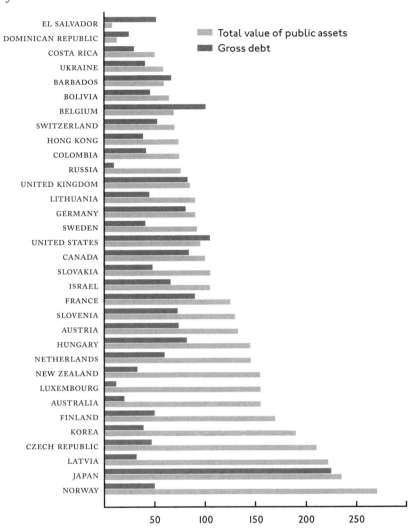

Source: Authors' compilation, based on International Monetary Fund, "Another Look at Governments' Balance Sheets: The Role of Nonfinancial Assets" (Washington: IMF, 2013). See Dag Detter and Stefan Fölster, *The Public Wealth of Nations* (London: Palgrave MacMillan, 2015), p. 51.

a. These figures contain some uncertainty. For example, New Zealand publicly reports net debt minus financial assets in the Super Fund, so the debt may not be comparable with many of the other countries.

Figure 4-2. *Value of Nonfinancial Assets as Percentage of GDP*

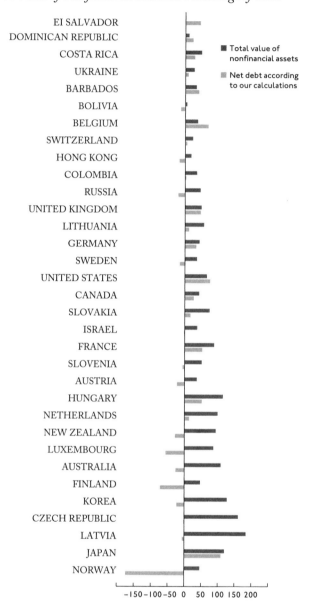

Source: Authors' compilation, based on International Monetary Fund, "Another Look at Government's Balance Sheets: The Role of Non-Financial Assets" (Washington: IMF, 2013). See Dag Detter and Stefan Fölster, *The Public Wealth of Nations* (London: Palgrave MacMillan, 2015), p. 51.

historic buildings, is estimated to exceed $75 trillion.[6] This is well over the current estimate for global public debt of $54 trillion. This estimate for public commercial assets, however, is book value and only partially captures local assets. The value of local government assets may be several times the holdings of national governments.

The market value of a city's public assets is most likely many times the value of the city's or metropolitan area's gross metropolitan product (GMP). A large share of these assets consists of commercial real estate. Since GMP, like GDP, is a statistical measure, whereas the value of assets and liabilities is a financial number, it would be more correct to compare financial numbers alone. To do this the more useful ratio is the net worth (total financial and nonfinancial assets) less total liabilities (debt and non-debt).

Focusing on the change in net worth over time would not only help governments focus on the management of assets, liabilities, and risk but would also incentivize investment in infrastructure. Better accounting and ways to improve city accounting today are so important to the asset-building approach that we need to examine it in greater detail.

FINANCIAL ACCOUNTING, ACCOUNTABILITY, AND THE RISE AND FALL OF CITIES

Accounting and accountability are intimately linked with democracy. In the ancient Greek democracies as in the early Roman Republic, accounting was held in high regard and was clearly connected to accountability. It would have been inconceivable to reach a higher office in these early democratic societies without being able to demonstrate a proper understanding of accounting. Even managing the resources of a major household was thought to require accounting skills. In fact, this is the source of the word "economy," from the Greek *oikonomia*, meaning "household management" (*oikos*, "house," and *nemein*, "to manage").

Managing these ancient empires would not have been possible without keeping detailed accounts of the resources needed to pay for the roads, water, and sanitation systems that made up the realm, as well as to support and pay the troops and feed the people.

In *The Reckoning: Financial Accountability and the Rise and Fall of Nations*, Jacob Soll describes how accounting shaped kingdoms, empires, and entire civilizations throughout the course of history.[7] Data have shown that one of the greatest historical challenge governments have had is to adopt double-entry bookkeeping as their management tool, and then to maintain it. Only with the advent of double-entry bookkeeping, in the Middle Ages, did it become possible to understand wealth and profit and weigh current investment expenditure against the benefit of future returns.

Effective accounting and political accountability made the difference between the rise and fall of many a society, from Renaissance Italy to the Spanish Empire, to Louis XIV's France, to the Dutch Republic, to the British Empire and the early United States. History has clearly shown that we ignore and fail to appreciate this connection between effective accounting and political accountability at our peril. The crucial next step is to keep track of wealth, not just revenue and expenses.

SINGLE-ENTRY BOOKKEEPING ONLY CAPTURES MONEY FLOWS

The way many local governments keep their books today is reminiscent of ancient accounting systems. One of the first originated in Mesopotamia as a system of tokens almost ten thousand years ago, long before numbers and letters had been invented.[8] Merchants trading up and down the Euphrates and Tigris Rivers kept track of the assets they sent with boats in the form of the tokens that were held in a clay envelope. Single-entry bookkeeping was born.

Five thousand years later numbers and words replaced the tokens and created a system that records the flow of income and expenses through the use of a daily summary of cash flow—cash receipts and disbursements. The concept behind this single-entry bookkeeping system survives to this day, for example in the statements reflecting the transactions on a bank account or credit card for a household. This system, although very rudimentary, still serves its purpose even for microbusinesses, such as garage sales, that do not require an understanding of wealth or profit.

The ancient Greeks and Romans fought a constant battle against corruption, waste, and fraud. Emperors were repeatedly forced to restructure the finances of the empire and were constantly criticized for increasing taxes, which further weighed down both business and the general population. Emperor Vespasian (A.D. 9–79) is claimed to have responded, "Money doesn't smell" ("Pecunia non olet") when he was criticized for levying a tax on urinals to fund more monuments to glorify his reign, such as the Vespasian Amphitheater, more commonly known as the Colosseum.

As mentioned earlier, the single-entry bookkeeping available to the emperors Augustus and Vespasian was a purely cash-based system. The main disadvantage of this system is that vital data are not available for effectively planning and controlling a business or government. The lack of a more systematic and precise bookkeeping method led to inefficient administration and a small likelihood of detecting theft and other losses. More important, it was not able to evaluate the financial position or the actual wealth at any given moment. Doing that required the invention of the balance sheet, which requires double-entry bookkeeping

The limitations of single-entry bookkeeping weakened empires, kingdoms, and civilizations. When rulers on top of that disregarded accounting altogether and failed to recognize the importance of accountability and saw themselves as only answerable to God, self-destruction and decline were usually not far off.[9]

The important missing links to better financial management and accountability were the two fundamental pillars of modern capitalism: Hindu-Arabic numerals and double-entry bookkeeping.

DOUBLE-ENTRY BOOKKEEPING AND THE BIRTH OF CAPITAL INVESTMENTS

A fresh approach to accounting finally developed during the Renaissance in Europe, urged forward by hard-nosed merchants in the booming Italian city-states. These merchants, well versed in the various forms of barter trading, a complex skill that also included the exchange of money, saw the need for an improved bookkeeping and accounting system for their expanding mercantile and financial empires.

The first piece of that puzzle was discovered by accident. As a young boy visiting what is now Algeria around 1190, the Italian Leonardo of

Box 4-1. *Double-Entry Bookkeeping*

Double-entry bookkeeping system is so called because every financial transaction generates an entry in one account and an equal, offsetting entry in another account, or column. The technical terms for these offsetting entries are called debit and credit columns. For any time period, the sum of all debits must equal the sum of all credits.

The Accounting Equation

The double-entry system provides several forms of internal controls. It also enables a proper balance sheet that works according to the accounting equation. This holds that all assets equal all liabilities, plus the equity paid in by the investors.

The accounting equation: Assets = Liabilities + Equity

Any departure from these equalities in a double-entry system is a signal that a transaction entry error has been made somewhere.

Debit and Credit

A double-entry system keeps in view a company's entire charts of accounts— both the income statement accounts and the balance sheet accounts. For

Pisa, also known as Fibonacci, discovered the existence of the Hindu-Arabic numerals, a notation system actually invented by Indian mathematicians but now more commonly known as Arabic numerals; it is the notation system most widely used today. He realized that these figures not only would be much more efficient for mathematics but also would greatly facilitate commerce. In 1202, he wrote the *Liber Abaci* (Book of Calculation), which introduced to Europe the concept of using these numerals to replace the old system of Roman numerals.

An increasingly complex trade and monetary system in medieval Europe also required a more sophisticated management system of bookkeeping that would better convey a universal system of accountability and trust. The first known use of the double-entry bookkeeping system example, suppose the company receives cash through a bank loan. In the double-entry system a record is made of increases in two accounts:

1. Asset account—debit (such as the cash account)

2. Liability account—credit (such as the account for bank loans)

Matching Concept

Related commercial transactions often occur at different times, such as when a product is delivered today, but paid for at a later date. Double-entry bookkeeping allowed for the introduction of the matching concept, whose purpose is to avoid misstating earnings for a period. Reporting revenues for a period without reporting all the expenses that were incurred could result in over- or understated profits.

Accrual Accounting

In contrast to simple cash-based accounting, applying the matching concept requires accrual accounting, the practice of recognizing revenues when they are earned and expenses when they are incurred—not necessarily when cash actually flows in those transactions.

was in the Giovanni Farolfi ledger of 1299–1300, a neat and well-preserved set of accounts.[10] Double-entry bookkeeping not only provided an enormous boost for the ability to handle complex transactions involving both money and barter, but was also very useful for increasingly sophisticated bank financing and management of wealth (see box 4-1 for an explanation of basic bookkeeping and accounting principles).

Partnership arrangements built on a universal language of accounting enabled the growth of complex trading companies and banking activities across a larger geographic area than the world had ever seen before. Banking families such as the Medici in Florence and the Fuggers in Augsburg built large trading and banking empires that often bore their family name. These international empires were often built through partnerships with a local merchant, held together through a controlling stake in each partnership. This expansion required a common, reliable accounting system.

Although there is no direct relationship between algebra and bookkeeping, the teaching of the two subjects and the books published during this time often were addressed to the same audience. One such was Luca Pacioli's *Summa de Arithmetica, Geometria, Proportioni et Proportionalita*, which deals with algebra as well as double-entry bookkeeping. The book had an important influence in both domains. Children of merchants were sent to reckoning schools in Flanders and Germany, or to *abaco* schools in Italy, where they learned the skills useful for trade and commerce.[11]

These intellectual inventions facilitated the development of some of the fundamentals of modern society. The new mathematical and accounting system eventually paved the way also for a more advanced debt-financing market.

THE MUNICIPAL BOND MARKET—EARLY FRUIT OF VALUING CAPITAL

The double-entry bookkeeping system and accrual accounting made it possible to introduce the concept of profit and loss as the sum of all costs and income over the same accounting period. They also took into account cash that was not yet received or paid but was due during the period in the statement of profit or loss. With this accrual accounting, recognizing revenues when they are earned rather than received and expenses when they are incurred rather than paid for, it was possible to better understand the value of assets, as well as that of liabilities and equity. Thus the invention of accrual accounting made it possible to create a balance sheet, in essence a summary of the values of assets and liabilities. These innovations laid the foundation for the development of a sophisticated bond market in twelfth-century Italian city-states and established the dominance of Venice, Genoa, and Florence in the maritime environment of the Mediterranean and made possible their trading connections with Asia through the land-based Silk Road.

When, in 1453, Constantinople and the eastern part of the old Roman Empire finally surrendered to the Muslim Turks, Christian rule in the whole of the eastern Mediterranean ended. Trade with Asia using the land-based routes became much more difficult for Christian Europe. This set the stage for the Age of Discovery, when larger sailing vessels and the discoveries of the sea routes to the Americas and India inevitably moved much trade away from the Mediterranean to the world's oceans.

These historical developments gave the opportunity to maritime nations such as Holland in the seventeenth century and England in the eighteenth to further develop capital markets, and helped set these countries apart from the rest of the Western world. These early mercantile successes gave the Dutch and English sustained financial and commercial advantages for centuries.

The industrial revolution, large-scale manufacturing, improved logistics, and—perhaps most important—the introduction of the limited liability company, which allowed many to invest in risky ventures without becoming liable for all losses. This helped spur global trading and commercial activities, creating a demand for further development of capital markets, a modern legal system, and the advanced accounting system that we are still using today, including methods for assessing how much assets lose value over time—asset depreciation—that are necessary to value an inventory.

With a growing market for trading of bonds and shares to finance the industrial revolution, a reliable accountancy profession assumed ever increasing importance. Modern accounting required the ability to measures the results of an organization's economic activities and convey this information to a wider variety of global users and stakeholders, including investors, creditors, managers, and regulators.

It took the private sector accounting and financial information some seven hundred years of hard-earned experience garnered from booms, busts, mismanagement, and fraud to become an integral part of the global business and the financial system. Through continuous technological improvements, innovations, and challenges the accounting profession developed still further in order to even better measure and communicate economic activity to all its stakeholders.

For the public sector, the impetus to develop proper public sector accounting has just started. It aims to improve currently substandard financial management tools and recognize the concept of accountability to its primary stakeholders, taxpayers and bond holders.

ANTIQUATED DEBT AND ASSET CONTROL

The booming industrial cities of Britain's industrial revolution such as Manchester and Liverpool depended on capital from the financial markets in the City of London to feed their vibrant growth. The same was true for the cities in the industrial heartland of the American Gilded Age, such as Pittsburgh, Philadelphia, Boston, and Detroit—they relied on the financial know-how and clout of New York's Wall Street.

The development and expansion of financial institutions such as banks and stock markets has since far outpaced the growth in underlying global GDP. Today global capital markets are almost three times the size of global GDP, handling debt and equity instruments and their derivatives worth \$212 trillion annually.[12] This financial deepening is beneficial to the economy and society, giving investors such as households and businesses more choices for investing their savings and raising capital, as well as promoting a more efficient allocation of capital and risk.

Raising funds for a private sector venture relies on the trust and accuracy enabled by modern accounting and financial information, be it to an unknown start-up or well-known corporations such as Apple, GE, and Exxon. Ultimately these transactions occur between individuals who are total strangers to each other, yet they are willing to part with their capital to invest in a business venture that they trust will enhance their wealth in the future. These transactions are surrounded by a specialized ecosystem of professional advisers, regulators, and media and financial experts, scrutinizing the integrity and every detail of the financial information and process, as well as the performance of the investment in real time and with full disclosure.

However, the equivalent process in the public sector has not followed the same trajectory and requirements for universal standards as the private sector. Quality of financial information is in most places still very much based on cash flows and single-entry bookkeeping. The lack of transparency and public scrutiny allows for financial mismanagement without any consequence, until it is too late.

Rhode Island is one of the smallest states in the union, whose population, of around a million people, is slightly more than that of Austin, Texas. Yet, this state with a GDP of $56 billion has $11 billion in debt issued by more than one hundred entities.[13] These run the gamut from the state itself to the thirty-nine municipalities to twelve quasi-public agencies and nearly one hundred special districts, such as fire districts and housing authorities. Not only is this debt uncoordinated, but because there is no proper consolidated balance sheet, the ultimate guarantor, the state, is unable to understand and even less to manage the consolidated fiscal risk for the state as a whole. For example, the municipality of Central Falls nearly went bankrupt in 2012 and had to be saved with help from the state and by means of drastic cuts in pensions.

Transparent and good-quality financial information to enable a better management of public wealth is often completely nonexistent. That lack of sophistication in public sector accounting has caused waste and huge misallocations of capital, ultimately resulting in the underinvestment and lack of maintenance in vital infrastructure that we face in our cities today.

The public sector manages perhaps greater wealth than the private sector put together, but without the equivalent sophisticated financial information. Is this because modern rulers share the sentiment of medieval kings and feel themselves to be "answerable only to God?" Are today's citizens really content with being uninformed and unable to hold their politicians accountable?

A proper balance sheet is a crucial part of all financial management, but is an important missing link in public sector management. Historically, it is good news that improvements of city accounts have been important ingredients in the rise of prosperous cities. Already, quite a few countries, including New Zealand, Australia, and the U.K., are adopting international accounting rules even for local governments.

The Texas state comptroller of public accounts has started the "Transparency Stars" program, which recognizes local governments for going above and beyond the bottom-line transparency requirements by providing clear and meaningful financial information and opening their books not only in their traditional finances, but also in the areas of contracts and procurement, economic development, public pensions, and debt obligations.

IMPORTANCE OF THE PUBLIC BALANCE SHEET

Seen from a financial point of view, the public sector needs to have a strong balance sheet and sustainable levels of debt to pay for promised benefits such as pensions, health care, and care for the elderly. If the public sector balance sheet is weak, an aging demographics process, as we have in some developing countries, can create enormous stresses in the government's finances, and potentially in financial markets. This requires that we not only understand the true value of the commitments made for maintaining a sustainable level of well-being for the people, but also make them transparent and make them factors in the political debate.

While the size and cost of the debt, including the present value of future payment commitments such as Social Security and Medicare benefits, are now becoming more transparent, the broader consolidated balance sheet remains veiled, and this includes the valuation of public assets with commercial value. Public assets are often hidden or valued incorrectly. Because of a lack of transparency, it is hard to surmise what yield assets might generate that could supplement the government's tax revenue.

Academics have for decades argued for more comprehensive balance sheets in terms of intergenerational equity.[14] Others want government balance sheets that are more comprehensive in bringing on to the balance sheet items that do not meet the accounting definitions of assets and liabilities, such as social policy obligations.

At the core of good financial statements is accounting for assets and wealth. Integrated reporting seeks to broaden reporting from financial capital to include a number of other types of capital: intellectual capital, natural resources, and so forth. Irrespective of how desirable some of this reporting might be, the situation in the public sector is that these issues are distractions from the most critical task, getting high-quality, conventional financial statements according to a commonly understood set of standards, namely, those of the International Public Sector Accounting Standards Board (IPSASB).

For the public sector to have proper financial statements would be a huge step forward, and is far less problematic to argue than is the case for any particular enhancement to existing financial statements. In working on integrated reporting, governments should not consider this development until and unless they produce high-quality financial statements. Not the least, because many governments would use these alternative forms of reporting as a smoke screen to avoid producing good financial statements.

TURBO CITIES FOCUS ON STOCKS, TREADMILL TOWNS ON FLOWS

Almost all fiscal analysis refers to flow variables such as government revenue or expenditures, or the budget surplus. A city budget is the main instrument through which fiscal policy is implemented, monitored, and communicated. However, a city budget only tells us something about the flows in any given year, perhaps complemented with some short-term projections of these flows in the next few years. A budget does not give us visibility on implications of long-term political decisions, or the structural impact of all the accumulated annual fiscal balances and policies and policy implications over time.

Public accounting focuses largely on flows, and these do not say much about the real state of the financial affairs in the public sector and nothing about wealth. For a government official or politician with a responsibility for a budget, esteem and power may be measured by the size of that flow. This mind-set assumes that assets are intimately linked to their current use, and this is why fragmentation and lack of visibility are not seen as problems in public financing.

However, such hidden resources have a financial value that is demonstrated by potential supplemental income, through leasing property to the private sector and random privatizations, sometimes risking outright rent seeking, clientelism, and corruption. Once property is seen as a commercial asset that represents an opportunity cost, the focus shifts entirely toward its best use. Allowing for value maximization as an objective for commercial assets makes every asset a fungible resource and the concern of the entire city management. Managing an asset better in one part of the city could help fund the investment needs in a different area, to the long-term benefit of the entire city and its people and not just to a small segment of the bureaucracy.

WHAT GETS MEASURED GETS DONE

Making assets visible requires using the modern accounting standards that have been used in the private sector for centuries, such as double-entry bookkeeping and accrual accounting. The latter is the practice of recognizing revenues when they are earned and expenses when they are incurred—not necessarily when cash actually flows in those transactions. The financial management benefits of such international accounting standards provide significant value to a budgetary management framework in the public sector (see box 4-2).

ing treatment and original text of the IFRS unless there is a significant public sector issue that warrants a departure from those standards. The board adopts a due process for the development of IPSAS that provides the opportunity for comment by interested parties, including auditors, finance ministries, and other practitioners.

Many governments say they intend to introduce IPSAS because they are considered to be good practice. However, very few governments have actually adopted the standards. No country has as yet adopted the cash-based IPSAS standard. The main problem is the key requirement to produce consolidated financial statements for all controlled entities. Consolidating government business entities with ministries and departments is claimed to be very time consuming and not worth the very real costs.

The number of governments that have adopted the full accrual basis for their financial statements of their central government ministries, or even the entire public sector, is also very limited; it includes the U.K., Australia, and New Zealand. For some countries developing even functioning cash-based accounting is a challenge and a necessary first step.

Some governments at the national level are slightly ahead of other countries and are more progressive than most cities. Among them, especially New Zeeland, but also the U.K. have been in the process of adopting international accounting standards since 2000. Although there are still substantial issues that need to be ironed out to ensure consistency in financial reporting, it is important to understand the scale of the challenge for governments at the national or local level that are considering implementing a more modern system of financial management.

The United Kingdom has adopted the Whole of Government Accounts (WGA) approach, which refers to consolidated and audited accounts of over 5,500 organizations across the U.K. public sector in order to produce a comprehensive, accounts-based picture of the financial position of the U.K. public sector.[15] WGA is based on international accounting standards used internationally by the private sector.

Although the system has been under development since 2006, substantial measurement challenges and inconsistencies are still being addressed by the U.K. government, particularly in the inventory and valuation of assets, but also in public sector pensions and more commercial types of assets such as real estate and public utilities that provide water or electricity.[16]

The financial management benefits of accrual accounting can be separated by stages of implementation including:

Accruals-based income and spending, using a definition of working capital—delivers significant improvements in financial management and better decisionmaking

Operational assets and liabilities—a greater understanding and more complete picture of government ownership and, in particular, a clearer view of the liabilities that a government is carrying, which was a crucial discussion point for those countries that suffered following the financial crisis

Commercial assets and liabilities—clarity on commercial opportunities and revenue-raising assets that might generate more income for government

Balance sheet risks—clarity on the role of government in standing behind critical national assets, its lender-of-last-resort responsibilities, and the guarantees and commitments that it offers or is required to issue through its policy implementations

Wellington City Council in New Zealand has used international accounting standards for decades. This does not mean their asset management is always as good as it could be. But New Zealand as a whole and Wellington in particular could nevertheless serve as an example of exceptional accounting at the local government level, which is the first critical step toward better balance sheet management.[17]

Most other cities do not use international accounting standards, hence are working without the benefit of a balance sheet. The lack of a proper balance sheet and market valuations ultimately leads to unnecessary divestitures, often at the wrong time and at a substantial discount to market value at best use, in essence transferring public money to the private sector.[18] Instead of using accepted international accounting standards most of the public sector uses antiquated and misguided valuation systems.[19] In the United Kingdom, this has been criticized by the Public Accounts Committee.[20]

In fact, very few cities can produce a proper consolidated public sector balance sheet that reflects the true market value of its entire portfolio of commercial assets.[21] These problems often originate from a perspective where governments do not make a distinction between policy assets and commercial assets and thus fail to assign market value to their vast port- folios of real estate assets, which could generate an income if properly managed. Without assigning a value to a government's portfolio of assets, there is consequently no need for a consolidated ownership management, nor even for a consolidated list of assets that have no value. Maintaining fragmented ownership of commercial assets leads to a lack of transparency and prevents governments and their stakeholders from ever understanding the scope and value of their portfolios.

This is not helped by the fact that many real estate assets are not even on the government books nor even listed in the U.K. government's Land Registry. Real estate is a not insignificant segment of the portfolio of public assets. Recent research of Land Registry data in the U.K. show that the public sector is a significant owner of real estate, holding some 6 percent of all land, split approximately 1:2 between central and local government. The Ministry of Defence stands out as the single largest landowner in the U.K., owing over 1 percent of the national land area. The other central depart- ments own a further 1 percent between them, with the National Health Service (NHS) being by far the most significant and most important—not the least because its holdings are in many of the major urban areas and have significant potential for redevelopment to residential and commercial uses.

The proportion of publicly owned real estate in the major urban areas is even higher. Around 15 percent is freehold. Eight local governments— Brighton and Hove, Barking and Dagenham, Eastbourne, Rushmoor (Aldershot and Farnborough), Gosport, Leicester, Portsmouth, and Stevenage—own more than 40 percent of the land.[22]

In the Greater London area the figure is on average over 20 percent, with some boroughs owning around 40 percent of the land area in their jurisdiction. These figures are indicative of the magnitude of public sector land ownership, subject to detailed cataloguing of health and emergency services, such as the NHS, which are not categorized by the Land Registry.[23] In London as in most cities the government does not have a consolidated list of public assets, owing to the fragmented ownership and focus on expenditure and revenue rather than on the value of assets. The fact remains that even despite many laudable efforts to compile such a list, there is not one successful unified attempt to do so and even less to put a market value on the public properties in London at current use, not to mention at best use. Part of the reason might be the lack of transparency on the public housing segment, or simply the lack of political will.

UNDERESTIMATING MARKET VALUE AND MISUSE OF ASSETS

Public institutions often use public commercial assets without understanding their proper market value or alternative use, and they consequently neglect to set a cost for that use. This lack of information creates the wrong incentives and encourages government to be wasteful in its use of public assets.

But some cities are making an effort to comply with international accounting standards. As an example, Cleveland has put together a list of its assets and accounts for them in the annual report. However, the list is incomplete, partly because of the lack of data in the land registry and also due to a legal quirk whereby many assets acquired before 1980 are not accounted for at all.[24]

Interestingly, Cleveland distinguishes in its annual report between what it calls "business type" and "governmental type" assets, but nevertheless fails to follow up by valuing its assets at market value. Instead it values its assets at historic cost. This is only possible according to the official public sector accounting standards in the United States, which have not yet reached the international level despite ambitions to do so. In the United States, generally accepted accounting principles (GAAP) for the private sector are set by the Financial Accounting Standards Board, GAAP for the states and cities by the Governmental Accounting Standards Board, and GAAP for the federal government by the Federal Accounting Standards Advisory Board.

In Sweden, some local governments have for generations had the laudable habit of managing their commercial assets in separate and seemingly more commercial holding companies. Nevertheless, local governments in Sweden are for unclear reasons prevented by law from applying international accounting standards and account for their assets at market value (see box 4-3). This position prevents professional management of the portfolio of assets.

Regulation also prevents proper risk management and public governance of fiscal risk. The public sector in Greater Stockholm is the largest owner of commercial real estate in Sweden, as well as by far the largest employer in the country, employing 7 percent of the workforce in the region, represented by both the County of Stockholm and the City of Stockholm. Yet neither government follows IPSAS or IFRS.

Consequently, none of the entities consolidate their pension liabilities or account for their commercial assets at market value. With a market value of its real estate at least twice that of the book value, partly held through their respective urban wealth funds (UWFs)—Stockholm Stadshus AB, the city holding company, and Landstingshuset i Stockholm AB, the county holding company—their balance sheets misrepresent not only a vast opportunity cost on the asset side but also any potential risk on the liability side, through its pension obligations and other future commitments.[25]

In sum, not many modern cities compare well with the private sector in terms of transparency, accounting standards, and financial management. What is prudent or even required for a private sector employer can be disregarded in the public sector. What in the private sector is a basic level of professionalism to maximize the value for the owner of assets and avoid fire sales or selling below market value is not recognized as mismanagement in the public sector as a result of inadequate accounting.

Box 4-3. *Sweden's Municipal Accounting Law*

Government accounting in Sweden is seen to have a different purpose from private sector accounting, since it is considered that the primary objective of the government at a national or local level is not to make a profit nor generate a return on capital, but to meet political policy objectives and provide goods and services to citizens. Even commercial assets owned by a government are seen as public resources to be used to provide public goods and services to citizens and users. Sweden sees IPSAS (International Public Sector Accounting Standards) and IFRS (International Financial Reporting Standards) as suitable for short-term market considerations only and counterproductive for application to the public sector, especially regarding measurement (valuation), disclosure, and consolidation.*

Consequently, Sweden's Municipal Accounting Law of 1997 does not recognize the concept of public assets as commercial assets, but views all assets as extensions of government policy that therefore should not be assigned a market value, as they are not intended to be sold. The law considers the budget and the profit-and-loss statement the main instrument of accounting and financial information.† Future pension liabilities are not allowed to be fully consolidated in the balance sheet.

THE ELEPHANT IN THE ROOM

The global financial crisis highlighted the significant gaps and weaknesses in public sector accounting practices and underscored the need for more comprehensive, reliable, and timely financial reporting by governments. These concerns were echoed by the G-20 meeting in Moscow in February 2013, when representatives called on the IMF, the World Bank, and the Organization for Economic Cooperation and Development (OECD) to work to improve the transparency and comparability of public sector financial reporting.[26]

Fiscal reports should provide a comprehensive, relevant, timely, and reliable overview of the government's financial position and performance. Understanding the risk factors behind particular elements of government

Local governments in Sweden introduced accrual accounting in 1986 but are obliged to follow local government accounting standards, regardless of whether operations and assets are held directly by the city or via a corporate holding company. Swedish municipalities—in theory funded mainly by taxes and supposedly only holding assets to meet policy objectives—cannot file for bankruptcy and are strictly required to maintain a balanced budget. This aims to prevent the city from making a loss. However, if a loss should occur, it must be covered within three years, through the budget.

The Swedish government has proposed a new law that would allow local governments to fully consolidated their pension liabilities onto the balance sheet, but without allowing for a market valuation of the assets.[‡]

*Eurostat, Assessment of the suitability of the International Public Sector Accounting Standards for the Member States—Swedish response, May 2012.

†Swedish Parliament (website), Svensk författningssamling, 1997:614, Lag (1997:614) om kommunal redovisning [Swedish Code of Statutes, 1997:614, Law on Municipal Accounting] (www.riksdagen.se/sv/dokument-lagar/dokument/svensk-forfattningssamling/lag-1997614 -om-kommunal-redovisning_sfs-1997-614).

‡Government of Sweden (website), "En ändamålsenlig kommunal redovisning" [Expedient municipal accounting], official report of the Government of Sweden, document no. SOU 2016:24 (www.regeringen.se/rattsdokument/statens-offentliga-utredningar/2016/03/sou-201624/).

assets and liabilities is very helpful in assessing fiscal risks and the solvency of public finances.

The global financial crisis also demonstrated the need for a risk-based approach to fiscal policymaking that applies a systematic analysis of potential sources of fiscal vulnerabilities, currently outside of the normal budget. This would include potential external shocks such as a decline in macroeconomic activity, with its consequences for tax and benefits, as well as acknowledging fiscal exposures to the banking sector, public commercial assets (including government-owned enterprises), and local governments.

A public sector balance sheet would be able to capture this risk exposure and quantify and publish specific fiscal risks such as guarantees and other contingent liabilities, as outlined in the third pillar of the IMF's Fiscal Transparency Code and the related evaluations.[27]

Again, New Zealand is ahead in this respect: the Public Finance Act 1989 requires that its Statement of Specific Fiscal Risks set out, to the fullest extent possible, all government decisions and other circumstances known to the government at the date of the finalization of the fiscal forecasts that may have a material effect on the fiscal and economic outlook, but are not certain enough in timing or amount to be included in the fiscal forecasts.[28]

A PROPER PUBLIC SECTOR BALANCE SHEET AS A PROMOTER OF ECONOMIC GROWTH

Amid discussions over the lukewarm worldwide economic recovery after the Great Recession of 2008, it is commonly claimed that infrastructure investment financed by new debt could stimulate growth. The worry with this otherwise good idea is that funds will be squandered on assets that do not generate sufficient value.

A public sector balance sheet would be an excellent instrument to bring into this discussion. It would provide the data to answer the question, how do new investments affect public sector net worth? The debt would rise, but assets in the form of capital stock would no doubt also increase. And if these investments are cannily managed, monitored, and maintained, the potential earnings capacity of the economy would rise in the future—leading to a stronger primary fiscal balance.

The measure of net worth in a credible balance sheet could be an invaluable tool for coordinating efforts to boost economic growth. Although every city has different circumstances, the net worth reflected would provide insight as to where such infrastructure investments could be most effective in generating real public wealth. Currently, this discussion is mostly political. A public sector balance sheet would also greatly improve transparency about the risks a city is running with its combined liability and asset structure. Even the liability side needs to be accounted for better.

DEBT, THE WHOLE DEBT, AND NOTHING BUT THE DEBT

Since the Asian financial crisis in the late 1990s, more attention is being paid to debt issued by central governments. Most countries have also consolidated liability management under one centralized national debt office. However, both national and local governments still focus on ratios such as gross debt to GDP, which provides no information about the ability of the government to service the debt nor the efficient use of the funds.

Although local government bankruptcies are not a widespread problem, many struggle to meet the needs of their residents. The concern, as *Governing* magazine put it, is "the ones on the edge—the 'distressed cities' . . . that likely will never declare bankruptcy but are nonetheless struggling to become economically viable again." There are myriad examples of municipalities and counties in serious enough fiscal distress to erode critical services and hamper the community's ability to thrive.[29]

The perception in the United States is that municipalities have rarely defaulted on their debt and actually have to seek permission to file for bankruptcy. As a consequence, municipal debt is regarded as having an extremely low risk for investors. Over the past sixty years, only sixty-four counties, cities, towns, and villages have filed for bankruptcy.[30] That is in part by design, as twenty-one states do not allow local governments to file for bankruptcy, and several others place conditions on these filings.[31] However, several prominent recent cases of municipal bankruptcies since New York City in the late 1970s have slowly changed the perception of local government risk. These bankruptcies include Stockton, San Bernardino, and San Jose in California; Jefferson County, Alabama; Harrisburg and Scranton in Pennsylvania; and, most recently, Detroit.

The combination of the weak U.S. economy, high municipal debt levels, and large underfunded pension liabilities coupled with unfunded retiree health benefits raises the need for both local governments and states to improve their ability to monitor fiscal risk and their financial well-being in a much more professional way.

State governments should have a keen interest in the fiscal health of local governments. James Spiotto, a lawyer specializing in municipal distress, stated when he testified before Congress that although states do not necessarily take on the financial liabilities of local governments, they are ultimately responsible for the disposition of failed municipalities. In other words, "The state is always going to be responsible if the local government fails. The state is the parent."[32]

The United States also faces colossal fiscal pressures, including mounting public pension obligations. However, state governments currently cannot use the federal bankruptcy system to reorganize their collective debt. Also, the U.S. Constitution prohibits state governments from "impairing the obligation of contracts." As originally understood and enforced, this clause prohibits state legislatures from passing laws to relieve any debt, private or public.[33]

Puerto Rico is an incorporated U.S. territory that has been struggling with a high debt burden. Much of the debt is in the form of municipal bonds issued by the Puerto Rico government and its various agencies and utilities to help cover revenue shortfalls and current expenses. The debt is tax-exempt for investors throughout the United States and pays higher yields than other municipal bonds. This made it attractive to investors, despite the increasing financial troubles of the island; in fact, the good yields could be part of the reason Puerto Rico amassed so much debt.

Unlike American cities such as Detroit, Puerto Rico is not allowed to file for a court-arranged bankruptcy reorganization. And unlike sovereign nations such as Greece, it can't seek emergency assistance from the International Monetary Fund. That is why it has asked Congress to give it extraordinary powers to reduce its debt without declaring bankruptcy (which it cannot do).

The current financial pressure has led to a series of debates on bankruptcy processes, including a debate about whether states should be allowed to file for bankruptcy. Some argue that passing a federal law allowing states to declare bankruptcy would increase interest rates, rattle investors, raise the costs of state government, and create more volatility in financial markets. Either way, local governments and American states would benefit immediately from improved transparency that would result from such a federal law. Others argue it would take Washington to introduce legislation that forces U.S. cities and state governments to audit their debts, thereby making their finances accessible, as well as to create a process that would enable municipal debtors and creditors to find a collective solution to excessive debt situations, rather than a piecemeal approach.[34]

In the absence of accounting methods such as those that are used internationally by the private sector and by a few national and local governments, the understanding is still limited as to the extent of total public debt, including that of government at all levels of government-owned enterprises and other commercial assets—indeed, even the central bank (the Fed is not owned by the state, but the state is its beneficial owner). Furthermore, the extent of future liabilities that the public sector has committed to with regard to pensions is just beginning to be discussed at a political level, but in the absence of reliable financial data.

Absent a consolidated balance sheet, such financial data are viewed piecemeal, both overlapping and falling between chairs of responsibility and accountability. The situation is becoming serious: we have witnessed the severe consequences of inability to keep promises made in Detroit. Other U.S. cities and states currently suffer under the severe pressure of too much debt.

CONSOLIDATING ASSETS AND ACCOUNTS
It is a given that administrative divisions between various levels of governments are often complex. Despite the challenge of this complexity, local governments would benefit from the consolidation of both accounts and asset management at some level to clarify responsibility and accountability.

Complex ownership can lead to serious mismanagement, such as in the example of New Jersey's Pulaski Skyway: repairs and maintenance were not done because neither side took responsibility or was held accountable. Other examples of potential mismanagement or years-long inaction are land parcels—often located along a waterfront—that have federal, state, and city owners. Gathering all relevant assets under the umbrella of a holding company with a pro-rata ownership would force all entities involved to settle any differences upfront, instead of having the lack of clarity continue to shape the day-to-day management and decisionmaking process. This holding-company-as-umbrella concept has been used successfully in Europe by many real estate developments in and around harbor areas and other waterfronts, as well as areas around railway stations (described in detail in later chapters).

In the United States, New York has been on the forefront of consolidating the management of vital commercial assets, although commercial and policy objectives are often in play, too, which makes their approach less effective than it might be, and brings with it a high risk of mismanaging public funds. One such example is Empire State Development (ESD), the umbrella organization for New York's various economic development public-benefit corporations and its nine subsidiaries. Its stated goal is to create and retain jobs, particularly in distressed areas, and to undertake projects that would not be financially or organizationally feasible for the private sector alone. Since 1997, over 9,300 projects have been approved, totaling more than $8.3 billion in grants and $2.8 billion in loans. ESD issued more than $17 billion in state-supported debt to finance state projects, including correctional facilities, youth centers, sports facilities, technology centers, and community enhancement facilities.[35]

ESD also formed the Lower Manhattan Development Corporation (LMDC) in November 2001, just a few months after the September 11 attacks, to plan the reconstruction of the World Trade Center site and distribute nearly $10 billion in federal funds aimed at rebuilding downtown Manhattan. However, the LMDC did not originally own the World Trade Center, which created some problems in its dealings with the Port Authority of New York and New Jersey and Larry Silverstein, a private property developer who had recently acquired the lease to the site.[36] Recently, the largest private real estate development in the United States, Hudson Yard, is also being built, partly thanks to significant tax breaks and city funding. These examples show how U.S. development corporations often are not given a clear mandate to generate value, but instead pursue vague policy directives that open the gate to political meddling and inefficient use of public funds.

The line between politics and business often seems less clear in the United States. For example, ESD is empowered to act as both a public body and a commercial entity, issuing bonds and notes, granting loans and, acquiring private property, but also issuing tax exemptions, exercising the right of eminent domain, and overriding local laws, ordinances, codes, charters, and regulations such as zoning.[37] Like all New York State public-benefit corporations, it can issue bonds without a voter referendum, bypassing the state's constitutional limits.[38]

The Port Authority of New York and New Jersey is another hybrid: a quasi-commercial government vehicle with a mixed mandate. It has its origin in the fact that New York was the main point of embarkation for U.S. troops and supplies sent to Europe during World War I. The government saw the need for an agency to supervise and regulate the extremely complex system of bridges, highways, subways, and port facilities in the New York–New Jersey area and to manage the logistical challenges. The result was the creation of the Port Authority in 1921, under the supervision of the governors of the two states. It became the first bi-state agency in the United States.[39]

The Port Authority was initially set up to be financially independent of both states by being able to issue its own bonds. These are paid off from tolls and fees, not from taxes. Soon, this financial independence helped it to become one of the major agencies for the development of large-scale infrastructure projects.

With its multiple objectives the agency has built-in conflicts of interests, including commercial management of assets and acting as a supervisor-regulator of the same assets. On top of all this, it is also a law enforcement agency, with its own police force.

As a manager of commercial assets it is neither equipped with the required governance structure, including a clear objective of value maximization, nor the proper transparency. Furthermore, the ownership of many assets the Port Authority operates has not been transferred to it; they are still owned by city, state, and federal governments, making it impossible for the agency to manage the assets professionally. With fragmented responsibility and accountability, transparency is often the first casualty, with the risk of mismanagement and corruption not far behind.

Not surprisingly, the Port Authority is subject to constant criticism regarding both its management of assets and its business operations, as well as the lack of democratic accountability.[40] Apart from the assets it operates but does not own, it also does have a real estate portfolio, but value maximization of the portfolio is not its sole objective. The Port Authority remains a highly politicized body, where any real estate sale will always be complicated by the perceived benefit to politicians on either side of the Hudson River.[41]

The administrative structure is outdated and inappropriate as an instrument to carry out a commercial objective. The importance of such a portfolio of commercial assets to the metropolitan area and U.S. economy warrants the best possible professional governance in order to help make the region and the nation more competitive with the rest of the world. Professional management of commercial assets could also help fund further infrastructure investments and much-needed maintenance.

Instead, the lack of proper financial management and transparency, such as the unfunded pension liabilities of $81 billion plus total liabilities of $28 billion on total assets of only $44 billion, presents an apparent fiscal risk to the local governments involved, and potentially to the federal government.

Many of the Port Authority's operations are seen as performing at substandard levels. The New York airports often get rated as some of the worst airports in the world. The commercial management of the portfolio compares badly not only with equivalent assets in the private sector, but also with other public sector owners.

The obvious remedy would be to break up the Port Authority into its three constituent parts: asset management, supervisor-regulator, and law enforcement. This way, New York could once again lead the way in progressive institutional development. Transferring all commercial assets into a commercial holding company, with proper governance, transparency, and a clear objective of value maximization, would make it possible to help develop the portfolio and the entire metropolitan area into a truly competitive region.

In the next chapter we will look more closely at how such a more independent governance of city assets can be implemented.

CHAPTER 5

The Urban Wealth Fund:
A Conduit for Maximizing Value

EVEN POOR CITIES own large swaths of commercial assets. Most of these cities could be well served by more professional governance of these portfolios of assets. "Commercial assets" means mainly operational and real estate assets. The most visible part of the portfolio consist of operational assets including incorporated or non-incorporated activities such as electricity and water utilities, waste management, and transportation-related infrastructure such as ports, airports, and mass transit systems. Less visible, but almost always more important from a value perspective, is the real estate portion. Real estate assets generally make up the lion's share of the portfolio's value.

In the United States publicly owned water utilities serve 87 percent of people who have piped-in water service.[1] More than 60 percent of all electricity providers are publicly owned electric utilities; the providers provide more than 15 percent of the electricity generated and sold inside the country.[2]

On the transportation side, all commercial airports but one are government owned, and these account for more than 7 percent of national GDP and employ more than 6 percent of the country's workforce.[3] Most of the ports in the United States are owned by the public sector; they handle almost 95 percent of the nation's imports. Almost a third of GDP is derived from international trade, the bulk of which is waterborne.

It is easy to see that these publicly owned operational assets form the backbone of the U.S. economy, and their effectiveness is crucial for economic growth and the well-being of the entire country. Real estate assets, though less visible, are also a vital part of the U.S. economy. They make up the largest slice of the public portfolio of commercial assets in economic value terms. In addition, many cities continuously undertake strategic acquisition and administration of tax-delinquent residential and commercial properties, which adds to the size of this portfolio, although they have little capacity to manage the portfolio professionally. Nevertheless, the portfolio has significant impact on the local economy.

The main challenge to maintaining and developing vital infrastructure is to identify when and where to expand capacity, and to determine how to fund such development. We argued in the previous chapter that a crucial first step is a proper understanding of the city's balance sheet. With this in hand, taxpayers, politicians, and investors can better recognize the long-term financial consequences of political decisions and make choices to mobilize returns instead of to levy more taxes, increase debt, or impose austerity measures.

But understanding a city's balance sheet will not do the trick by itself. Unlocking the value of public assets as a core urban strategy requires professional expertise: investment specialists with some measure of independence in day-to-day operations from all special interests that try to influence city politics. In other words, the key to unlocking this wealth lies in the distinction and separation of governance of commercial assets from a city's other policy and governance functions.

Achieving a reasonable yield on publicly owned commercial assets could free more resources than most cities' total current investment in infrastructure, including roads, railroads, bridges, water, electricity, and broadband. As demonstrated earlier, most cities could more than double their investments with smarter use of their commercial assets.

Managing the city assets smartly through our proposed urban wealth funds, managed at arm's length from short-term political influence, will enable cities to ramp up much needed infrastructure investments, as well as reduce fiscal risk.

PUBLICLY OWNED COMMERCIAL ASSETS

This idea rests on one key calculation: governments around the world have an estimated $75 trillion of public commercial assets—roughly equivalent to GDP and ranging from government-owned enterprises and real estate—which are often badly managed and frequently not even accounted for on their balance sheets.[4] A higher return of just 1 percent on this portfolio of global public commercial assets would add some $750 billion to global public revenues (see figure 5-1).

Commercial assets owned by governments can be a goldmine way beyond the obvious assets, public enterprises and official building, and include a mass of less visible assets. Many pieces of this vast portfolio—such as buildings for what was once used for telephone exchanges, post offices, heavy industries along the waterfront for easy access to transportation as well as vast spaces formerly used for administrative work—predate the arrival of modern technology and can be put to new uses. Abandoned sites, undeveloped land, and brownfield spaces, if professionally managed, can be made into attractive and valuable assets, as can the land in harbor areas or around and above railway tracks and stations.

Giant retail firms such as Walmart, Tesco, and IKEA own vast real estate portfolios and are active investors and developers of both residential, office, and retail properties. The stock market value of Tesco indicates that investors value it as a real estate developer with a lesser retail operation attached, as this retail operation actually has a negative value compared to the value of the property portfolio. The same could perhaps be claimed for cities. If cities' commercial portfolios were transparent and professionally managed, cities could be seen as investment companies with a wide range of holdings of real estate assets and operational enterprises, helping to fund a lesser welfare division.

In subsequent chapters we provide international examples of cities that have funded important parts of their transport infrastructure through professional development of their real estate assets, as well as contributed to the welfare of future generations and consequently enabled to lower taxes and reduce debt.

Figure 5-1. *Global Wealth Segments*

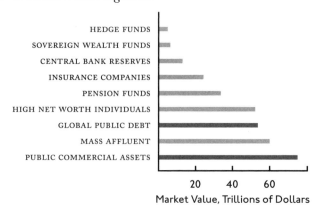

Source: Dag Detter and Stefan Fölster, *The Public Wealth of Nations* (London: Palgrave Macmillan, 2015), p. 53.

THE REAL ESTATE CHALLENGE

Real estate is often the largest part of a government's commercial portfolio, and it presents the biggest challenges. The first challenge is that of pulling together a proper balance sheet of the entire portfolio of real estate assets. Transparency for this segment requires first of all a modern cadastral map—a land register map showing land ownership and as many further details about the property as possible. A cadastral map shows the ownership of land parcels and provides unique identifying numbers for parcels, certificate of title numbers, and positions of existing structures. The cadaster is a fundamental source of data in claiming legal title to a piece of property for the purpose of a mortgage or the resolution of disputes and lawsuits between landowners.[5] But many city cadastral maps are incomplete, which makes the compilation of a list of city-owned real estate more challenging. A modern alternative might be to use block-chain technology to replace traditional land registries and serve as an open source of information administration of both public and private land. Block-chain technology does not allow any single authority or user of the cadaster to manipulate its contents without consent from the other main participants. In this way it can provide some protection from corruption or illegal leakage of assets to other owners.

The United Kingdom is generally regarded as one of the pioneers in public accounting and transparency, yet real estate owned by many government entities is not even included in the Land Registry. A case in point is the National Health Service, the government-owned health service provider. Furthermore, the NHS does not have a proper understanding of its property portfolio, despite the fact that it may be one of the largest property owners in the country. With a better understanding of where the assets and what potential they have the NHS could most likely begin to manage its balance sheet more professionally and thereby hope to solve its financial problems. The redevelopment of St. Bartholomew's Hospital in London offers an example of the potential value that rests within these assets—and the types of transformative investments that returns on those assets can enable.[6]

ASCERTAINING THE REAL VALUE OF REAL ESTATE

Fully embracing the term "commercial" in the phrase "public commercial assets" opens up a whole new line of thinking. Such assets should be viewed the same as if they were privately owned, having value maximization as the sole objective of any decisionmaking about them. The opposite—treating commercial assets as political instruments—distorts competition, investments, economic growth, and ultimately consumers' interests. Misallocation of public capital inevitably leads to waste, corruption, and crony capitalism.

Local governments often fail to recognize the market value of their real estate and consequently lack incentives to maximize value. Once acquired, real estate has typically not been recorded at all or else has been depreciated according to book value that has no relation to market value. The cost associated with the original development of these assets was often booked so long ago that there is no perceived need to maximize the return on the original investment.

Every penny generated from an increase in yield is a penny less that must be wrung from budgetary cuts or increases in taxation (see figure 5-2). Any government spending review should, in parallel, determine the extent to which additional yield can be generated from the government's asset portfolio.

Figure 5-2. *Better Management of Public Assets Can Generate Big Returns*

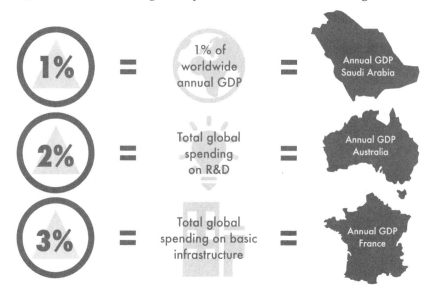

Source: Authors' calculations.

Fully effective exploitation of public commercial assets should be transparent, and the implicit opportunity costs should be made visible to the public services and government departments using these assets. It is crucial to understand how to put each one to its most productive and best use, or at least make visible the cost of using the asset in a sub-optimal way.

INSTITUTING PROFESSIONAL ASSET MANAGEMENT IN CITIES

Some real estate assets in a city are not immediately understood as having a commercial value because they are the locus of activities related to public policy, such as schools or hospitals. Even if a city has no intention of changing the function carried out in a building, it still benefits from separating the value of real estate assets from the policy activity using the property. The real estate regarded independently could be considered as a commercial asset, with only a contractual relationship between the asset and operation.

Figure 5-3. *Rio de Janeiro's Escola Municipal Cícero Pena (far right), Flanked by Five-Star High-Rise Hotels*

Escola Municipal Cícero Pena is a public school in Rio de Janeiro, Brazil, located right on Avenida Atlantica, the famous stretch facing the Copacabana beach. Surrounded by high-rise five-star hotels, on perhaps the most expensive land in the country, is suddenly this school, dwarfed by all the surrounding real estate (see figure 5-3).

This property is being used by an activity that, though socially important, could be located a couple of blocks away on much cheaper land in an environment perhaps more beneficial to the students' learning. Such relocation would release the property occupied by the school for use with the highest market value, while still being owned by the city. Such a change would no doubt improve the general welfare because it would raise city income while affording the government the possibility to build an equivalent or better school with part of the revenue from developing the more valuable property.[7]

These kinds of opportunities abound, but they are often not taken advantage of in a comprehensive way because political and administrative institutions are not geared toward exploring how public assets can generate greater value, nor do they have the information at hand that would enable such planning and professional asset management. That outcome requires a more systematic approach with some kind of professional engagement. Examples of successful relocations and redevelopment of attractive properties include famous cases such as the Ministry of Finance in Paris, which up until 1986 occupied what is now the Museum of the Louvre. The Lanesborough Hotel, a five-star hotel opposite Hyde Park and reputedly the most expensive hotel in London, was originally built as St. George's Hospital in 1733. The existing building was ready and operational by 1844 and served as such for more than a hundred years. In the 1970s the hospital was moved out of Central London, leaving the house vacant for years. A hotel chain eventually purchased and renovated the empty building and opened the facilities as The Lanesborough Hotel in 1991.

Many opportunities may not be as glamorous as these examples, but could nevertheless present even greater economic benefits to society. Such forward-looking development of public assets can be even more important in the coming decades. For example, self-driving vehicles may require municipal investments, but they also have the potential to free road and parking space that a city government can turn into valuable commercial or residential property.

One of the crucial prerequisites for opening this path to a higher degree of financial independence for the city is the creation of a public sector balance sheet for the city itself, a process that treats the city more like a commercial enterprise. This is not a new idea nor is it heretical or counterintuitive to the government's purpose as the purveyor of the common good. On the contrary. The ancient city-states of Athens and Sparta and the medieval versions in Florence and Venice had to rely on their wit and strong finances to survive and prosper. In fact, the historic center of London and the location of much of the U.K.'s financial sector even has this claim in its formal name, the City of London Corporation. It claims to be the world's oldest continuously elected local government body; both businesses and residents are entitled to vote in elections. The corporation is just one of thirty-two boroughs that make up the greater metropolis of London, but it has professionalism in managing its assets and finances rarely if ever seen in any other Western city or metropolis. Its professional approach mirrors that of the much larger and well-known successes of modern city-states in Asia, such as Hong Kong and Singapore.

With a proper understanding of the entire balance sheet of a city, also including contingent future commitments and revenues that are not normally capitalized and included among the liabilities of a city, taxpayers, politicians, and investors can better understand the consequences of long-term political decisions.[8]

DEVELOPING THE REAL ESTATE PORTFOLIO
AND MAXIMIZING VALUE

Proper accounting is the prerequisite to maximizing value of both operational and real estate assets.

With operational assets it is first of all important to benchmark the operational and financial efficiency with private sector peers to better understand the performance gap with the best-in-class. Second, proper accounting allows the government to optimize the capital structure and set up a relevant dividend policy, in line with its private sector competitors. Third, through business development it will maintain the focus on the core business and invest only when profitable. This has proved to be an important strategy, as government-owned operations tend to become unwieldy conglomerates with a poor allocation of capital and overburdened by non-core assets. The reason that government-owned enterprises end up a hoarders of assets with poor return on capital is partly because they can only raise additional equity through a very painstaking political process in which their commercial requirement for additional capital will compete with the need for social spending and other public welfare requirements. Consequently, leaders of government-owned enterprises are incentivized to minimize earnings in order to avoid paying dividends altogether. To be sure, there are endless ways to show a loss and avoid paying dividends, including diversifying and making investments regardless of whether they will give a positive return or not and then cross-subsidizing within the group. The result is that public enterprises often end up as ill-defined and opaque operations with poor return on capital and wasteful capital allocation.

In the context of publicly owned real estate, value maximization can be achieved through a similar process making the best use of each asset and the portfolio as a whole, through a process starting with commercialization and optimization, and ultimately with a potential rationalization. Commercialization requires that a comprehensive business plan assess all assets, including assets that are unused, used by third parties, or directly used in the provision of public services, but that can either be relocated to more cost-effective and beneficial locations, or used to generate ancillary income, such as through additional or alternative use of the property.

A second focus should be optimization of economies of scale to be achieved across the entire portfolio, as well as with each real estate segment, not just maximization of yield from each individual asset.

Third, rationalization assumes a professional capacity to develop assets to reach their best use and potential. Developing a portfolio also requires the skill of determining which assets have reached maturity, meaning that they have reached a fair value, and therefore can be sold in order to use the proceeds to reinvest in assets that are capable of yielding a higher return. Mature assets could be disposed of at the relevant point in the market cycle, as part of the broader business plan for maximization of yield across the entire portfolio, but not in isolation as this could lead to similar destruction of value as in a fire sale. Monies generated from rationalization of activities should first be made available as a source of funding for achievement of the business plan and could ultimately be used to fund other government requirements such as infrastructure investments.

THE BALANCE SHEET: PREREQUISITE OF AN INDEPENDENT URBAN WEALTH FUND

The call for better management of commercial assets raises the obvious question as to why government departments charged with managing the entity's assets have not done it better already. The reality is that governments have for decades made continuous attempts to improve management of their commercial assets, within the structures of government.[9]

A government bureaucracy within the government structure is, however, simply not designed to manage commercial risk, since its purpose is the direct opposite, to avoid risk. The whole purpose behind the invention of the limited liability company was to encourage further entrepreneurial activity by limiting investors' risk to the actual amount of money invested in the company. By the same token, a way must be found to distance a city from commercial and financial risk and thereby also limit fiscal risk. A city administration not only lacks a proper balance sheet, which is required to understand the concept of financial risk in the first place, but is also lacks the mandate, institutional setup, and capacity to take on administrate commercial risk.

Separating the management of commercial assets from the short-term political cycle has important benefits for the government and the economy in general. First, the separation between regulation and ownership of commercial assets inside the government administration helps the government create a more level playing field within each sector. Second, placing the financial risk in a dedicated balance sheet in a ring-fenced vehicle at arm's length distance from short-term political interference, while maintaining government ownership, minimizes the fiscal risk the portfolio of commercial assets represents to the government and the economy.

Third, the ability to use a balance sheet allows for much closer alignment of the life cycle of the assets with the management of the investments, to the benefit of the economy and the entire society. The initial costs of an asset, such as design and construction, are usually only a fraction of the total cost over its entire life, with the main costs being maintenance and operations. Since the life of most assets such as real estate is measured in decades rather than years, it is vital to align the management of such long-term projects with the life cycle of the assets rather than the life cycle of the significantly shorter political term, in order to secure the necessary investment in maintenance.

Cutting the ribbon of a new project might have political advantages, while spending valuable taxpayer money on maintenance of assets when the benefits are not visible is politically risky—unless you have a balance sheet to demonstrate that you have used the money wisely and increased net wealth. Managing such expenses is better turned over to professional investment managers incentivized to maintain or increase the net worth of assets.

PUBLIC-PRIVATE PARTNERSHIPS: MORE CONS THAN PROS

Cities and governments sometimes engage in commercial ventures directly with the private sector through public-private partnerships (PPPs). This can end up being more expensive for the public entity and hence the taxpayers than is originally perceived.

PPPs involve a contract between a public sector authority and a private party, in which the private party takes on the management responsibility to provide a public service or undertake a construction project and as such assumes contractually a substantial financial, technical, and operational risk. The concept has been criticized since it started to become popular in the early 1990s. The main criticism is the ability to take what is essentially government debt off the public sector balance sheet, to what are often more expensive covert obligations.

Overall, the situation exacerbates the inadequacies of government accounting.

Another problem with this type of financing is that it lays bare the inability of a government bureaucracy to manage commercial risk. Due to its inherent commercial incapacity, the government is due to give away risk to the private sector partner. This results in a potentially correspondingly larger profit for the private partner, while the public sector partner often is left with the ultimate financial risk should the project fail.[10]

The inability of the public sector to oversee, manage, and negotiate long-term commercial contracts with vast commercial and financial consequences means that the public sector often loses considerably, with the subsequent political criticism from the public about the use of taxpayer money to enrich the private sector.

History has shown that negotiating these contacts requires the very commercial skills that are lacking in a political organization. This is why the results of such arrangements have been quite mixed and would ideally require the kind of professional organization that is represented by an independent holding company set up for the sole purpose of managing commercial assets while retaining public ownership. And this needed type of professional organization is the urban wealth fund.

A BETTER WAY TO MANAGE COMMERCIAL ASSETS: FUNDAMENTALS OF AN URBAN WEALTH FUND

The best way for a local government to manage commercial assets is instead to put them into a type of commercial holding company called an urban wealth fund (UWF). A UWF is an incorporated holding company that acts as a professional steward of public commercial assets and is maintained at arm's length from short-term political interference. The idea of a professional steward of public assets, maintained outside of the government bureaucracy, is not new. It has been used for centuries.

One of its earliest examples is the Swedish Kammarkollegiet, established in 1539 by King Gustav Vasa as an effort to further strengthen the country's financial management and newly won independence from its debtors and military foes in the Hanseatic League. The Kammarkollegiet was charged with a number of tasks by the government, including managing and increasing the wealth of its financial assets.[11] Today it is the oldest public agency still active in Sweden. An even earlier example of the need for external management is the sanctuary on the island of Delos in the fifth century B.C., which acted as the common asset manager for Athens and its allies in the war against Persia.

Properly structured, a UWF can be charged with developing and managing assets and realizing their best value through potential sales that maximize long-term economic value consistent with the principles of rationality, public interest, and transparency. The holding company is also a better vehicle to improve the management and access to debt financing and potentially reduce the fiscal risk and the cost of borrowing in the capital markets—for financing infrastructure projects or other commercial ventures.

The professional independence of a UWF is bolstered by the clear objective of maximizing value and ensuring it acts openly and transparently. This is to demonstrate it is truly responsible and held accountable for the management of the portfolio and remains free of short-term government meddling, in order to gain credibility with stakeholders and the international capital markets.

As with a government pension fund that invests in a private equity fund and contracts with the "general partners," a government owner of commercial assets can hire professional "corporate governors" to achieve more efficient utilization of their invested capital and higher returns.

Active governance is not simply a question of avoiding waste, corruption, the influence of vested interests, and crony capitalism. Maximizing value means developing the business using a competitive operational strategy that is funded by an optimal capital structure with the aim of yielding financial returns similar to comparable assets in the private sector. The gap in yield otherwise seen between a publicly owned company and its private competitor is a loss of income to taxpayers.

FUNDAMENTAL PRINCIPLES OF PROFESSIONAL ASSET MANAGEMENT

In a market economy, the government acts only as an independent referee aiming to reduce monopoly profits and inefficiencies, lowering prices for end-users, increasing investment and productivity, and encouraging competition in the sector. This stance is irreconcilable with the government having direct involvement in commercial enterprises that risk crowding out private sector initiatives. If the government nevertheless does own commercial assets it needs to pay special attention to three fundamental principles in order to mitigate this contradiction and conflict of interest: transparency, clear objective, and political independence.

1. **Transparency.** Achieving the same standards of transparency for the UFW and its portfolio of holdings as for a listed holding company.

2. **Clear objective.** Having value maximization is the sole objective. Policy objectives are outsourced through a competitive procurement process and paid directly by the government.

3. Political independence. The UWF and the portfolio are kept at arm's length from short-term political influence.

These three principles are connected; like the spokes of a wheel, all must be equally strong and tight in order for the wheel to turn smoothly and with least wear. Otherwise the wheel soon bends. Political independence without transparency will create a behemoth lacking checks and balances; political independence without a clear objective becomes a wrecking ball against fair competition and efficient capital allocation. Keeping a clear objective is not possible without both transparency and political independence. Each principle must be carefully reflected in the governance structure and continuously upgraded and refined with the test of time.

TRANSPARENCY

Transparency and disclosure are essential components in any modern corporate governance framework. They are the map to improving quality and effectiveness of oversight. This includes applying international standards for accounting and financial reporting, as well as being subject to annual external audits.

Transparency is also a prerequisite to assign responsibility and accountability for operational efficiency, capital structure, and a competitive business model. Having the relevant information in the open and accessible by the general public is the best insurance against assets being captured by vested interests. Using a private sector holding company enables the government to borrow the tools from the private sector and take advantage of hard-earned governance experiences developed over centuries.

A critic might argue that the private sector is not the ideal role model to learn from as it seems to be delivering a never-ending stream of booms, busts, and corporate scandals. But these could instead be seen as a sign of progress, analogous to the way the medical profession is improving its ability to detect and treat illnesses and injuries. Hiding and keeping quiet about a tumor will not improve the survival rate, nor return the body to health.

Transparency concerning the commercial assets of a city should reflect the highest international accounting standards and be no different than that of a listed company, since this is truly a public asset. IFRS accounting standards should hence be used for the consolidated annual report of the UWF, as well as every subsidiary holding. Each annual report should provide a fair picture of the development of the portfolio, every major holding, its commercial activities, financial position, and bottom line in accordance with laws and accepted practice in the private sector. An example of such transparency can be found with Solidium, the national wealth fund in Finland, or Temasek, the UWF of Singapore, or listed private sector investment companies such as Industrivärden and Investor AB in Sweden.[12]

All financial relationships between the government and public holdings, including government guarantees and other warranties, should also be transparent to ensure the efficient use of government funds, enable the assessment of total fiscal risk, and prevent corruption.

CLEAR OBJECTIVE

Pursuing a single objective, such as value maximization, is the most effective way of achieving a target, be it strategic, commercial, or financial. Before the distinction was made between commercial assets and policy assets, use of public assets often had multiple goals, such as acting as an employment resource and providing goods and services at below-market price, while pretending to be for profit. Not surprisingly, this ultimately led to market failures, bankruptcy, and a constant replenishment of fresh equity, using tax money. For example, the government-controlled mortgage companies Fannie Mae and Freddie Mac blend political objectives and value maximization, which is a root reason why a bailout was needed after the fiscal crisis of 2007–08.

A clear objective for a commercial asset is to embrace, implement, and communicate value maximization as the sole objective for the public portfolio of commercial assets. A clearly defined and quantifiable objective is the prerequisite for any owner to align his interest with the company's, from the board to management and every employee. Multiple and even contradictory objectives for a commercial asset or enterprise means unclear results and ultimately losing the way. When Alice in Wonderland asks the Cheshire Cat, "Would you tell me, please, which way I ought to go from here?" the Cat says, "That depends a good deal on where you want to get to." Alice's reply, "I don't much care where," prompts the Cat's entirely reasonable response: "Then it doesn't matter which road you take."

Being focused and knowing your targets is everything—in business, in sports, in life. What's more, you want to get there as efficiently as possible. Strolling around aimlessly without a map is fine if you are on vacation, but is a huge waste of taxpayer money for a government-owned business.

A clear objective is also fundamental for transparency and oversight. Easily quantifiable targets allow corporate governors to measure financial performance.

In the event that a government wants a commercial company operating in a deregulated sector to carry out a policy objective that cannot be sufficiently covered by user fees, such as the universal service obligation for a post office, this should be viewed as a subsidy that should be procured in an open competition among several bidders, in order to ensure the most efficient use of taxpayers' money. For example, a public railroad such as Amtrak should be explicitly paid to inherently loss-making routes only if procurement of such services is carried out in competition. If ultimately carried out by a government-owned enterprise, these aims must be made transparent without confusing them with the objective of value maximization.

POLITICAL INDEPENDENCE

A separation between commercial assets and policy assets is the first fundamental political decision, paving the way for the professional management of commercial assets. These two different types of assets require completely different types of governance and management capabilities. Policy assets can be managed by civil servants with the relevant policy experience, within the governmental framework. Commercial assets, on the other hand, must be governed within a separate framework and management structure, away from short-term political influence, on similar terms as private sector competitors.

This is necessary to ensure a level playing field and avoid market distortions where publicly and privately owned assets compete in the same market. Commercial assets, regardless if public or private ownership, should all be subject to the same legal framework and requirements. Establishing a level playing field for private and publicly owned companies ensures that both are subject to the same legal framework, and that publicly owned commercial assets are also able to use all the tools of the private sector.

Additional steps to help strengthen political independence could include broadening the stakeholder base by raising debt based on an independent credit rating, as well ultimately listing the equity of each holding on the stock market when suitable.

The benefit of political independence of a UWF works in both direction. It also prevents the public commercial assets from competing at a disadvantage with the private sector and protects the political establishment from becoming embroiled in corporate troubles, as well as from the temptations of clientelism and corruption.

To solidify its independence, the UWF should operate under a corporate governance structure based on the highest international standards, where the directors of the company are entirely responsible and held accountable for the company's performance and for ensuring the efficient value creation and competitive yield of the portfolio.

Introducing an ownership policy that clearly establishes a chain of command that disseminates responsibility and accountability at every level of governance will help strengthen political insulation.[13] Outlining and making the limits of political involvement transparent, including its responsibility to set out the company vision, appoint external auditors, and nominate the non-executive directors is a crucial demarcation for establishing political independence. The policy could also state that any communication between the board, through its chair and representatives of the owner(s), should be limited to issues of critical importance and, if necessary, resolved through a resolution at the shareholders' meeting.

The strength of any governance structure is also dependent on the local legal and institutional framework where each legal tradition interprets the four basic governance functions—ownership, supervision, decisionmaking, and execution—differently.

Terms such as "director" and "board" have different meanings in different legal environments and can be misleading. Regardless of the terms used, the important thing is to set out a clear division of responsibility that can ensure proper supervision and checks and balances are maintained, and to prevent short-term political interference. Proper internal controls and competence is a key component for the UWF to demonstrates its independence, rather than relying on, or even being seen to rely on, the government as the ultimate guarantor of risk.[14]

HOW TO CREATE AN URBAN WEALTH FUND

Creating the fund is a four-step process:

1. Compile a list of assets and conduct an indicative valuation of the portfolio of assets that allows an informal review of the portfolio and attracts public support for professionalizing the management of the portfolio.

2. Set up a proper balance sheet that will form the basis of the first audited annual report, the starting point for the new board and management (an obvious first step for any private sector owner).[15]

3. Incorporate the fund, transfer all assets, and appoint a professional board and auditors, so that the government can fully delegate the management of the portfolio.

4. Produce a comprehensive business plan for the portfolio as a whole and for each underlying segment, such as real estate and government corporations, to understand how to put each asset to its most productive use, making clear the opportunity cost of using the asset in a suboptimal way.

Depending on the strength of political will, the process can start either with the incorporation of the fund or with the transparency initiative, which is the compilation of the list of assets. In practical terms it would be easier to set up the holding company first and let the appointed professionals manage the inventory of assets. However, in the absence of financial urgency, there may be a need to explain to the public that the city owns a whole range of commercial assets and that managing these properly requires an independent and more professional governance structure.

In order to obtain public support for a more professional management of the assets, it makes sense to produce and publish an annual report "lite," an unaudited brochure highlighting the total value and yield of the entire portfolio of commercial assets.[16]

APPOINTING AND EVALUATING THE BOARD

Along with actually transferring the legal ownership of the assets to the holding company, there needs to be an actual transfer of the legal responsibility and accountability for the assets to the board of the UWF. Subsequently, in addition, responsibility and accountability must be delegated by the UWF to the board of each enterprise they hold in their portfolio. This requires a professional and institutionalized nomination process that can win the confidence of all stakeholders that the ultimate selection criteria are based on merit and the relevant competence.

The optimal combination of competence will change over time, depending on the situation in the market and within the company. Therefore, a proper board nomination process not only must be based on a professional board evaluation but also must be grounded in the current business plan and adjusted as requirements change.

The performance and suitability of each director should be assessed once a year in a comprehensive evaluation process against the requirements of the business plan and market analysis. This evaluation can lead to changes in the composition of the board to ensure that relevant competences are always at hand and are aligned with objectives and the relevant market outlook.

Trust in the governance structure of the UWF rests in no small part on the independence and credibility of the supervisory function of the UWF board of directors, regardless of the legislative model. It is crucial for a functioning governance structure that this board be clearly established as the main body responsible for the portfolio. Unless this responsibility is fully vested and clearly understood and communicated, the government will not be able to transfer its responsibility for the assets, but will instead always be seen as ultimately responsible for the portfolio.

The credibility of the board is also dependent on the quality of the legal and regulatory framework. An economy underpinned by a weak legal system and government institutions makes it easier to appoint friends and family to the boards of public assets—reminiscent of the days when royal bequests of land were used to create allegiances and an additional source of income for an ally.

Conversely, in an economy dominated by a single political party, the nomination function becomes a tool to extend party influence; for example, the Organization Department of the Central Committee of the Chinese Communist Party retains the privilege of appointing the executive chairmen and top managers of government-owned companies and banks. In practice, the Organization Department appoints the party committee within each asset or bank. Because the chairmen of the party committees must be given senior roles, they tend to be appointed as the executive chairmen. The chairman and the party secretary often being one and the same, reports directly to the party rather than to the nominal owner—the government or holding company—while the supervisory board reports directly to the government entity responsible for the holding. Consequently, these boards are weak, and the combined power of chairman, CEO, and party head makes any ownership vehicle or holding company less effective.

By contrast, successful family businesses often share the ability to appoint the best possible managers to run their empires and the underlying holdings, limiting the influence of the wider family. This has not only helped preserve family fortunes over several generations and limits family disputes to sharing the dividends, but also insulates the owners from being directly implicated when scandals hit any of its holdings.

Board nominations can be used as a tool to help change the course of a company or even an entire portfolio. One such case was the restructuring of the Swedish government portfolio in 1998. Here active governance included introducing a more professional nomination process of non-executive directors and subsequently the senior management to each corporation. More than 85 percent of the non-executive board members and 75 percent of the CEOs as well as half of the CFOs in the portfolio were replaced over a three-year period, a total of several hundred people. One important factor that made possible this vast cultural transformation of the leadership from self-serving elite to dynamic group focused on serving the company was that almost 30 percent of the new leaders were women. This arose not from a misguided principle but from a desire to reinforce meritocracy and help change the corporate culture in the entire portfolio.[17]

In a political environment, controlling appointments is the backbone of a political platform. Therefore, giving up the ability to influence board appointments for a large corporate portfolio is perhaps the single biggest reason why politicians resist moving ownership away from the political domain. Even in developed economies with politicians otherwise keen to be seen as champions of meritocracy, the reluctance to relinquish control over this powerful tool persists. Politicians' focus on power and not on wealth creation might explain why this vast pool of wealth remains hidden and mismanaged.

It is time for this to change!

PROFESSIONAL MANAGEMENT

Apart from a board of directors legally responsible for the portfolio, the UWF also needs to attract the right business management talent to execute day-to-day business. To do this requires the relevant incentives to be in place in order to attract the best professionals. But even more fundamental to attracting topnotch professionals is recognition that the quality of the governance structure ensures management's independence from short-term political meddling and that the professionals who accept the challenge will actually be allowed to act with the best commercial interest in mind and answer only to a professional board. The winning combination for successful hiring of professionals is freedom to act and appropriate compensation for success.

In general, the challenges of setting up a UWF are similar to setting up a private equity fund, which is why there is much that can be learned from the private equity sector. The initial management team does not need to be very large: a limited group of around ten to fifteen professionals depending on the breadth of the portfolio, supported by external advisers able to assist on a project-by-project basis. The team could then grow over time at a measured pace, by taking on more functions internally that were previously outsourced. A UWF, like a private equity fund, should have the ability to compensate professionals at market rates. However, with a UWF having a political master, it should act responsibly and avoid being the market leader in pay compensation to avoid controversy with its ultimate owners, the taxpayers.

The senior management team is led by the chief executive officer (CEO), who is ultimately responsible for the execution of the strategy. The chief operating officer (COO) is responsible for compliance and risk management. The chief financial officer (CFO) should have a treasurer and a debt-structuring specialist on the team, as well as professionals with responsibility for investor relations and communications. The CFO must also oversee the fund's IT systems in order to have full control of the system used for accounting and cash management.

The portfolio should be divided into relevant sector teams for the operational side of the portfolio (for example, transportation, utilities, general industry) and the real estate (for example, residential, commercial, office, services, and so forth). Each sector team should consist of an investment executive and one or two investment managers. The team members should have international experience in the relevant industry, either as executives or as advisers with a professional service firm operating in the sector. A network of senior industrial advisers, with experience from the relevant industries, could also be a useful support to both the management and the board, also as non-executive directors on the boards of each holding.

Apart from being the actual owner of each asset, the UWF will act as a sounding board providing expertise and support so that each holding can grow and develop through the implementation of its business plan. Execution of strategies laid out for each portfolio company is the responsibility of the CEO of the holding. The board of each holding is best led by an independent non-executive chairman and other external non-executive members, with perhaps only one professional from the

UWF together with the relevant industrial adviser. For holdings listed on the stock exchange, the UWF might even benefit from refraining from a presence on the board and perhaps only nominate an industrial adviser from the network of advisers as a non-executive director.

Although the similarities are abundant in so many ways between a private equity firm and a UWF, the board and executive management of a UWF must maintain constant vigilance against short-term political influence.

CHAPTER 6

Succeeding with Urban Wealth Funds: Some Case Studies

MANY CITIES ARE MOVING in the right direction to improve transparency, with the local governments in New Zealand perhaps still being the most advanced, and Australia and U.K. close behind. Cities from Sweden to the Persian Gulf have used the holding company model for decades, with varying results and effects to society. A few cities stand out as especially successful in setting up independent and professional holding companies and urban wealth funds to manage their commercial wealth to the benefit of the entire community. In this chapter we spotlight some specific cases that are instructive.

SINGAPORE: TEMASEK

One of the world's leading urban wealth funds, Singapore's Temasek, is sometimes seen as an outlier and an almost impossible precedent to emulate. It has boasted an average annual financial return on assets of 15 percent since its inception in 1974 and has helped fund the development of the city-state and the net worth of the public sector balance sheet to the benefit of current and future generations.

With today's view of Singapore as a self-evident champion of good governance and wealth, it may be hard see it as an example worth studying and even harder to see it as a model to learn from. As with a star athlete who seems to be winning effortlessly, the hard struggle and grinding discipline it took to reach this stage gets much less attention. It is, however, worth remembering that Singapore was hardly a very promising place back when it first started its journey in the early 1960s. Rather, it was filled with more danger and risk than most cities face today.

At the time, few expected Singapore to survive, let alone prosper. As early as 1957, Singapore's first prime minister, Lee Kuan Yew, is often quoted as having said that the idea of a potentially independent Singapore was a "political, economic, and geographical absurdity." It is not hard to see why when you look at the situation of the small island at the tip of the Malaysian peninsula and just across the Malacca Strait from Indonesia, a territory of about 224 square miles at low tide—about the size of Greater Chicago and considerably smaller than New York City's 304 square miles. Singapore had no natural resources, no hinterland, no industry. It depended on the outside world not just for food and energy, but even for water.

In 1968, the British government announced a withdrawal of its troops from Singapore, leaving the city strategically vulnerable, and also leaving thousands of workers without a job and as much as a fifth of the economy at risk of grinding to a halt.

The new independent Singaporean government decided to make some strategic decisions sharply at odds with the conventional economic wisdom at the time: a shift away from import substitution in favor of export-led industrialization and attracting global multinational corporations as the vehicles to achieve industrial growth.

But Singapore did not only pursue a radical economic policy to generate economic growth and wealth. The government also made a commitment to provide three basic public services—housing, education, and health care—and to make them affordable for all citizens, with subsidies as needed to achieve this goal.

The Singapore Housing and Development Board (HDB), the public housing authority, committed to provide housing for all, had already been set up in 1960. Over time, poor-quality overcrowded housing and a mass of temporary self-help housing in unimproved squatter settlements was progressively cleared and replaced by high-rise accommodations and improved facilities in public housing estates and new towns. As a result, the public housing sector has grown to become the predominant housing sector, controlling the stock of affordable housing in Singapore. This has encouraged the formulation of public policies aimed at reducing the cost of housing and easing access to owner occupation in public housing, even for lower-income residents.

The proportion of the resident population living in public housing has risen to more than 80 percent, and 90 percent of residents own the flat they occupy.[1] HDB provides Singaporeans with affordable homes, through its role as the master planner and developer of Singapore's public housing estates. It also encourages Singaporeans to become home owners by subsidizing flats with price discounts for new flats and by offering a variety of housing grants and housing loans at concessionary interest rates to help eligible Singaporeans own their own homes. For needy Singaporeans, the HDB provides heavily subsidized rental flats.

HDB is also involved in commercial and industrial property development and management to provide a range of amenities and employment opportunities in HDB-owned towns.

SINGAPORE'S PROACTIVE, UNORTHODOX ECONOMIC STRATEGY

One decisive factor in Singapore's unorthodox economic strategy that resulted in such success was no doubt the idea of professionalizing the governance of commercial assets to independent holding companies, leaving the government free to focus on overarching economic issues. The Singaporean government took a proactive role in establishing government-owned enterprises in key sectors such as manufacturing, finance, trading, transportation, shipbuilding, and services. Early companies were the Keppel, Sembawang, and Jurong shipyards. Another example was Neptune Orient Lines, established as a shipping company to leverage the island's strategic location in one of the world's busiest passages between Europe and the Middle East and North Africa and East Asia. Some of the assets were consolidated under holding companies such as MND Holdings and Sheng-Li Holdings (now Singapore Technologies); others were directly held by the Ministry of Finance.

THE CREATION OF TEMASEK

Temasek was established in 1974 as a separate holding company, in order to enable the government to maximize long-term shareholder value, as an active investor and shareholder of commercial enterprises and real estate. Temasek consolidated under one roof all of the commercial assets owned by the government: existing holding companies and state-owned enterprises; previously existing monopolies and utilities that had recently incorporated and still resided within the respective ministries; and some real estate. Temasek was used to separate the regulatory and policymaking functions of government from its role as a shareholder of commercial entities (the role of providing public housing was left with HDB).

To maximize wealth and reduce risk, Temasek has expanded internationally through its initial holdings in other operational assets outside of Singapore, as well as making financial investments within its core sectors. In addition, it has diversified outside of its original core sectors. Today Temasek has major holdings in some seven sectors, including financial services; telecommunications, media, and technology; transportation and industrials; consumer and real estate; energy and resources; and life sciences and agriculture (see table 6-1).

Temasek's three largest holdings are Singtel (51 percent), DBS Group (30 percent), and China Construction Bank (5 percent), representing some 26 percent of the value of the portfolio.

The geographic diversification strategy has had the aim of reducing Temasek's dependence on Singapore itself and expanding across Asia. It is now very active in North America and Europe; Australia and New Zealand; Africa, Central Asia, and the Middle East; and Latin America (see table 6-2).

Temasek's Net Portfolio Value amounted to S$242 billion (US$194 billion) as of March 31, 2016. The total shareholder return in Singapore dollar terms for the year ended March 31, 2016, was 15 percent. Many of Temasek's holdings are now world-leading companies within their sector such as the telecom operator Singtel, DBS Bank, and PSA International, the port operator.

Singtel is the largest company by market capitalization listed on the Singapore Exchange. It controls 82 percent of the fixed-line market,

Table 6-1. *Temasek Distributions, by Sector, as Percentage of Total Distributions*

Sector	Percent 2014	2015	2016
Telecommunications, media, and technology	23	24	25
Financial services	30	28	23
Transportation and industrials	20	17	18
Consumer and real estate	12	15	17
Life sciences and agriculture	2	3	4
Energy and resources	6	5	3
Multisector funds	5	5	7
Other (including credit)	2	3	3

Source: Temasek Review 2016 (www.temasekreview.com.sg).
Note: Distribution based on underlying assets, as of March 31 of each year.

Table 6-2. *Temasek's Portfolio, by Geographical Area, as Percentage of Total Portfolio Value*

Area	Percent 2014	2015	2016
Asia (minus Singapore)	41	42	40
Singapore	31	28	29
North America	8	9	10
Australia and New Zealand	10	9	9
Europe	6	8	8
Africa, Central Asia, and the Middle East	2	2	2
Latin America	2	2	2

Source: Temasek Review 2016 (www.temasekreview.com.sg).
Note: Distribution based on underlying assets, as of March 31 of each year.

47 percent of the mobile market, and 43 percent of the broadband market in Singapore, and has a combined mobile subscriber base of 500 million customers from its own operations and regional associates in twenty-five countries, including 100 percent of the second largest Australian telecommunications company, Optus, and 32 percent of Bharti Airtel, the largest carrier in India.

DBS Bank is the largest bank in South East Asia measured by assets and is among the larger banks in Asia, with operations in seventeen markets.

PSA International Pte Ltd (PSAI) was formerly the Port of Singapore Authority, a statutory board regulating, developing, operating, and promoting the Port of Singapore's terminals. In 1996 it was split up into a commercial and regulatory part. The regulatory functions were handed over to the Maritime and Port Authority of Singapore.

PSAI is now one of the world's largest port operators, active across the globe in its primary business of integrated container terminal services. PSAI has major investments in nineteen countries around the world. The total throughput for the group was 64 million TEU (twenty-foot equivalent units, about the size of one container) in 2015, with the Singapore terminals alone handling almost half of that volume, or about a fifth of the world's trans-shipped containers.[2]

Other well-known brands within Temasek include Singapore Airlines, an international airline. Also, Singapore Technologies, or ST Engineering as it is now known, is one of Asia's largest defense and engineering groups, with 100 subsidiaries and associated companies in forty-six cities in twenty-four countries in the Americas, Asia, Europe, and the Middle East.

On the real estate side, the Singapore company CapitaLand is one of Asia's largest real estate companies with assets under management of $10 billion, including shopping malls, serviced residences, offices, and residential homes mainly in Singapore and China. Its portfolio includes private-equity-like real estate companies and other development companies as well.

Political insulation within Temasek is reinforced by professional boards and a risk management system that puts responsibility and accountability solidly with the board of each holding. These measures are often backed by independent credit ratings and even equity listings. The board of Temasek, as well as those of its holdings, consists of independent non-executive directors recruited on merit. Almost half of both the management and staff recruited internationally are non-Singaporeans.

Transparency and clear objective are also strengthened by the credit rating, a privatization of the debt through issuing bonds on the international capital markets. Only the choice of CEO represents a much-discussed inconsistency in its governance record. The fact that the Ho Ching, the CEO since 2002, is married to Singapore's prime minister has put a dent in the credibility of a governance image that is otherwise seen as best in class.

Singapore has taken the professional wealth management concept one step further by creating two major asset managers, or public wealth funds, for its assets: an urban wealth fund (UWF; also called a national wealth fund) and a sovereign wealth fund (SWF). Temasek, the UWF, is a private-equity-like fund managing operational assets as well as some real estate. GIC Private Ltd. (formerly known as the Government of Singapore Investment Corporation) is a hedge-fund-like fund managing the government's foreign reserve and other liquid assets. GIC has some $342 billion in assets under management as of March 2015.

The joint market value of the two public funds is well in excess of the public liabilities and more than 1.7 times the annual GDP of Singapore, which gives the Singapore government a very strong public sector balance sheet. Consequently, Singapore has consistently achieved the top credit rating AAA from the three main credit rating agencies. Both funds are delivering a significant surplus to the government, enough to continuously help fund the development of the city-state as well as to shore up the equity to increase the net worth of the public sector balance sheet to provide for future generations.

SINGAPORE AND JAMAICA: A COMPARISON

To help put the economic achievements of Singapore in perspective, we could compare it to the economic development of Jamaica. This might help rid Singapore of its undeserved image of having been born with a silver spoon in its mouth. Both are former colonies that became independent

Table 6-3. *A Comparison of World Development Indicators for Jamaica and Singapore, 1965 and 2014*

	Jamaica		Singapore	
	1965	2014	1965	2014
Population (millions)	1.8	2.7	1.9	5.5
Life expectancy	67	76	67	83
GDP, nominal ($ millions)	972	13,891	974	308,000
GDP/capita ($)	552	5,150	516	55,150

Source: Authors' compilation, based on World Bank, World Development Indicators (http://data.worldbank.org/?locations=JM-SG).

from British rule at about the same time in the 1960s, Jamaica in 1962 and Singapore in 1965.

In 1965, Jamaica had a peaceful and rapidly growing economy based on a successful mining, farming, and tourism industry in a stable Western Hemisphere environment. Singapore, an ancient port in Southeast Asia that had recently been a British garrison guarding a strategic harbor, in 1965 had been expelled from the Malaysian Federation, a federal constitutional monarchy with Islam as its state religion. The newly created city-state of Singapore found itself in the middle of a region of political, racial, and religious instability. Singapore and most of its neighbors had recently been liberated from both colonialism and the Japanese occupation of World War II.

In 1965 Jamaica and Singapore had roughly the same population, life expectancy, and GDP, although Jamaica had a slightly higher GDP per capita than Singapore. The situation today looks very different. Singapore not only has a higher life expectancy, but also a nominal GDP more than twenty times that of Jamaica and a per capita GDP ten times Jamaica's (see table 6-3). Rather than being the result of luck, Singapore's success demonstrates that such achievements are actually within the reach of any city willing to leverage the innovative institutions and tools available to the leadership of a city.

PORTFOLIO MANAGEMENT OF REAL ESTATE
VS. OPERATIONAL ASSETS

Concentrating the ownership of real estate and operational assets under one single holding company rather than several has both economic and financial benefits, including the ability to produce an integrated business plan that helps increase the yield. Economies of scale lower transaction and operational costs and enable better access to financial markets.

Even for larger metropolitan areas with portfolios equivalent to the size of national governments, it pays to resist the political temptation to create multiple holding companies. This may just result in competition between the entities seeking to represent the city to stakeholders and the world outside the metropolis.

Yet the realities of such real estate consolidation can be politically complex. The resistance from the political system should not be underestimated. Politics is all about power and influence, and for an entity or an individual representing an institution within a political system to relinquishing ownership and control of an asset is a real threat to such ambitions. Creating wealth will not be an item on the agenda in a political environment without a balance sheet, since politics is geared to reelection and popularity, not maximizing wealth. Hence, a city leader may have difficulty even finding all the real estate assets hidden within different departments. Consolidating and transferring them from the ownership control of colleagues in various departments currently acting as custodians can prove challenging, unless there is a financial crisis or a wider awareness among the general population supporting the purpose and benefits of reforms for better management of assets.

The main difference in the challenge to consolidate real estate assets is their different level of visibility compared to operational assets such as utilities, airports, trains, and bus and metro systems, which are often a part of the daily life of most residents. These are assets with which politicians can touch the lives of voters in order to gain their support. Operational assets also have employees and labor unions that give these assets their own relatively strong voice.

"Hidden" real estate, on the other hand, has no one to speak on its behalf, except in the occasional case of development where the populace feels affection for individual buildings or neighborhoods. Real estate is most often not even recognized as a commercial asset because it remains unregistered and hence unknown, undeveloped, and unappreciated. Without a visible value on a balance sheet it will remain seen as having little or no worth and will be ignored.

A tactical and strategic alternative to a full consolidation of a real estate portfolio would be a restricted consolidation of some kind: across asset classes; as a special-purpose company; or following segmental lines—for example, a consolidation of the holdings of one department. The fastest alternative is a holding company created for a particular purpose such as developing a waterfront district or a city center. Brownfield opportunities exists in many shapes and forms, including former industrial or commercial facilities, harbor areas and other waterfronts, hospitals, railway stations, and the air rights above railway tracks that can be upgraded and developed.

Using such a special-purpose holding company has many advantages. The main benefit with this type of restricted UWF is the relative ease and speed with which the government is able to react to a certain need or opportunity. The restricted scope means that only a limited number of stakeholders are affected and this makes it easier to communicate and negotiate the benefits of the proposal.

The other type of alternative consolidation is to incorporate along segmental lines—basically the same way a government department or ministry is organized. In Sweden this type of consolidation has been done for, respectively, educational and old-age care facilities and health-care assets in Stockholm, and for railway-related assets in Jernhusen. In the U.K., London Continental Railways used this structure (discussed in a later section of this chapter). A sector-based consolidation means that there is no change of ownership and so there is less internal political resistance from the current owners such as a government department, while transparency is improved considerably and irrevocably.

Our proposals extend beyond the governance of just commercial assets. An urban wealth fund with sufficient independence from governmental control could be allowed to rebalance its portfolio and not only help finance infrastructure investments but also act as the professional steward and anchor investor in potential infrastructure consortia. This could turn an urban wealth fund into a great boon to investment in much-needed infrastructure. MTR in Hong Kong is one of the most outstanding examples of this concept (see also the section on Copenhagen and its geographic UWF By og Havn I/S later in this chapter).

HONG KONG: THE MTR CORPORATION

Hong Kong's fast-growing economy prompted a study released in 1967 that suggested formation of a public transport company. This led to creation of the MTR Corporation (originally, Mass Transit Railway Corporation), established in 1975. The corporation could be described as a segmental UWF: it manages an integrated rail transit system that owns rail infrastructure, the adjacent land, and much of the adjacent real estate. It runs the subway and rail system in Hong Kong. Although MTR was listed on the local stock market in 2000, the government remains the majority shareholder. MTR operates a predominantly rail-based transportation system comprising domestic and cross-border services, a dedicated high-speed airport express railway, and a light-rail system. The entire system stretches more than 137 miles and has eighty-seven stations and sixty-eight light-rail stops. It also runs intercity services to and from the Chinese mainland, as well as a small bus operation providing feeder services in Hong Kong.

MTR has funded and managed vast infrastructure investments and is also a major property developer: it has helped to significantly increase the delivery of new residential homes in Hong Kong. Many of its stations are incorporated into large housing estates or shopping complexes.

Residential and commercial projects have been built above existing stations and along new line extensions.

The investment portfolio includes mainly shopping malls and eighteen floors of office space in the Two International Finance Centre office tower. Associated commercial services for the captive audience in and around the stations is also a vital business for MTR in Hong Kong, including the leasing of retail space, advertising space, automated teller facilities, and personal telecommunication services. In fact, the property holdings generate almost 60 percent of the total operating profit for the domestic business in Hong Kong—including property development and rentals and property management, by developing for sale mainly residential properties in partnership with private sector property developers— whereas the transport business contributes just 40 percent (see figure 6-1). MTR pays a substantial dividend to the city, providing an income for the government that has been deployed to pay off existing debt and develop other assets. How can MTR deliver this when other cities are struggling with both developing residential housing and making their metro system operate efficiently at a break-even point? The MTR business model is called Rail plus Property (R+P). When the government wants MTR to build a new metro line, it sells MTR land with development rights, including the air rights, at stations or depots along the route at market value zoned at "current use."[3] MTR develops the metro line and the adjacent property to "best use," as would any private sector developer. The profit more than covers the cost of the buildout of the metro line without the need for subsidies. So far it has successfully developed the "property"— that is, the air rights—over about half of the system's eighty-seven stations, amounting to 139 million square feet of floor area. New projects being planned or developed will add another 37.6 million square feet.

In 2006 MTR also took over the neighboring Kowloon-Canton Railway Corporation, which up until then had been using a different business model. It has managed this expansion efficiently while maintaining a profit.

Other city governments around the world may not have such a comprehensive real estate portfolio to use for development, but they could still learn from MTR and Hong Kong how thinking of land and real estate in commercial terms can be used for the benefit of the city and its

Figure 6-1. *Sectors Contributing to MTR Operating Profits*

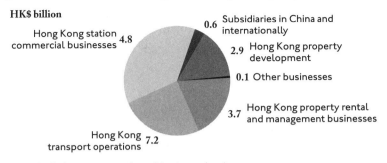

HK$ billion

Hong Kong station commercial businesses 4.8

0.6 Subsidiaries in China and internationally

2.9 Hong Kong property development

0.1 Other businesses

3.7 Hong Kong property rental and management businesses

Hong Kong 7.2 transport operations

Note: Excludes project study and business development expenses.

people. And it is not that the transportation business is performing poorly and requires the subsidy from the real estate business. On the contrary, the transportation system's fare-box-to-recovery ratio, the ratio of total fares to operational costs expressed as a percentage, which measures the efficiency of a railway's pricing, was 187 percent for MTR, the world's highest. In comparison, Singapore's stands at around 125 percent, while the London Underground and the New York subway come in at 90 and 51 percent, respectively.[4]

Hong Kong trains carry more people, suffer fewer delays, and arrive more frequently than most of the world's other mass transit trains. Purchasing power parity for fares shows that the fares are marginally more expensive than Singapore's, in line with New York's, but almost a third the price of London's.[5] More than one-third of revenues is spent on maintenance, renewals, and service improvements on the rail network. Half of that amount is devoted to daily cleaning and inspection; the other half, to capital expenditures such as routine replacement of cars and components.

MTR is now exporting its operational excellence by rapidly investing in railways in different parts in the world. In the U.K. it has obtained contracts to operate the London Overground and TfL Rail, the first phase of the future Crossrail (the Elizabeth Line) service. In Sweden, the Stockholm Metro and MTR Express operate an intercity railway between Stockholm and Gothenburg and the Stockholm Commuter Rails System (the Pendeltåg). In China, it operates the Beijing Metro Lines 4 and 14, the Hangzhou Metro Line 1, and the Shenzhen Metro Longhua

Line (Line 4). In Australia it operates the trains and systems for the Sydney Metro Northwest project.

Hong Kong and the MTR set an example to city leaders elsewhere to encourage commercial and residential development near transit hubs, which is something almost every city can achieve. Also, the efficient extraction of commercial revenues from the captive audience in and around stations is a valuable model, especially for cities that have banned commercial activities all together in their city centers, such as Washington, D.C. In 2015 MTR paid $590 million in dividends to the Hong Kong government.

This leads us into the other side of the equation, where real estate developers are potential contributors to fund infrastructure investments. Examples include Jernhusen in Sweden and London Continental Railways in the U.K., where railway-related properties and station projects have been undertaken together with private sector developers while still being able to capture all or at least a reasonable part of the upside. The Greater London Authority (GLA) has been less successful in using its property to fund infrastructure investments. Copenhagen, however, has apparently taken a leaf out of Hong Kong's MTR book.

COPENHAGEN: CITY AND PORT URBAN WEALTH FUND

Copenhagen's By og Havn I/S (City and Port) is a local government holding company and urban wealth fund established by the city of Copenhagen in 2007 as a general partnership (I/S stands for *interessentskab*), with 5 percent participation from the national government, to develop a number of specific urban districts. With a total area of 1,290 acres it is the largest UWF and urban development project in Europe, and the result of a number of mergers of several development companies and real estate assets owned by the local and national government. This includes water front districts in the Copenhagen harbor area totaling 518 acres, as well as the land-locked Örestad district of some 766 acres between the city center and Copenhagen's Kastrup Airport.

The successful development of these districts will enable the company to contribute more than 33,000 new residential housing units, 100,000 work spaces, and a new university for more than 20,000 students, as well as new parks and retail and cultural facilities. With the financial surplus from its operations, By og Havn has been able to help fund part of the extension of the local metro system as well as other infrastructure investments required by the developments and the city. It does this through a direct dividend as well as with investments in the various projects.

From a governance perspective, the company has been given a clear objective of maximizing value and maintaining international accounting standards of transparency. However, the government apparently did not intend to make the company politically independent, for political insulation has been nonexistent from By og Havn's inception. This is clear from its legal form, a partnership, whereby its members are fully liable for all of its obligations and through its politically dominated board nomination procedures. The owners' unwillingness to give the company a sustainable capital structure by setting it up with a negative equity since 2008, is a further testament to the fact. The founding legislation of the company stipulates that it is to fund itself through government loans and a government guarantee regulated by a tripartite agreement between the central bank, the Ministry of Finance, and the Ministry of Transport. This tether to government ministries makes By og Havn a less efficient management and funding vehicle of commercial assets than those of many of its international peers, by further increasing government debt and fiscal risk and not taking full advantage of a more efficient private sector vehicle.

HAMBURG: HAFENCITY

As Hamburg's extensive harbor facilities were modernized and made more efficient, a 157-square-mile large inner-city district with old harbor buildings was made available for redevelopment. HafenCity Hamburg GmbH is a holding company set up by the city to own and manage the urban regeneration of the port city's harbor district, whose goal is to develop the old port warehouses and repurpose them as offices, hotels, shops, office buildings, and residential areas. The plan, when the area is completely developed, is for more than 2 million square meters of gross floor area, to be used for 6,500 to 7,000 residential units for over 14,000 residents and business premises for some 35,000 people. Its governance structure, including political insulation, is unfortunately not known to the public, as the transparency of the company is managed like a state secret, even though the assets and the company are ultimately owned by the public and the taxpayers.

LONDON: CONTINENTAL RAILWAYS LIMITED

London Continental Railways Limited (LCR) was originally set up in 1994 as a holding company for the European Passenger Services to build the Channel Tunnel Rail Link from London to Paris. In 2009 the company ran into financial difficulties and was taken over by the U.K. Department for Transport. Having divested itself of the actual rail link, the company can be described as a segmental UWF with a primary focus on property development and land regeneration, such as the area around King's Cross Station in London. This was once an important industrial site in the middle of London, but by the late twentieth century the area, known as the railway lands, had devolved to disused buildings, railway sidings, warehouses, and contaminated land.

The decision in 1996 to move the Channel Tunnel Rail Link, connecting Paris and London, from Waterloo Station to the St. Pancras railway station, next door to King's Cross, became the catalyst for change, prompting the U.K. government to decide to develop the King's Cross site through an independent holding company. Argent, a U.K. property developer, acted as the partnership's asset manager.

In 2015, LCR sold its remaining 36.5 percent shares to Australian-Super for the equivalent of $400 million. Contrary to Copenhagen's By og Havn, the LCR group has no liabilities at all, which is not the most optimal capital structure and would not be an attractive way of capitalizing a private sector company. In 2015 it recorded a profit of $127 million, of which almost half reflects the increase in the valuation of investment properties, with the rest being the trading performance of the commercial office properties and a share of the profits of the King's Cross partnership of $22.5 million.

King's Cross has always played a vital role in the commercial life of the capital. The sixty-six-acre development has a total of 8 million square feet of gross floor space of mixed-use development, including 3 million square feet of new works pace; about 500,000 square feet of retail, cafés, bars, restaurants, and leisure facilities; up to 2,000 new homes; a new university; and a range of educational, hotel, and cultural facilities.

Many of the old Victorian buildings around the site, including the Great Northern Hotel, have been refurbished and reopened. Organizations such as Google, Louis Vuitton, Universal Music, Havas, and the University of the Arts London have chosen to locate here. New public squares, gardens, and parks have opened, as well as restaurants, shops, and cafés. By 2020 up to 50,000 people will be studying, living, and working in King's Cross.

LCR's other development projects include the $2.6 billion International Quarter project in Stratford, centered on Stratford Regional and International Railway Stations in East London. The project is a mixed commercial and residential development in partnership with Lendlease, a private property developer. It includes Chobham Academy, the East Village (previously the athletes' village constructed for the London 2012 Olympic and Paralympic Games) and the Westfield shopping center. Within Stratford City there is also provision for 2.9 million square feet of retail and leisure space, 1.3 million of hotel space, 6.6 million of commercial district space, and 16,400 new homes.

In addition, LCR is working with the Department of Transport and Network Rail to bring the Waterloo international terminal in central London back into use and is exploring the potential for transforming the railway arches at Leake Street into a new dining and leisure destination.

Another high-profile development project in the U.K. is the regeneration of the Mayfield Quarter in Manchester, including the site of the former Mayfield Railway Station. This is a mix of light industrial units and derelict buildings, where the aim is to create a mixed development expected to deliver 825,000 square feet of office space, 1,300 residential homes, a 350-room hotel, retail and leisure facilities, and a new 6.5-acre city park along the river.

JERNHUSEN: A PROPERTY DEVELOPER IN SWEDEN

Jernhusen in Sweden offers another example of how a segmental UWF can be used to develop a substantial railway-related real estate portfolio in a commercial and professional way, to the benefit of the economy and society as a whole. Jernhusen owns and develops a $1.8 billion urban real estate portfolio concentrated in and around railway stations in the three largest cities in Sweden: Stockholm, Gothenburg, and Malmö.

The portfolio had its origin in the deregulation, starting in 1988, that opened up the Swedish railway network to competition by separating railway operations from the rail-track network. In 2001 the real estate—mostly train stations—was separated from the rail-track network, and Jernhusen, a wholly owned government real estate company, was created to manage it.

Value maximization is the stated objective of the company. It adheres to the Swedish Corporate Governance Code and has a good transparency and risk management system. It is further boosting its independence from short-term political influence by issuing debt securities, but it does not have an independent credit rating. Most of the board members are recruited for their experience in corporate governance, apart from one civil servant from the government and the chairman from the political establishment.

JERNHUSEN'S PORTFOLIO

The portfolio consists of stations, depots, and cargo terminals, and develops commercial property around the main stations. The total area to let is 621 thousand square meters. The return on equity was 17 percent in 2015, achieved through active management of the portfolio. With an equity ratio of 41 percent, it made investments of around $170 million and divestments of $14 million. Since inception, Jernhusen has invested some $1.4 billion in transport-related infrastructure, especially in and around the Central Station in Stockholm alone.

The stations have a total of a half a million daily visitors, representing 48 percent of the total market value and 52 percent of the total turnover from predominantly retail outlets and restaurants, but there are also offices. Retailers at stations tend to be focused on fast-moving consumer goods such as snacks, newspapers, soft drinks, and so forth.

The development portfolio is around 22 percent of the total portfolio in terms of market value and 3 percent of turnover. Once fully developed, the property is often divested. Depots are critical for the operation of trains and generate some 39 percent of turnover and represent 24 percent of market value, while cargo terminals represent 6 percent of both the value and turnover.

For the last ten years the average return on equity has been around 11 percent. Vacancies are low and growing railway traffic has increased underlying demand for Jernhusen's properties. The company's balance sheet remains strong, with a reported loan-to-value ratio of almost 50 percent in the first quarter of 2016.

Stockholm represents more than half of the value of the portfolio. One if its major development projects, Station Stockholm City, will have a significant impact on the entire country. This is the development of a new station integrated with Stockholm's Central Station, designed for the Citybanan, the new 3.75-mile commuter railway tunnel beneath central Stockholm. Placing commuter rail traffic in a dedicated tunnel will significantly improve long-distance and commuter traffic through Stockholm, which today is still restricted to only two tracks, a limitation the system has had since its creation in 1871. This increase will impact the capacity of the entire national rail traffic system, since more than 80 percent of all railway traffic in Sweden passes through the Central Station in Stockholm.

Another project around the Central Station in Stockholm involves decking the railway tracks, in order to double the capacity of passenger in the station, developing a whole new area of office and commercial space right in the very heart of Stockholm.

PROJECTS OUTSIDE STOCKHOLM

Jernhusen has completed another vital tunnel project underneath Malmö connecting Malmö Central Station with the Öresunds Bridge, which links to Kastrup Airport and Copenhagen in Denmark and then the rest of Europe. This has led to development of the station and the related property. In Gothenburg there is a plan to deck over the station and develop new office and commercial space. Simultaneously Jernhusen is gradually divesting properties located in smaller municipalities.

LOCUM: A SPECIALIZED HEALTH-CARE REAL ESTATE MANAGER IN SWEDEN

Responsibility for health-care services in Sweden rests mainly at the county government level, but also to some extent on municipal councils that care for elderly and disabled people not requiring medical help. All other health-care services are the responsibility of the county council. While the privately funded health-care sector is still small in Sweden, an increasing share is now handled by publicly reimbursed private providers.

Locum is the dedicated real estate manager for the health-care sector in Stockholm. It is wholly owned by Landstingshuset i Stockholm AB (LIS), intended as the countywide segmental UWF of the Stockholm County Council.

HOLDING COMPANIES: A SWEDISH TRADITION

Local governments in Sweden, at both the county and municipal level, have a tradition of creating holding companies for their commercial assets and in particular the real estate segment. However, what could seem like a professional move to improve the professional management of assets has often been done with the purpose of avoiding transparency and gaining access to additional funds not included nor visible in the government budget.

With a holding company structure, the political owner is able to transfer and hide the cost of personnel and substantial external consultants— services that risk being reduced in budget spending reviews. More important, a holding enables the transfer of profits from profitable enterprises within the group to loss-making activities as a way of supporting vested interests and subsidizing politically motivated activities and relationships.

Public health services worldwide are often some of the largest property owners in a larger city. As discussed in earlier chapters, the U.K.'s National Health Service could redevelop substantial amounts of real estate for residential housing and commercial offices and earn a return, while still maintaining ownership if professionally managed. However, this will not happen without independent and professional property management.

A CAUTIONARY TALE

In this context, at first glance, Locum, the specialized health-care real estate holding company in Stockholm, could look like a progressive model for other public health services operations to follow on a national or local level. Worldwide, public services are crumbling under the austerity measures laid down by a government owner, such as the NHS in the U.K., even though it is sitting on a real estate gold mine. The governance structure set up by Stockholm County Council should act as a cautionary tale of how not to mobilize such wealth.

Locum AB was established in 1992 in response to the reorganization of the Swedish health-care sector. The aim was to consolidate the management of all real estate assets within the regional government in Stockholm County and introduce market rents with the purpose of increasing operational efficiency, not maximizing value.

Locum AB is one of the largest real estate managers in Stockholm, managing a portfolio of more than 2 million square meters with a potential market value of at least $2.5 billion.[6] Political insulation is almost nonexistent at the company, mainly due to the fact that the actual ownership of the real estate remains with the local government via Landstingsfastigheter AB (LFS), another corporate vehicle owned directly by the Stockholm County Council.

The fragmented governance structure and poor transparency is obviously meant to hide the financial reality and avoid accountability and responsibility for the performance and cost of managing the assets. From an accounting perspective, Locum is only carrying the cost of personnel for managing the assets while the actual balance sheet is with LFS. Neither of the three corporate holding companies has value maximization as an objective.

The fact that more than one third of Locum's portfolio has been privatized since its inception makes the entire system of holdings seem more like a privatization agency set up to avoid transparency and accountability that ensures that privatized asset are sold only when fully developed, at the best time and at full value. A system with fragmented responsibility and without the capacity to develop and sell assets when the full value has been reached could potentially open itself up to exploitation by vested interests, clientelism, and corruption—a potential that has been amply demonstrated in both Greece and Ukraine.

The complete disregard for any proper governance, including political insulation, transparency, and a clear objective, makes Locum unable to attract and retain professional management, or even to act as a professional counterpart in any commercial transactions. This is amply demonstrated by the process leading up to the biggest construction project in Sweden in recent times, the building of the Nya Karolinska Solna University Hospital, the $6 billion state-of-the-art hospital currently under construction to upgrade the Karolinska University Hospital in Stockholm County.

The county council took direct responsibility for this public-private partnership project, despite the fact that it had no previous experience in managing such projects—or any commercial project, for that matter. The political leadership was apparently undeterred by the fact that there were no competing bids and that only one private sector party bid for the project. Not surprisingly, it is ending up as one of the most expensive hospitals in the world. Nor has it responded to the claim that any changes required to the construction (which for a hospital is usually a large part of the total investment) must be done by the current private sector partner, unless the hospital can procure such additional investments in a competitive and truly cost-efficient way. This investment is almost twice the size of the value of the entire real estate portfolio held by the county.

Despite the relative size and the potential fiscal risk of the project, the process was managed in an entirely political structure and fashion. The result serves as an illustration of the limitations of the public-private partnership model and why a balance sheet and professional governance matter. Without a professional counterparty on the side of the government capable of managing commercial risk, too much risk will often be surrendered to the private contractor. When financial discipline remains inside the government bureaucracy instead of being delegated to an independent and professional UWF, politicians risk having to give away valuable tax money to the private sector in a wasteful and negligent manner.

The importance of proper governance and professional management of public assets must never be underestimated.

Managing commercial assets professionally with decent returns is not rocket science; it has been done successfully for centuries in the private sector and has also been proved possible in the public sector, given a political will to adhere to the fundamental governance principles of transparency, political insulation, and clear objective.

STOCKHOLM STADSHUS: A RESIDENTIAL PROPERTY HOLDING COMPANY

The greatest bottleneck for Stockholm's becoming a world-class innovation hub is residential housing. Stockholm Stadshus AB (SSAB), the UWF of the City of Stockholm, scores better than Locum on most of the three fundamental principles, but the situation is not helped by the antiquated approach forced upon local government by the national government's stifling accounting laws and housing regulations.

SSAB is a comprehensive UWF including both operational and real estate assets, consolidating some sixteen sub-holdings and their subsidiaries. Wholly owned by the Stockholm City Council, the UWF was established in 19991 to introduce more professional governance of commercial assets as a response to financial mismanagement that had laid bare the fiscal risks the city actually takes on through its commercial activities. Although the original intention with its creation has been fulfilled, it is questionable if the political owners are really using the wealth of the city's inhabitants to the benefit of the city and all of its citizens.

THE RESIDENTIAL MARKET AND PUBLIC HOUSING IN SWEDEN

The residential market in the City of Stockholm consists of 90 percent multifamily housing, of which 55 percent of the stock is tenant-owned and the remainder is rental apartments. Of the rental apartments, only

40 percent are owned by the city; the rest are owned by mainly larger private investors.[7]

Stockholm as a city and innovation hub is growing faster than probably any other city in Europe. It is also claimed to be the world's second most prolific tech hub (behind number one Silicon Valley) on a per capita basis. This could all come to a halt without sufficient residential housing for newcomers and the younger generation. As a result residential property prices have rising sharply over a long period of time, due to the low supply of new housing and inadequate housing construction since the early 1990s.[8] Part of the reason for the low level of supply and construction activity is that further investment would be unprofitable due to labor union resistance to full competition in the construction industry, as well as the underlying government regulations that keep rents artificially low. These regulations, originally intended as an effort to provide affordable housing for low income-families, have in effect created a housing bubble and a stumbling block to increase the residential stock of rental flats in one of the fastest-growing cities in Europe.

Unlike Singapore, the Swedish system has not been able to provide housing to a majority of the people, since the city owns housing assets representing only some 15 percent of the total housing stock. Nor is it able to provide housing for those who need it the most, since access is neither means-tested nor based on any proof of need. Obtaining a lease has instead become an economic privilege for a small portion of the population, and the system has led to a considerable illegal trading of rental apartments in return for political favors.

THE CITY COUNCIL'S SOLUTION

Enter SSAB, the UWF of Stockholm, which sees its job as by law to provide housing to its inhabitants. The real estate portfolio consists of almost 11 million square meters of floor space with a total market value of $17 billion, mainly multifamily residential housing, representing almost 90 percent of book value of the total portfolio and 70 percent of the turnover, the rest being a handful of operational holdings. This makes it the largest property owner in the country—it is more than six times the size of any listed real estate company on the Stockholm Stock Exchange.

Real estate is held in a number of segmented holding companies, including residential assets in Familjebostäder, Stockholmshem, and Svenska Bostäder; specific holdings for educational and care facilities; and segmented holdings for venues such as the Stockholm Globe Arena AB, one of three indoor stadiums in the city, and exhibition venues in Mässfastigheter AB, the largest trade fair in Sweden.

Operational companies include Stokab (broadband infrastructure company), Stockholms Hamn (commercial harbors), Stockholms Stadsteater (the largest theater in the city), Stockholms Stads Parkerings (parking lots), and two utilities, Fortum Värme (the district heating company) and Stockholm Vatten (water utility).

Return on capital for 2015 was only 2.5 percent, with the real estate portfolio practically subsidizing the operational portfolio, clearly demonstrating that its performance would not stand comparison with the best-in-class management within each segment. As currently structured and managed the housing portfolio would qualify neither as a good investment nor as an efficient policy instrument to provide affordable housing to the general public as is amply demonstrated by Singapore's HBD.

Improving political independence, primarily through the abolition of the rent control regulation and being freed of the misguided and antiquated perspective of the Swedish Municipal Accounting Law, which prevents both the use of market valuations and the business objective of value maximization (see box 4-3, on Sweden's municipal accounting law), would clarify the purpose of the owning the portfolio. This would also allow for a more professional board than the current one, none of whose members seem to be nominated on merit and all the non-executive directors are politicians. Some of these companies have more than twenty non-executive directors who are politicians—giving the impression that the board of directors exists more for the benefit of the politicians than for actually supervising and driving the performance in the company.

The question remains for this and many UWFs around the world, is there sufficient political will to manage such a vast portfolio professionally, for the benefit of taxpayers and society as a whole? Done properly it would boost the economy and help fund much-needed residential housing and other infrastructure assets.

London is another city that needs to develop residential housing and new transport infrastructure to continue to develop as a turbo city. This will require bold new ideas with regard to land development. Brownfield land alone will not be sufficient to plug the housing gap.

LONDON: POTENTIAL FOR AN URBAN WEALTH FUND

London possesses a substantial portfolio of public sector land and sites, including former military, transportation, and NHS sites, which could be developed. Furthermore, there is great potential to both increase the density of and developed further existing council housing estates.[9] Although this is a highly sensitive issue and politicians generally prefer to leave it outside the political debate, Lord Andrew Adonis, chairman of the UK Government Infrastructure Commission and Crossrail 2, has suggested some innovative development models to improve city estates in order to build more homes and better communities where people want to live and work.[10]

It is likely that a comprehensive London UWF that consolidated the real estate owned by the governments within the Greater London area and was put under professional management would make a meaningful funding contribution to infrastructure projects such as residential housing and Crossrail. Such an entity could also help supply the land for development and manage such major projects in a professional and sustainable fashion.

Data show that the public sector owns over 20 percent of the freehold property in Greater London—in some boroughs the figure is more like 40 percent (as discussed above in chapter 4).[11]

The sheer number and size of council estates in London, particularly in inner London boroughs, is far larger than commonly appreciated, although many boroughs lack proper lists of their assets. According to

Lord Adonis, Southwark Council owns 43 percent of the land in its borough, mostly council estates but also including 10,000 garages. Many inner London councils own 25 to 30 percent of the land in their borough. Islington Council alone owns about 150 council estates of fifty or more homes on some of the most expensive land in the world. However, data on these housing estates are not included in the Land Registry, which is one reason why the indicative value of this segment remain elusive as well as a politically sensitive issue to raise.

Where housing estates are combined with adjoining brownfield or other public sites, the development potential is larger still, and local authorities are in a unique position to promote this assembling of larger parcels.

Redevelopment of estates is sometimes assumed to mean that existing tenants and residents will be displaced, which is the main reason that this topic is regarded as politically explosive. However, Lord Adonis says this need not be the case, nor should it be, as redevelopment will usually mean a much better use of land with typically around twice the density of existing estates. This should offer ample opportunities for engaging residents in the design and redevelopment plans and provide an option to remain in new homes once completed. Where adjoining public and other brownfield land is also mobilized, a fourfold or even fivefold increase in the number of homes could be achieved.[12]

Recent studies in four London boroughs have shown that perhaps as many as 20,000 homes could be created by increasing the density of existing estates to "central" density levels, equivalent to 210 dwellings per hectare.[13] This would equal 50 percent of the Greater London Authority's ten-year target for new homes in three boroughs in the study.

Currently neither the Greater London Authority nor any of the thirty-two boroughs that make up Greater London has a consolidated list and market valuation of its real estate holdings. Having such a list would make it possible to fully realize the potential of its portfolio through a comprehensive business plan. The creation of a London UWF would provide the much-needed transparency concerning the land that is owned by the public sector. It could also support the funding, financing, and development of such real estate to the benefit of the economy and the people.[14]

Crossrail, the largest infrastructure project currently being undertaken in Europe, is an example of how a metropolitan-wide UWF would have been an extremely helpful source of funding, as well as a potential project coordinator. Crossrail 1 is a modern seventy-three-mile railway across London that will run from Maidenhead and Heathrow in the west to Shenfield and Abbey Wood in the east. It will provide a new, modern railway across London that will connect the outer suburbs to the City, Canary Wharf, and the West End, and link London's major financial, business, shopping, and entertainment districts directly with Heathrow Airport. Crossrail 2 is a proposed $29 billion second phase that will link southwest and northeast London.

Crossrail will increase rail capacity in London by 10 percent and alleviate pressure on the rail, Tube, Docklands Light Railway, and London Overground services. It will provide new connections with multiple interchanges with key Tube, DLR, London Overground, and national rail routes at Liverpool Street, Paddington, Stratford, Woolwich, Tottenham Court Road, Bond Street, Whitechapel, Farringdon, Custom House, Ealing Broadway, and Canary Wharf. It will also connect Heathrow, the West End, the City, and Canary Wharf via a single transport link.

Crossrail 1, estimated to cost $21 billion, is being financed by a combination of government grants, fares, and profits earned on enhancement of land values that arise due to the new railroad. The central government will supply one-third of the funds, and London businesses will contribute more than one-third, derived partly from new development above the stations and contributions from key beneficiaries such as Heathrow Airport and the City of London. The remaining third (or less) will come from Transport for London, the local government body responsible for the transport system in Greater London; funds will be raised through loans and paid for by the Crossrail operating surplus. More than half the cost for Crossrail 2 could be met from sources other than the taxpayer.

For Crossrail 2, several different methods were contemplated where value could be extracted from developments to make a contribution to the project. One idea was that the public sector could take a stake in developing land and apply the expected surpluses from sales to the Crossrail 2 project, as has been done by MTR in Hong Kong. A related idea was to establish a segmented UWF (called a mayoral development corporation in the U.K.). This had been done previously to develop the Olympic Park Legacy Corporation, in order to ensure the regeneration, development, and sustainability of the Olympic Park to deliver 2,500 new homes and create 13,000 new jobs by 2023.[15]

Such a restricted UWF for the Crossrail 2 route would develop a master plan for each area and ensure the provision of utility, transport, and social infrastructure to the developments as appropriate. However, the conclusion was that the limited scope of such a restricted UWF could struggle to find suitably large parcels of land along the affected route of Crossrail 2 to make a meaningful contribution to the project.[16] Where more transformational developments are taking place around Crossrail 2 stations, an active intervention by a restricted UWF could generate a more meaningful contribution to the costs of the project, but there is also significant risk associated with such developments. Therefore, it was judged that the limited scope of a restricted UWF would not be sufficient to fund Crossrail 2.

What is missing is a broader view of the potential to develop a common understanding for a comprehensive Greater London urban wealth fund. Such a common understanding would be able to generate the political will required to consolidate the vast portfolio of government-owned real estate, regardless of current ownership. The City of London and the invention of the limited corporation once changed the economic landscape of the Western world. Now, it's time for Greater London to take the lead in the Western Hemisphere with a demonstration of unprecedented political cooperation to mobilize its commercial assets to the benefit of the metropolis and its people.

CHAPTER 7

Shrinking the Social Debt of Cities

CONSIDER THE STORY OF LESTER. He sleeps rough, mostly under a bridgehead. During the days he walks the streets of Chicago, trying to pick up bottles, begging, sometimes stealing when there is an opportunity. When luck is with him, he scrounges enough to buy a bottle of booze or whatever drugs are available at the moment among his fellow homeless. Afterwards he is often picked up by the police and brought to a county hospital, which is good because those are the few times he receives a shower and clean clothes.

Through his various activities Lester, forty-four, cobbles together some $6,000 a year, but his costs to the public purse are about seven times that.[1] According to one North Carolina study, a chronically homeless person in the United States racks up a stunning average annual bill to society of $39,458 in combined medical, legal, and other costs.[2] The figures are similar in other studies around the country and, for that matter, in other rich countries.[3]

In the United States these costs are spread around different municipal and state actors, so no single entity is in a position to invest in promising ways of reducing these costs. But the story of Lester is not just about what can be done now to reduce his cost to society—and improve his own quality of life. Lester's life history makes it clear that his record of petty crime and homelessness has prevented him from obtaining employment over the past twenty years. How did it all start?

Lester was a high school dropout. He is dyslexic and never really had a chance to keep up with the pace of homework. He grew up in Chicago's South Side in a neighborhood where young people are drawn into gangs of unemployed youngsters. If Lester lives to the age of sixty, the life-time costs to the taxpayer for his aimless and some might say botched life will amount to more than a million dollars. That is not counting the tax revenue that he might have generated if his life had developed more productively. An investment in terms of special training for dyslexics early on in Lester's school career just might have had a significant positive effect on the trajectory of his life.

Suppose such a social investment would have cost $10 000. This would have been worthwhile even if it had raised Lester's chances of leading a normal life by just a single percentage point, since $10,000 is 1 percent of $1,000,000. A canny city has institutions that allow these choices to be made rationally.

In political debates, social spending is generally viewed as a form of consumption. Transfers to low-income earners, better housing standards, and higher teacher wages are proposed to better the lot of the less well-off, but some oppose such expenditures as wasteful.

Our approach is based on viewing social capital just as we would view a share in a company or an item on the balance sheet, rather than a flow. And we have our own definition of social capital. Unfortunately, the term "social capital" has been used loosely, and measured and compared by means of indices that lump together different kinds of social outcomes, such as the Petris Social Capital Index (PSCI), which combines poverty rate with other presumed factors that may improve social outcomes, such as wage levels of preschool teachers. The problem with these approaches is that the definition of social capital is vague and such definitions imply that more spending on social programs generally increases social capital.

Instead we aim for a clearer definition of social capital that naturally promotes the use of evidence-based social investments. In theory, the most meaningful way of viewing social capital would be the present value of the expected stream of future social costs. Since expected future social expenditures are costs, they should more appropriately be called *social debt*.

But this approach is cumbersome in practice. For one, it is time consuming to continually update such a calculation. New Zealand, which initially championed this approach at the national level and published the results of its ambitious attempt, now mainly emphasizes the use of evidence and long-run cost-benefit calculations to guide social investment.[4]

The goal, after all, is not to predict future events exactly, but rather to value social investments in a way that is roughly on target and is not easily manipulated by advocates of different initiatives. We favor a pragmatic approach that at the same time is simple to use for all decisionmakers in a city administration, and is transparent for those affected by these decisions. This approach would be packaged in a tool that anyone can use after just a few minutes' acquaintance with the way it works.

One such tool is the Public Health Calculator, launched by Uppsala University in 2011 in cooperation with the insurance company Skandia (see figure 7-1). The calculator's purpose is to help public entities use the data they have to tailor their social investments in public health to where the investments are most needed and will do the most good.[5] The screen shot in figure 7-1 shows (upper left) that the user—such as, for example, a city administrator—seeks some health projections for the Stockholm greater metropolitan area. The table's column labels give the option to select, for example, the share of the population in different age groups engaged in various forms of lifestyle risks, such as alcohol abuse.

The program can then supply projections as to the change in the incidence of various types of diseases in five years' time. An extension of this program, made in cooperation with the insurance company Skandia, shows the actual costs to municipalities in terms of health care, social insurances, and employers. It also shows how much each municipality could expect to save in the coming years if public health were to improve along one of the dimensions.

This model is easily extended to other areas of social investment. Essentially this kind of tool creates a baseline calculation into the future in order to assess the benefits of various social improvements, building on the research and other information one would need for a full-scale social cost-benefit analysis. Yet it is all made so user-friendly that a school

Figure 7-1. *Skandia and Uppsala University's Public Health Calculator*

The following table represents the calculator interface shown in the figure.

	BMI > 30 (%)				Daily tobacco smoking (%)				Phisical inactivity (%)				Risky alcohol use (%)			
	2014		2019		2014		2019		2014		2019		2014		2019	
Age / Numbers — Men / Women	M	F	M	F	M	F	M	F	M	F	M	F	M	F	M	F
20-44 — 1629855 / 1561289	9	8	12	8	7	8	7	8	14	13	14	13	22	17	22	17
45-64 — 1228289 / 1205769,	19	17	19	17	12	16	12	16	14	15	18	15	18	11	18	11
65-84 — 788907 / 867493	17	17	17	17	8	12	8	12	16	17	16	17	11	6	11	6
Total: 3647051 / 3634551																

	New incidence				Sum
Diabetes type 2	274	0	292	0	566
Cardiovascular disease	53	0	153	0	206
Stroke	1	0	7	0	8
Lung cancer	0	0	0	0	0
Colon cancer	1	0	8	0	9
Breast cancer	0	0	0	0	0
Prostate cancer	0	0	0	0	0
COPD	0	0	22	0	22
Depression	10	0	25	0	35
Hip fracture	0	0	29	0	29
Alcohol-related disease	0	0	0	0	0
Total	339	0	536	0	875

New incidence	Employer — Taxes	Health care	Municipality	State insurance

The Public Health Calculator is a tool that makes it easy to estimate the cost-effectiveness of public health investments. It contains information on the demographics in regional districts, their health status, and the costs of poor health to various levels of government. A user can, for example, enter the estimated effect of an alcoholism-oriented public health investment in terms of reduced risk drinking. The program then calculates the estimated effects on incidence of disease, the cost reductions for employers, and the revenues and costs for various levels of government.

Source: Shutterstock.

principal, a city administrator, or a local politician can use it to assess the long-run consequences of various actions.

For example, city administrators in Uppsala wanted to invest in a mobile technology that would allow people to test alcohol levels using a breathalyzer attached to a dedicated mobile phone. This would enable people who needed to prove sobriety to keep their driver's license, child custody, or social assistance to conduct these tests at home or at work, rather than coming in to a lab or having a social worker visit. There is some clinical evidence for the effectiveness of this kind of tool for reducing heavy drinking. In the short term the investment would have cost more than the direct short-term savings to city administration. So it probably would not have been implemented if the long-term social cost tool had not been available showing the projected savings. But using this and the Public Health Calculator, it could easily be ascertained that investment in this technology was worthwhile in the long run.[6]

In the latest extension, Skandia is working on additions to the tool that incorporate the consequences of actual interventions or programs for which the effects have been adequately documented in evaluations and the research literature.[7] Our proposal is that cities should use similar tools and require their administrations and political processes to use them to rank choices and interventions. This is a rational way of assessing the effect of different policy choices on a city's social debt, or on the value of their assets.

Such tools can enable a new approach to making social policy. They make it easier to argue for spending on social investments to improve long-run social wealth and outcomes. And they also provide data to support cutting programs that are dear to various interests but that achieve few long-run improvements. In this chapter we present evidence concerning various types of social investments and how some cities achieve better health results and fewer social problems using this approach.

SOCIAL INVESTMENTS

The central idea behind social investments is that sizable future social costs and mishaps can be avoided by larger investments now. For example, a greater investment in training a dyslectic four-year old may reduce the risk of this child becoming unemployed, or even an addict or a criminal twenty years later.

INVESTING IN SOCIAL ASSETS DURING CHILDHOOD

In 2010 the government of New Zealand adopted an approach to social investment that is similar to the Public Health Calculator. First they calculated future expected social costs, what we call social debt. Then they focused on improving the lives of New Zealanders by applying rigorous and evidence-based investment practices to social services.[8] This approach favors early investment to achieve better long-term results for people and help them to become more independent.

As a result, fewer New Zealanders will rely on social services, and the overall costs for taxpayers will be lower. This is of course good news for the Treasury: "Social Investment puts the needs of people who rely on public services at the centre of decisions on planning, programs and resourcing, by setting clear, measurable goals for helping those people; using information and technology to better understand the needs of people who rely on social services and what services they are currently receiving; systematically measuring the effectiveness of services, so we know what works well and what doesn't; purchasing results rather than specific inputs, and moving funding to the most effective services irrespective of whether they are provided by government or non-government agencies."[9]

Based on this platform they discovered many surprising facts about lifetime social costs of various social conditions and promising measures to reduce these costs. For example, 1 percent of five-year-olds are known to Child Youth and Family Services, have been supported by benefits for more than forty months, and have a parent who has had contact with Corrections. This 1 percent consists of around 600 children per year, which over twenty years creates a pipeline of 12,000 at high risk. Of an average group of 10 of these five-year-olds, 7 will not achieve a high school degree. By the age of twenty-one, 4 will have been on long-term benefits. At thirty-five a quarter will have been in prison.[10]

In addition to the poor life outcomes for most of these children, there is a substantial cost to the community and society as a whole. On average, each child in this group will cost taxpayers about $200,000 by age thirty-five, and some over $1 million.

At least since 1968 it has been documented that long-term social investments make a big difference in social outcomes.[11] But much of the more detailed results of what works and what doesn't have more recent origins. Some of the most striking empirical evidence about the potential benefits of early intervention come from the long-term evaluation of Perry Preschool, a small-scale, intensive early childhood experimental program launched in the 1960s for disadvantaged African American children in Ypsilanti, Michigan. Children have now been followed through age forty, and the data for the members of the program group show much lower arrest rates, better schooling attainment, and higher incomes.[12] A benefit-cost analysis of the Perry program suggests that it may have generated nearly thirteen dollars in benefits for every dollar spent on the program, with much of the gain attributable to reductions in criminal behavior.

Results such as these and the New Zealand approach could give some clear answers as to what kinds of investments are worthwhile in order to achieve greater social mobility and also to head off some of the problems that children in disadvantaged neighborhoods can experience. One could call these micro-programs that at the macro-level can lead to dramatic differences between cities in the lifetime prospects of children (discussed in chapter 2).[13]

SOCIAL INVESTMENTS IN FIGHTING CRIME

Investing in social assets during early childhood may also be a very cost-effective way of reducing crime—especially when compared to the many costs associated with incarceration. Unfortunately, many cities have invested in reducing crime primarily through more policing.

Lower crime rates reduce social debt through many channels. Waiting for investments in young children's capacity to pay off should of course not be the only strategy. Many U.S. cities have in recent decades succeeded in reducing crime, but researchers still struggle to identify all the underlying causes for the reductions.

One source of the difficulty is that there are large, and largely unexplained, fluctuations in crime rates over time. In fact, it is even hard to measure crime rates, apart from murder. Crime rates tend to be higher in bigger cities, but differences between similar-size cities and differences over time can be huge. In the United States the murder rate fell by 30 percent between 1930 and 1960, and then rose again, reaching the same level again in 1975. In New York the murder rate rose fourfold, to twenty-two murders per 100,000 people in 1975. But after 1975 the murder rate in

New York fell just as much as it had risen. By 2005 it was down to six murders per 100,000, and other serious crimes fell by as much. Other cities' murder rates have also fallen since then.[14] Some external causes have been suggested. John Donohue and Steven Levitt find that legalization of abortion plays some role.[15] Another hypothesis that finds some support is lead paint poisoning that may have detrimental effects on mental development in children. But increased incarceration and more police on the streets are also found to have some effect.

Another hypothesis is that local crime cultures arise just like trends in music or clothes. Therefore, it should not come as a big surprise that some short-term interventions that influence youths (who are responsible for a disproportionate fraction of crimes) can be surprisingly effective. For example, three large-scale randomized controlled trials in Chicago of two different interventions show evidence of substantial behavioral impacts for disadvantaged youth. The core of each intervention is what psychologists call cognitive behavioral therapy, which is designed to reduce automaticity, or violent responses to perceived provocations. Participation in programming reduced arrests over the program year by 44 percent for violent crimes and just about as much for other crimes.[16]

Two cost free strategies may work, but the statistical evidence is not very clear: Innovative data-driven systems helped target police resources toward troubled areas. New York introduced a system called CompStat that allows police chiefs to see exactly where crimes occurred, and pinpoint those spots. The other policy is community policing, which in practice is more difficult than one might expect from the theory. These initiatives have contributed to reduced crime. According to Franklin Zimring, a law professor at the University of California, Berkeley, the rate of serious crimes such as murder, rape, and burglary in New York has fallen twice as much as for the country at large, to about a fifth of the 1990 level.[17] But what is easily missed is that New York has spent nearly three times as much on public safety as most other cities.[18] Clearly some short-term interventions can be quite effective, but investments in long-term measures may be even more cost-effective.

SOCIAL INVESTMENTS TO HELP THE MIDDLE CLASS

Much focus in recent decades has been on crime reduction, and most attention has been given to the most disadvantaged neighborhoods. This is also where many cities have made investments of different kinds, and in many cases they have results to show. For example, in the nation as a whole the life expectancy of disadvantaged minority groups is converging to the average.

Meanwhile, under the radar, many formerly middle-class areas have deteriorated, or formerly middle-class people have been forced to move to cheaper neighborhoods. The results of this neglect of middle-class people on chutes in deteriorating neighborhoods is seen in falling life expectancy for white men over the past decade, which is a uniquely American phenomenon—that is, in no other developed country is the life expectancy of white men falling.

It is natural for a city that is building its social assets to focus on lifting the poorest. But it may be even more even more cost-effective to avoid downward spirals for middle-class segments of the population. To this end a good strategy is to use city assets to blend high- and low-income areas by creating attractive hubs—such as colleges, hospitals, and start-up incubators, in middle-class neighborhoods on the slide.

This kind of action can provide a more varied neighborhood and open possibilities for young people, but will usually have to complemented with various social investments. Some examples of social investments that can be worthwhile are training programs for people who have lost their jobs. But much of the middle-class slide is also correlated with health issues such as alcohol and drug abuse, overweight, and mental health issues.

In Britain, a sobering report from the Royal Society for Public Health recommends a radical change of British drug policies based on the research that exists today. It shows that there are good evidence-based justifications for mandatory drug education in schools and for replacing the present drugs classification with one based on evidence of harm. The report's writers point out that imprisoning the young damages their development, severs their ties with family and community, and brings trauma and exposure to gang violence. There exists, they say, "an emerging body of evidence that criminal sanctions are not effective" in deterring illegal drug use. The impact of imprisonment on drug users is, however, hugely damaging, particularly on the young. Among the most striking examples of positive action is Portugal, which in 2001 took the bold decision of focusing on harm-reduction and health promotion, while removing criminal sanctions on personal possession of drugs. The results included an 80 percent decline in drug-induced deaths by 2012, a 94 percent reduction in new cases of HIV among those who inject drugs, and a decline in cases of hepatitis C and B. Drug use in Portugal is now below the European average, and social costs, including costs to health and to the legal system, have fallen significantly.[19]

Psychological disorders are also closely tied to middle-class decline— among other things, psychological disorders such as schizophrenia and even less serious disorders can lead to homelessness and affect an individual's ability to hold down a job. It is already well known that milder disorders can be significantly mitigated with early cognitive behavioral therapy. A more recent and surprising insight is that the same holds true for some serious afflictions such as schizophrenia. There is now strong evidence that early detection and treatment can cure or mitigate the disease, which can save considerable amounts later on.[20]

HELPING THE HOMELESS AS A SOCIAL INVESTMENT

In recent years a number of studies have indicated that it is significantly cheaper to house the homeless than to leave them on the streets. For example, studies tracking chronically homeless adults who were helped with housing seem to indicate dramatic cost savings that more than paid for the cost of putting them in decent housing. In Charlotte, North Carolina, a program to house the homeless was started in 2012 and initially housed eighty-five chronically homeless people. Savings have included $1.8 million in health-care costs realized from 447 fewer visits to the emergency room per year (a 78 percent reduction) and 372 fewer hospital days (a 79 percent reduction) for the population that had been housed. There was also a 72 percent drop in arrests, and the new tenants also spent eighty-four fewer days in jail than they had in the year previous to moving into the housing.[21]

The housing cost $6 million in land and construction costs, and tenants are required to contribute 30 percent of their income (which consists mainly of benefits) toward rent. The remainder of the rent per tenant is covered by donations and local and federal funding. The Charlotte initiative also helps the formerly homeless to find their own sources of income. Without housing, just 50 percent had been able to generate some income through work. One year after move-in this share had risen to 82 percent. After an average of seven years of homelessness, 94 percent of the original tenants retained their housing after eighteen months, with 99 percent of the rent being collected.

The program has been so successful that Charlotte's Urban Ministry Center is planning a $4 million expansion to bring the total capacity from 85 to 120 units. More than 200 chronically homeless people in the county qualify for such housing. It is desperately needed to bring down Charlotte's homeless population, which had risen at twice the national rate in the years 2010–2013. Although the rate of homeless individuals without children dropped significantly, "On any given night, about 2,418 people in the community are homeless, including 952 in emergency shelters, 1,183 in transitional housing and 283 without any shelter."

WORK PROGRAMS AS A SOCIAL INVESTMENT

Work programs that give long-term effects can also be good social investments. For example, traditionally governments have focused on getting newly unemployed people back to work, as unemployment is one of the biggest welfare costs. But analysis of lifetime costs of people who receive welfare benefits of one kind or another found that one of the most expensive groups comprises people who have recently returned to work from being on unemployment. This is because they are likely to become unemployed again. In any given month, 70 percent of people who sign up for a benefit have received a benefit before. This suggests that more attention should be paid to helping those people stay independent. The crucial issues are the costs, and what the long-term benefits are.

In some cases, there may be alternatives to actual social investments that can reduce the number of people who live on unemployment benefits or food stamps. For example, in the United States, since 2009 the

When Boris Johnson took office as mayor of London in 2008 with a promise to lower youth crime, he asked his top aides to identify the best youth services programs. It turned out that no one knew which ones were best. Youth services provide lifelines and enrichment, often serving the most troubled and disadvantaged. Yet as Johnson found out, the success of these programs—unlike road construction or crime fighting—is exceedingly difficult to measure.

Johnson assigned a top lieutenant to the project who consulted with experts around the world. Based on this research, a five-level "standards of evidence" framework was created. The framework—dubbed Project Oracle—is cumulative, meaning that it is necessary to get one and then two of them right before advancing to higher levels. Level 1 is a basic theory of change, a simple articulation of the organization's goals, which remarkably few nonprofits have. Level 2 is a straightforward evaluation plan. From there, additional levels become increasingly thorough in their ability to measure impact.

With the framework in hand, the mayor converted an advisory board of London grant providers and academics into a governing consortium for the entire

number of "able-bodied-adults" without dependents receiving food stamps has more than doubled. Part of this increase is due to a federal rule that allowed states to waive the program's modest work requirement. According to a report from the Foundation for Government Accountability, only 21 percent of food stamp recipients were working at all.[22] This had very negative long-term consequences for them and for municipal and state social expenditures.

However, Kansas and Maine chose to reinstate work requirements. Once work requirements were established, half of all recipients left the food stamp program. Forty percent of these found employment within three months, and about 60 percent found employment within a year. Furthermore, with the implementation of the work requirement in Kansas, the caseload dropped by 75 percent. By January 1, 2016, work requirements were being enforced statewide in sixteen states.

effort. The consortium devised a bundle of supports and incentives. All non-profits can access highly subsidized training in evaluation methods. Now the mayor-led consortium of foundations and universities in London is moving all nonprofit youth organizations toward consistent, academically rigorous evaluation measures, a revolutionary turn away from the norm in performance monitoring of social service providers. The new system will for the first time enable the city to gauge and compare the relative progress made by publicly funded entities who work with disadvantaged teens and families. Rather than forcing evaluation on nonprofits, the mayor introduced a uniform and easy-to-use evaluation system within a supportive environment. Every participating nonprofit receives subsidized training and is matched with university professors and college students. Successes are celebrated through interagency competitions and cash prizes. This has provided a common framework for assessment that allows the public and philanthropic sectors to determine which social service programs are working, while allowing nonprofits to analyze what's making a real difference and what needs to be addressed operationally.

But improved social outcomes mostly also require social investments. For example, the state-led work-first welfare reforms of the 1990s moved millions of Americans back into the labor force, spurring greater economic growth.[23] But they combined demands and incentives for welfare recipients to seek work with social investments in work-fare and training programs. Welfare caseloads plummeted, employment rose, and poverty rates dropped, particularly among the most at-risk populations. Such examples illustrate social investments as part of an evidence-based mix of work programs and incentives. This is quite different from wholesale increases in social spending. In fact, investing in social assets today aims to reduce social spending tomorrow.

In some cases, it may be more difficult to track and evaluate the long-term effects of programs. Box 7-1 describes how a former mayor of London, Boris Johnson, tackled this issue.

These examples from developed countries show how evidence-based social investments can over time have large effects on a city's social assets or debts, and can reduce its social expenditures, freeing more resources for investments. This self-reinforcing process is a key for a treadmill town to transition to being a turbo city. In emerging-market countries, the basic questions are in principle similar, but solutions often need to be much cheaper. In addition, lawlessness, corruption, and institutional decay or a lack of needed institutions are much greater challenges.

SOCIAL INVESTMENT IN EMERGING-MARKET CITIES

Chongqing is the setting for China's most ambitious and creative social investment. Chongqing's efforts to achieve this have gone further than anywhere else in the country. Though called a municipality, Chongqing comprises 12 million villagers who live in the rural countryside, along with another 18 million who live in the core city and in other widely scattered towns. However, there is a constant stream of villagers leaving the rural countryside and settling in the city. Once they get there they have multiple problems, and so do the city administrators.

To manage the influx of villagers better, in 2007 Chongqing persuaded the central government to let it test out new ways of handling the newcomers and of making good use of the land they leave behind. Under its Communist Party secretary, Bo Xilai, the municipality's government touted what admirers called the "Chongqing model."[24] This involved three main initiatives. First, the government built apartments to rent to the urban poor, including rural migrants, and allowed tenants to buy their homes after they had lived in them for five years. Second, the government gave full urban status to millions of migrants, meaning they would get access to subsidized urban health care and education. Third, the government announced changes to the urban-planning system to allow land left behind by migrants to be traded: land used for housing in faraway villages can be converted to use for farming, and a corresponding amount of farmland near towns can instead be used for urban expansion. It was a breakthrough in a country that still officially disapproves of selling farmers' property. Farmers who want to sell their rights to their village land are given what is called a land ticket, or *dipiao*. Developers who want to build, say, a twenty-five-acre project on farmland can buy twenty-five acres' worth of *dipiao*. The tickets do not have to be owned by farmers of that very plot. The farmers get to keep 85 percent of the sale price of the *dipiao*. Their village administrations get the rest.

While these reforms have not quite lived up to the initially stated ambitions, they have helped Chongqing's economy to see GDP growth of several percentage points above the national average and better than most inland cities.[25]

In other emerging countries other types social investments are needed to tackle more deep-seated problems. In fact, some cities are in danger of reaching a tipping point where criminal elements are taking over. Most of the world's most dangerous metropolises are scattered across Latin America and the Caribbean, but some remarkable turnarounds show that such a fate is not inevitable. Medellín, Colombia, and Ciudad Juárez, Mexico, have succeeded with similar declines in murder rates as New York. São Paulo went from being one of the most dangerous cities in Brazil to one of its safest. Rio de Janeiro was known for legendary gang and police violence. After years of incremental experimentation, serious reforms were implemented from 2009 onward. Political leaders at the state and municipal level began investing in new approaches to law and order and social investment. More than 9,000 of the city's 43,000 military police started using proximity policing techniques, essentially having a visible presence in the proximity of known criminals. Murder rates fell 65 percent between 2009 and 2012. Investment and tourists returned.

But best of all has been the development in Medellín. We already described how Medellín used city planning and asset development to help reduce crime. But this was only possible because Medellín freed itself from entrenched interests. And some other cities are succeeding as well.

FREEING SOCIAL INVESTMENT
FROM ENTRENCHED INTERESTS

Leoluca Orlando, the mayor of Palermo, Italy, gave his city a new lease on life by taking on organized crime. This was a social, not a physical, infrastructure issue that needed attention—one that Orlando took on at the risk of his own life. When Orlando ran for the job of mayor, organized crime had displaced democracy, equality, innovation, and freedom.

In Palermo, on the island of Sicily, the special interest group that Orlando battled was the Mafia. The grip of special interests on a city's social policy are not always as ruthless as the Mafia's, but still they must be recognized as such. A special interest can be defined as groups that manage to exert a large influence on policies and use that toward their own interests rather than city development in the interest of the large majority. In some cities special interests can be groups of property owners; in others they can be teachers or police unions. Even when entrenched interests are not hired killers, the city politicians who manage to break their destructive stranglehold are exceptional.

In the United States the duo of Rudolph Giuliani and Michael Bloomberg, mayors of New York City, may constitute such exceptional politicians. A wide range of groupings from traffic cops to civil liberties opposed Giuliani's campaign to curtail crime.[26] Michael Bloomberg quickly expanded on the city's progress during the 1990s, after being elected New York City's mayor in 2002. He combined the reforms of his predecessor, in welfare and policing with his own. He re-zoned land for needed housing, reduced public school inefficiencies, and advanced major transportation projects like the seven-train extension and rapid buses. In addition, he pioneered changes in the urban fabric—from the High Line Park to an automobile-free Times Square—that may have seemed insubstantial to outsiders, but were appreciated by New Yorkers.

Some think Bloomberg went too far in social pragmatism. Examples included a defeated measure to ban large sodas. But this particular proposal was quite in line with other aims from the board of health to target, for example, trans fats in cooking, Styrofoam containers, and salt.

Ideally, however, cities would adopt rational, long-term social policies that are not dependent on uniquely courageous and competent individuals. Our preferred model conveys powers to a social investment fund for social investment with some political independence, as a sister organization to the urban wealth fund for governance of economic assets.

In our view a social investment fund should borrow some features from the consortium Boris Johnson put together for Project Oracle. It would continuously calculate the city's social debt and develop a simple calculating tool like the Public Health Calculator (see figure 7-1) and require its use for investment decisions. Using such transparent tools, it would rank and suggest programs that more efficiently reduce social debt. It could administer an actual fund to be drawn on by city administrators to fund social investments that are not covered by the ordinary budget, and that are expected to yield a return later on.

A number of Swedish towns have implemented experimental versions of social investment funds. One of the first, the town of Norrköping, south of Stockholm, pioneered the use of a social investment fund in Sweden in 2010.[27]

The most interesting feature was the methodological development of the fund concept. The emphasis was on identifying social investments that sometimes can take years to earn a return. With only $2 million dollars in the fund, a limit was set that projects should repay investment costs within five years. Much effort was put into identifying and codifying ways of measuring returns on social investment. Most of the initial projects concerned innovative ways of getting school dropouts back to school or into work. In 2014, two separate evaluations of the social investment fund were published in 2014. They concluded that the projects that the fund had initiated did indeed lead to large returns, or municipal cost savings. Funds similar to Norrköping's have now been implemented by about half of Sweden's municipalities.[28]

Our vision is to give such funds wider powers and the same political independence as urban wealth funds (described in greater detail in preceding chapters). This would make political short cuts that cost cities dearly in the long run much more obvious and more difficult to get away with.

A city's social costs are increased when residents are struggling in the labor market. Therefore, it is crucial for a city to nurture its human wealth. That is the topic of the next chapter.

CHAPTER 8

Boosting the Value of Human Assets

WHILE HAVING A LARGE SHARE of college graduates on average appears to be a good thing for growth, a surprising number of towns with few college-educated residents do better than cities that are populated by creative and intellectual people. The dividing line between successful and failing cities seems to hinge crucially on the ability to supply intellectual capital in the form of entrepreneurial skill or particular types of competence that are currently in demand by local growing industries.[1] Sometimes, this goes hand in hand with attracting many college-educated academics. And many studies have shown that, on average, cities with a growing number of college-educated residents also enjoy subsequent employment growth.[2] But these studies don't tell the whole story. In fact, other studies show that some cities also do well and grow with fewer college-educated inhabitants but with residents who have a knack for entrepreneurial growth.[3]

In this chapter we show how cities that grow and successfully provide high living standards have found unique selling points to attract the human capital they need, and how they have managed to build competence among the inhabitants they already have.

THE EDUCATION-AS-INVESTMENT FALLACY

Decades of research and policymaking to improve cities' human capital has been, we would argue, based on blurred thinking. Human capital has simply been assumed to be the same as years of schooling, and sometimes, years of work experience. Based on this fallacy a huge research literature has found correlations between years of education and national and regional growth.[4]

Yet this approach is probably highly misleading, and has led many cities down a garden path. Assuming that more input, in this case in the form of years of schooling, leads to higher capital value is based on a long gone industrial logic. Today huge investments can become worthless quickly, and small investments can become very valuable.

Traditionally human capital is measured in terms of years of schooling. Our claim is that cities that do well do not try to aim mainly for their residents to accumulate years of education and work experience. Rather they focus on quality, treating their citizens' intellectual ability or skills as assets that can be made more or less valuable. We use the term "human assets" to differentiate from commonly used, but misleading, measures of human capital in terms of years of schooling. The value of human assets is easily measured. Basically it is the price that employers are willing to pay for human assets above and beyond pure muscle power. This is captured reasonably well by the average hourly wage per person of working age.[5] The value of a city's human assets to the city can be pushed up in cities that attract many high-income people that move in. The argument could be made that a basic dynamic to increase human assets is to attract the kind of people who possess high assets to begin with. But the real achievement is to help people who already live in a city to be able to sell their skills for a higher wage.

THE VALUE OF HUMAN ASSETS

The bottom line for human assets is how they are valued in the labor market. Therefore, total wage income divided by the number of inhabitants of working age is a pretty good measure of the yield that a city's skills assets provide.

This may seem highly unjust. High-tech metros like Silicon Valley have high and skyrocketing values of human assets. Such "nerdistans," defined by their industrial or tech parks and suburban-style housing, are meccas for engineers and high-tech professionals who prefer suburban living.[6] Many upscale suburbs are composed almost exclusively of high-skilled, high-income, high-human-capital individuals and households.

But the purpose of valuing human assets is not to be fair, but to be right. And there is hardly any better measure than how many people employers hire and are prepared to pay. For a city like Detroit that does poorly on this measure, the point is not to compare itself with others, but to have an up-to-date picture of the direction it is heading and to be able to gauge progress.

While the value of human assets to a specific city is not as volatile as the stock market, it does vary over time. In thinking about the value of human assets, there are three principal considerations:

1. How much knowledge do citizens actually possess? Years of education and experience are no guarantee for top class skills or intellectual prowess.

2. Human assets are more valuable to both the city and its inhabitants if they are geared toward local employers' needs.

3. Human assets become more valuable if a city can increase demand for its citizens' skills by encouraging new employers and attracting an inflow of employers.

Let us look at how cities have succeeded in boosting their human assets.

GROW HUMAN ASSETS WITH BETTER
LIFELONG LEARNING

Actual knowledge is a composite of the quality of education and how much people learn throughout their work lives, from either workplace-related training or activities outside of work. One of the most established researchers in the field, Eric Hanushek, has shown that actual knowledge, not the number of years of formal education, are important for individual success and regional economic growth.[7]

If the number of years of formal education is not key, then what is key is to improve school results for the period of time that people are in school. Germany is a good example of maximizing educational benefit. In 2000 Germany had very poor results in the PISA (Program for International Student Assessment) ranking, the international comparison test of the OECD. Yet within fifteen years Germany managed to turn around its dismal PISA results, so that as of 2016 it now ranks among the best in Europe. Particularly noteworthy is that the weakest students' performance has improved the most in Germany, whereas it has deteriorated sharply in some other countries, including Sweden. Even the children of immigrants have improved significantly, which is interesting because both Sweden and Germany are large refugee and immigration receivers. Immigrant children in Germany now reach the same average performance in mathematics as the average for all children in the United States and Sweden.

How did Germany do this? After the shock settled for Germany in 2000, when the first PISA measure indicated terrible rankings, German states focused on what the research findings implied about successful schools. Germany has not poured more money into schooling, reduced class size, nor restricted the freedom to choose schools.

In Germany the students are more segregated by ability than in the United States, as students are streamed, starting with the fifth grade, according to their intellectual ability and interest, into either a nine-year or a twelve-year school. This streaming is not new, and is not the basis of Germany's reforms or of its success.

The important reforms were taken directly from experimental school research. Exactly how this was done varied from state to state, but in all cases followed roughly similar patterns. First, much attention was lavished on teaching techniques and training teachers to use evidence-proven tools for cognitive activation. Second, Germany introduced early assessment of children and, where necessary, invests in special support measures to try to involve parents in their children's education and even train them as well. Third, there came a more systematic evaluation of student progress and schools' success. National tests are supplemented early with regular spot checks to ensure that measurement results are correct. Cheap, effective approaches, such as using older children to tutor younger ones, are also used.

In chapter 7 we saw that early extra attention can reduce crime rates and increase incomes later on, as evidenced by the Perry Preschool experiments in Ypsilanti, Michigan, which were begun in the 1960s. Early extra attention can do wonders also for school results even many years later. One of the most successful interventions in the Perry Preschool was hiring teachers to work solely on language and communication in the early years, since most of the pupils don't speak English as a first language.

In sum, Germany did not invent anything new, but implemented proven research results systematically throughout the school system. Improving school quality is an obvious, but often neglected, way of building a city's human assets, and it does not even have to cost a whole lot.

TAILOR LEARNING TO EMPLOYERS' NEEDS

As we, and many educators, propose, many years of schooling do not automatically translate into great, or the most valuable, learning. Acquiring a lot of valuable knowledge, rather than attending school for many years, is only one step toward boosting the effectiveness of a city's human asset management. A crucial but often unasked question is whether the workforce's skills match the demand of employers. Only then do human assets become economically valuable.

According to the American economist Edward Glaeser, in an age of knowledge and information, cities where more than 10 percent of the population have college degrees statistically speaking tend to grow twice as fast in terms of population as those with fewer college educated.[8] But that is a correlation, not a statement of cause and effect. People with college degrees also move to cities that they find attractive even if job prospects are worse. Most important, employers in growing cities do not attract college-educated people in general, but those with the particular college education who fit their specific needs. This has an important implication. A city cannot hope to succeed better just by increasing the supply of college educated at large—that is, by inducing more of its residents to go to college.

The key is, instead, to ask how the needs of current employers can be better met. The small Swedish town of Edsbyn is brimming with successful smaller industrial firms that have a hard time finding engineers and skilled workers. Firm owners lament the fact that universities in faraway cities lure their children into college programs that give them careers that pay worse than what would have been on offer in Edsbyn. Often the children meet partners at these faraway city universities who have no interest in moving back to Edsbyn. The end result is that the university cities grow, but endow many young people with a skill set that is not best for overall growth of the country. But it may be that the firm owners in Edsbyn partly have themselves to blame. Perhaps they didn't communicate strongly enough that they offer opportunity for the college educated right at home. Perhaps they could have offered an apprentice system of some kind to channel the right students to their firms. Towns that help schools to cooperate closely with employers often give young people a much better understanding of what is in demand, and end up with growing businesses and lower unemployment.

The city of Coimbatore in the state of Tamil Nadu, on the southern tip of India, boasts impressive private sector growth, which appears to be directly linked to its thriving vocational training institutions, which produce a workforce with skills relevant to industry needs.[9] Some of the prominent manufacturing companies in Coimbatore are the local Sakthi Group and German Bosch. With a population of just 3 million in the greater metropolitan area, Coimbatore has ten universities, sixty engineering colleges, and thirty polytechnic and industry training institutes that prepare graduates with technical skills and specialize in fundamental disciplines such as physics and mathematics. Coimbatore's engineering schools produce engineers and managers as well as shop supervisors and machine operators. In fact, about 10 percent of India's engineering colleges are located in Coimbatore, putting it on par with or ahead of many cities in India that are larger in size, including Jaipur and Pune.

Coimbatore's institutions of higher education were created by the city's family-owned firms and thus are shaped directly by current industry needs, in addition to helping to develop future potential in new areas. The praxis-oriented technical curricula are developed in consultation with firms. Local engineering students spend part of each school day on the shop floor as well as in class. Firms are involved in devising curricula, sponsoring internships, and even in running some university departments. Students graduate with relevant applied skills and extensive manufacturing experience.

The entire setup is distinct from schools elsewhere in Tamil Nadu. Training programs and universities are created to produce a workforce with practical skills to meet expected local demand. This is quite different from the strategy in many less successful cities that pride themselves on universities that may be academically successful but do not educate in skills that local employers are looking for.

Finally, human assets become more valuable if a city can raise demand for its citizens' skills by encouraging new employers and attracting an inflow of employers.

INCREASE DEMAND FOR CITIZENS' SKILLS

Cities, as well as countries, grow richer when their people learn how to produce more valuable stuff per person. Cities in which many who think up how to produce more valuable stuff find it easy to start businesses will also pull up wages for the people who possess the skills they need. As a result, a city's total human assets become more valuable. As firms struggle to find all the skilled people they need, they also invest more in upgrading skills for their current workforce and keeping them at the cutting edge.

Sadly, many advanced economies seem to have lost the knack for increasing workers' productivity. Except for a brief spurt around the turn of the millennium, productivity has grown painfully slowly in rich countries in the four decades since 1986. But different cities do quite differently in this respect.[10]

In the 1970s, experts would have predicted that Los Angeles would outpace San Francisco in population, income, economic power, and influence. Actually the opposite happened: San Francisco outpaced LA. The usual factors used to explain urban growth—immigration, local economic policies, and the pool of skilled labor—do not account for the contrast between the two cities and their fates. So what does? In one detailed comparison, the respective cities' institutions and leadership is found to explain much of the difference.[11]

Experience has demonstrated that pouring tax money into new business in the form of subsidies or public risk capital does not work very well. Josh Lerner shows persuasively in his 2009 book, *The Boulevard of Broken Dreams*, that clusters of new entrepreneurship are very difficult to set in motion with such directed initiatives. One reason for failure is that these measures are born of a political process that usually gets things wrong, or is derailed by regulatory capture: various entrenched interests try to divert funding or get governments to impose regulation that furthers their own beliefs or interests, but harm others much more. One or another initiative may work, but knowing which one will work requires careful and independent evaluation.

Some researchers have found that, rather than promoting certain businesses, a city's efforts to improve its general business climate can make a big difference, in particular for the employment prospects of immigrants or other groups whose members struggle to find jobs.[12] One study compares nine different indices of business climate for American states.[13] It finds that indices that focus on wider issues such as quality of life or knowledge jobs tend to be poor predictors of employment growth, whereas indices that focus on the cost of doing business as influenced by regulation and taxation tend to be better predictors.[14]

A study in Sweden found that the local business climate was very important for immigrants' job prospects.[15] Entrepreneurs were asked to assess sixteen different areas that directly reflect how their particular municipality affects local business climate. These areas capture how well the municipal administration deals with licenses and permits, tendering and competition, schooling, and other issues that might be important to local business.[16]

It turned out that these factors had an important impact on employment rates, in particular of non-European immigrants to Sweden who often ended up in a particular town because they were refugees rather than because they were offered a job. A different way of putting this is that municipalities' improvement of business conditions encouraged and supported more businesses, and this in turn raised demand for the skills that immigrants had and thus made them more valuable. That is how cities that provide good business conditions boost the value of their human assets.

POLITICAL BARRIERS TO INCREASING THE VALUE OF HUMAN ASSETS

The three approaches to raising skill value described in this chapter have robust evidence to support them, yet they are pursued vigorously by just some cities. In many others, all kinds of vested interests have other agendas, or are simply not well informed about the evidence.

So it is important to ask whether there is a recipe that works even for cities with a divided or haphazard political landscape. In fact, some cities have good experience with somewhat politically independent organizations or even municipal companies that are partially owned by the business community and partially by the municipality. Sometimes these can act as "one-stop shops" for businesses that have routine technical queries on topics such as licensing. They can also coordinate issues that get lost between different departments of the city administration. In fact, they can actually take over responsibility for some administrative processes that are important to businesses, such as documentation, inspections, and some licensing.

This further supports the general gist of our argument, that a number of specialized functions related to asset governance should be handled more professionally and given greater political independence. In fact, as we argue in the next chapter, this may actually strengthen democracy.

CHAPTER 9

Reinventing City Democracy

AROUND THE TURN OF THE MILLENNIUM a series of protests, among them the "Occupy" movement, erupted in many Western cities; protesters claimed community ownership of public spaces and resistance to corporations, globalization, cars, and a diverse basket of other perceived threats. Underlying these protests was also a feeling that many cities do not live up to their task of enabling their inhabitants to carve out a high quality of life.

This protest movement fizzled out largely because it provided few solutions to how cities and countries can be governed better. This book formulates a recipe for success in the city that has rarely been formulated coherently, even though successful cities around the world have discovered some of the ingredients. We argue that cities do well that manage their wealth wisely—their social wealth, human capital, and economic assets. Those that succeed provide an exceptional quality of life for their inhabitants, and act as a magnet for newcomers.

We have found examples in cities all over the world. We argue that even though cities face different challenges at different stages of development, successful governance principles remain quite constant. In fact, some cities that started out poor but governed their assets wisely are now wealthy and are still served well by the same principles.

In many of these cities leaders have had an intuitive understanding of what it takes to make their city prosper. But it has been difficult to transfer this often tacit insight of particularly talented leaders to wider groups of city politicians and administrators. A good first step to wider implementation—in addition to reading this book!—is to train city administrators in the asset-based approach and in the use of the necessary tools, perhaps along the lines of the Peak Academy in Denver (see box 9-1).

But better information and training alone may not be enough to turn a treadmill city into a turbo city. Cities that focus on becoming rich in social, human, and economic assets rather than on trying to make ends meet may need to find institutional forms where city politicians formulate goals, overall directives, and citizens' interests while leaving as much as possible to independent and professional management of the city's assets.

Our argument is that delegating tasks to a more independent, professional organization such as an urban wealth fund not only can turn a treadmill town into a turbo city but also can actually improve democracy.

implementation of dozens of common sense cost-saving reforms. In one session, staff from the police, the 911 emergency call center, and license departments realized that manually inputting alarm permit data was wasting time, leading to missed data and needlessly costing the city thousands of dollars. In a few days at the academy, they charted an automated and coordinated approach. Eight colleagues at the city's human services agency realized that their myriad contracts with nonprofits lacked clarity of purpose, data, and expectations. The workers created consistent, cross-silo forms and procedures. Salary increases for the agency's management personnel are now tied to the number and quality of innovations advanced by their employees. In addition, ideas are profiled monthly on the city's website.[†]

*For further information on the academy's programs, see the Denver Peak Academy website (https://denpeakacademy.com).

†See Denver—the Mile-High City (website), "Mayor's Office, Peak Academy" (www.denvergov .org/content/denvergov/en/mayors-office/programs-initiatives/peak-performance/peak -academy.html).

The cause of democracy was served in one previously dysfunctional city in South America when the elected mayor became a political independent.

CASE STUDY: JAIME CASTRO'S THREE LONELY YEARS IN BOGOTÁ

In the late 1980s, Bogotá, the capital of Colombia, was a city in chaos. The city's administration, corrupt and dysfunctional, had no way of managing Bogotá's social and economic problems; years of mismanagement, corruption, drug cartels, and poverty had taken their toll. Yet entrenched interests blocked many attempts at reform.

In 1986 Virgilio Barco Vargas, the president of Colombia, who had been the mayor of Bogotá, lamented, "Of that booming city that I governed, today all that is left is an urbanized anarchy, tremendous chaos, immense disorder, a colossal mess."[1]

The turning point arrived in 1992, when Jaime Castro, a reform-minded lawyer, was elected mayor of Bogotá. Corruption in Bogotá seemed beyond help, but Castro had a unique quality: At the age of fifty-three he was willing to sacrifice his political career to create order and stability. A change in the legislation relating to term limits meant that the mayor could be in office for just one three-year term. That meant that Castro had just three years to turn the situation around, and then he would retire from office. He could afford to be unpopular because the law allowed him just one term anyhow: he was a so-called lame duck from the get-go. He was strongly committed to enacting change, and he could act without regard to all the interest groups—including criminal organizations, businesses, and unions—that normally are crucial for a mayor's political future. In effect, the term limit constraint turned Castro into a political independent.

Castro understood that it was not a coincidence that Bogotá was failing. The main problem was corruption. The city council held a great deal of power over the detailed management of the city, and its members relied heavily on extensive patronage networks to remain in power. They ran the city's agencies and publicly owned companies for personal benefit and to enrich their supporters. To deal with this corruption it is notable what Castro did not do: he did not appoint a blue-ribbon commission or hire expert consultants. Instead he used his experience as a constitutional lawyer to design a new law for how to govern the city. "Since the first day I walked into City Hall," Castro later said, "I began to take notes on small cards regarding what the statute would be, drawing on the difficulties I encountered along the way and my own observations."

Castro was ridiculed as a haughty mayor who did nothing but take notes on slips of paper. This view changed, however, when he not only wrote a document on how the city should be governed, but also had it enacted into law through a national presidential decree.

Castro set the stage for reform in Bogotá and became the first of a series of mayors who succeeded in turning the city around. In 2002 the city had improved to the point where the United Nations selected Bogotá as a "model city" to be emulated throughout Latin America. But implementing change was neither easy nor popular. The title of Jaime Castro's memoirs is revealing: *Three Years of Solitude*. The book's cover shows a picture of him standing alone, looking out his office window.

Jaime Castro had the nerve and skills to impose functional reforms during his limited three-year term. Voters rewarded him by voting for Antanas Mockus and Enrique Penalosa as his successors—men who, while in some ways quite different from Castro, continued in his spirit to change Bogotá for the better.

Like Castro, Mockus and Penalosa also came from nontraditional parties, which meant that they had a certain freedom in choosing the members of their administrations. Their teams were made up of young academics and professionals, including many women, and this rejuvenation in City Hall made it possible to move toward a more ethical and professional way of running the city, one that is much more in the interest of the large majority of the people, and therefore more democratic.

CITIES THAT GET STUCK

Politicians often believe that voters will not accept the kind of reforms that build assets. Jean-Claude Juncker, the current president of the European Commission, is often famously quoted for framing the worry of political leaders that voters are frightened by audacious reform when he said, "We all know what to do. We just don't know how to get reelected afterwards." That is why the term limit constraint on Bogotá's mayors actually frees them to be more audacious.

But—contradicting Juncker's point—politicians who reform often *are* amply rewarded. One empirical study focusing on the pace and direction of reforms in twenty-nine OECD countries since the mid-1990s showed that, despite the difficulty of introducing reforms geared toward economic development, voters often reward governments that do implement them.[2]

In spite of this surprisingly positive result, cities as well as countries can get stuck in a destructive downward spiral. In their 2012 much-acclaimed book, *Why Nations Fail: The Origins of Power, Prosperity, and Poverty*, Daron Acemoglu and James Robinson broaden the "conflict of interest" thesis into a far-reaching argument about how institutions determine the development of different countries. They illustrate how countries with "extractive" institutions generally remain poor. The elites in these countries find it profitable to suppress their populations and enrich themselves by abusing tax revenues or state monopolies to their own ends.[3] The same can happen in cities.

For decades, economists have been pessimistic about the prospects for effective government reform. Albert Hirschman detailed all the hurdles for reformers in his widely read book, *The Rhetoric of Reaction: Perversity, Futility, Jeopardy*.[4]

Yet people are becoming more aware and demanding change. There is also an interesting institutional competition between nations, states, and cities. We already saw how Bogotá got help from the national government to revamp its institutions. A similar mix of voter revolt and national intervention has led to the current revamping of Rome. Rome is plagued by overflowing rubbish bins, untended parks and gardens, inadequate public transport, and roads dotted with potholes. City politicians from the mainstream parties are on trial along with organized crime figures, all of them accused of jointly skimming municipal contracts. Romans are not accustomed to being ashamed of their city. But in 2016 it was subjected to the sort of direct, central-government administration normally reserved for Mafia-riddled villages in the rural Mezzogiorno, Italy's south. Fed-up Romans are also looking for an alternative. The Five Star Movement (M5S) started just a few years ago by the comedian Beppo Grillo seems to be winning the mayoral election by running as its candidate Virginia Raggi, a thirty-seven-year-old lawyer and consumer activist. Raggi's very lack of experience in office may in this case be an asset to her political future.

But institutional competition can also go the other way. When national governments appear unable to reform, cities will increasingly demand more leeway to find solutions or find creative ways to circumvent national regulation. In fact, this is already occurring in both North and South America.

Rodrigo Guerrero, the mayor of Cali, Colombia, from 1992 to 1994 and again from 2012 to 2015, and Antonio Villaraigosa, mayor of Los Angeles from 2005 to 2013 and as of 2017 a gubernatorial candidate, are examples of how a radical change is possible. They borrowed ideas and practices from around the world and worked with different layers of government to design integrated violence prevention strategies. There are encouraging examples across North America and Latin America and the Caribbean of mayors who open channels of communication with violence-plagued communities. Their goals are not only to put a halt to gang violence but also to introduce social policies to help crime-affected areas and underserviced communities and households and to redress extreme wealth inequality.

But for many cities, the advent of an exceptionally courageous and gifted mayor will in fact be an exceptional occurrence, and should not be hopefully awaited while remaining idle. Institutions must work when average people are called upon to run a city.

FROM "SOFT CITY" TO MORE DEMOCRACY

One common reason for lack of reforms and sound asset governance is a balkanization of local government. Many cities are actually complex organisms based on entities that function as though they were independent and siloed, yet in reality they are interdependent. For example, in Los Angeles County, as in other California cities, schools are the province of a school district with separately elected school boards; many other functions such as corrections and public health are provided by the county. These jurisdictions are not unified and often function at odds with each other. New York City is almost unique in that it owns and runs its own schools, water and sewer systems, sanitation, police and fire departments, jails, and health administrations, even though it also has to coordinate with five counties (for each of the five boroughs) on other issues. Jacksonville and Indianapolis are examples of cities that have merged city and county into metro jurisdictions in order to achieve administrative unity.

While a more unified city government probably helps, a common misconception is that a strong city is one in which politicians take charge and manage city affairs hands-on. In fact, the opposite is more often true. Just as "strong" states such as China or Russia are also weak in their ability to manage their country in the people's best interest, cities that do not delegate some realms of decisionmaking to professionals usually fail. The People's Republic of China is what Gunnar Myrdal termed a "soft state": one in which the potential for state action in the common interest is undermined by cadres of state employees who can make a fast buck by ignoring pollution regulation or by taking a bribe to ignore others' pollution.[5] Similarly, many cities are "soft cities" that consequently fail in their basic mission of providing sound services and a good quality of life.

Many of our examples from treadmill towns illustrate how public wealth can pervert democracy, an issue that has received much less attention than mere mismanagement of a public monopoly. When public wealth is within easy reach of city administrations or governments it creates incentives for abuse and corruption: buying political favors in exchange for lucrative contracts or positions in state-owned firms; offering organized interests free access to federal land or water from public water companies in exchange for political support; buying support of unions by allowing greater wage increases in state-owned companies; caving in to vocal minorities that oppose city development projects. In all these ways democracy for the common good degenerates into clientelism or worse. Politicians are rewarded who deftly buy support from various groups instead of enacting reforms in the wider public interest. That is the essence of a "soft city."

Even in cities with less outright corruption or clientelism, publicly owned firms force politicians toward a producer perspective. In cities as diverse as Berlin and Calcutta, leading politicians have rarely been interested in formulating consumer demands for more reliable infrastructure or better opportunities for those who create jobs.

In our previous book, *The Public Wealth of Nations*, we showed that democracy is vastly strengthened when the state has little wealth at its direct disposal. A truly strong state is one where politicians have to compete with agendas for the common interest, instead of competing by dishing out favors in the form of access to the public trough. The same is true for cities.

In a clientelist soft city, leaders have little interest in making city assets transparent. And they have little interest in ceding control of anything to professionals. It is hardly an accident that neither Greece nor Detroit has consolidated accounts of their respective considerable state assets, and have only incomplete records that are fragmented among several institutions. As long as city ownership of assets remains murky it is easier for local governments to distribute favors without being scrutinized. Even cooperation with neighboring municipalities is mostly spurned because it requires greater transparency and allows less meddling. After Detroit went bankrupt, an initiative for development of entire sections of Detroit took hold, led by an eclectic consortium of philanthropies such as the Kresge Foundation and corporations such as Quicken Loans, who work with urban development professionally. Obviously it would have been much better to invite this independent professionalism earlier in Detroit.

A "soft city" that can relinquish balkanized, clientelist decision structures also makes the first and most important move from a treadmill town to a turbo city: moving toward transparent professional governance of social, human, and economic assets, slightly removed from the political whims of the day. That is also the best way for different local government entities to cooperate in developing their city together. Transparency and professionalism are basic requirements for municipalities to trust each other.

Countries in which many cities modernize their governance will thrive, grow, and see democracy and civic engagement evolve.

Notes

PREFACE

1. Dag Detter and Stefan Fölster, *The Public Wealth of Nations: How Management of Public Assets Can Boost or Bust Economic Growth* (London: Palgrave Macmillan, 2015). The book was included in both the *Financial Times*'s and the *Economist*'s lists of Best Books of the Year 2015.

CHAPTER I

Chapter opening image: Crumbling overpasses and bridges in New York City (Jo Ann Snover, Shutterstock).

1. Anne Case and Angus Deaton, "Rising Morbidity and Mortality in Midlife among White Non-Hispanic Americans in the 21st Century," *Proceedings of the National Academy of Sciences* 112, no. 49 (2015): 1–6.

2. In 2014 the urban population accounted for 54 percent of the total global population, up from 34 percent in 1960, and this percentage continues to grow, according to the *Demographic Yearbook 2014*, "Table 8—Population of Capital Cities and Cities of 100,000 or More Inhabitants: Latest Available Year, 1995–2014" (link at http://unstats.un.org/unsd/demographic/products/dyb/dyb2014 .htm).

3. See, for example, Edward Glaeser, *Triumph of the City: How Our Greatest Invention Makes Us Richer, Smarter, Greener, Healthier and Happier* (New York: Penguin, 2011).

4. See, for example, McKinsey & Company, "Värdet av digital teknik i den Svenska vården" [The value of digital technology in Swedish health care], report (Stockholm: McKinsey & Company, June 2016).

5. Robert Kiyosaki and Sharon Lechter, *Rich Dad, Poor Dad: What the Rich Teach Their Kids about Money That the Poor and Middle Class Do Not!* (New York: Warner Business Books, 2000).

6. Most of the reforms that economists have recommended for decades are listed in the annual surveys by the OECD such as *Economic Survey of the US 2016* (Paris: OECD, 2016).

7. Daron Acemoglu and James Robinson, *Why Nations Fail: The Origins of Power, Prosperity, and Poverty* (New York: Crown, 2012). The book opens with a description of Nogales on both sides of the border.

8. According to Chang-Tai Hsieh and Enrico Moretti, "Why Do Cities Matter? Local Growth and Aggregate Growth," NBER working paper 21154 (Cambridge, Mass.: National Bureau of Economic Research, May 2015), almost half of aggregate U.S. growth was driven by growth of cities in the Global South. Many of these are not hubs for industries with the highest productivity, but they provide an environment where many newcomers are offered better jobs than they had before and there is an ample supply of housing.

9. The median city is the one in the middle between an equal number of those that performed better and those that performed worse. In recent years some cities in Florida and California, such as Tampa and San Francisco, have been making up for lost growth. See, for example, Ross DeVol, Minoli Ratnatunga, and Armen Bedroussian, "Best-Performing Cities—Where America's Jobs Are Created and Sustained" (Santa Monica, Calif.: Milken Institute, December 2015).

10. Swedish Agency for Growth Policy Analysis (Tillväxtanalys), "Digitaliseringens bidrag till tillväxt och konkurrenskraft i Sverige" [The contribution of digitization to growth and competitiveness in Sweden] (Stockholm: Rapport, 2014), p. 13.

11. Many studies show that a city that has twice the population of another has wages that are 2 to 10 percent higher than those in the smaller city. See, for example, Gilles Duranton, "Growing through Cities in Developing Countries," Policy Research Working Paper 6818 (Washington: World Bank, 2014) (http://documents.worldbank.org/curated/en/727191468326108729/pdf/WPS6818.pdf).

12. World Bank, "Competitive Cities for Jobs and Growth: What, Who, and How?" (Washington: World Bank Group, 2015).

13. Michael Storper, in "Why Does a City Grow? Specialization, Human Capital, or Institutions?" (Paris and London: Institut d'Etudes Politiques de Paris and London School of Economics, July 25, 2008), shows in detail why empirical

studies have provided so few insights. Apart from the long time lags between changes in city policies and outcomes in terms of better city development, specialization, human capital, and institutions are all endogenous explanations of growth with recursive relationships that are difficult to disentangle.

14. This case study is described in Jan Ekberg and Mikael Ohlson, "Flyktingars arbetsmarknad är inte alltid nattsvart" [The labor market is not always poor for refugees], *Ekonomisk Debatt* [Economic debate] 28, no. 5 (2000): 431–39.

15. Bruce Katz and Jennifer Bradley, in *The Metropolitan Revolution* (Brookings Institution Press, 2013), provide a fascinating description of the rivalries between local governments in the Denver metropolitan area, and what it took to overcome some of them.

CHAPTER 2

Chapter opening image: Abandoned dwellings in Detroit, Mich. (Alisa Farov, Shutterstock).

1. Christopher Berry and Edward L. Glaeser, "The Divergence of Human Capital Levels across Cities," NBER Working Paper 11617 (Cambridge, Mass.: National Bureau of Economic Research, September 2005), document the finding that the distribution of human capital has gone from relatively even among U.S. metropolitan areas to increasingly divergent.

2. *Wikipedia*, s.v. "2005 Levee Failures in Greater New Orleans" (https://en .wikipedia.org/wiki/2005_levee_failures_in_Greater_New_Orleans).

3. See also *Wikipedia*, s.v. "U.S. Army Corps of Engineers" (https://en.wiki pedia.org/wiki/U.S._Army_Corps_of_Engineers_civil_works_controversies _(New_Orleans)). Other scandals are described in Detter and Fölster, *The Public Wealth of Nations: How Management of Public Assets Can Boost or Bust Economic Growth* (London: Palgrave Macmillan, 2015).

4. Wowereit is the eponym of the story title "The Glamour Guy," *Time* (European edition), August 5, 2005.

5. For urban areas with a population greater than 300,000 people in 2014, see "Urban Policy—How to Shrink a City," *The Economist*, May 30, 2015.

6. One might fall for the temptation of trying to discern trends in preferences. For example, in the decade from 2000 to 2010, suburban growth in the United States sharply outpaced city growth. But in recent years, city growth may be holding up better.

7. Detroit gets most of its revenues from income tax, which is something of an anomaly in American cities, where property taxes are generally the main source of revenue. See Matt Helms, "Why Detroit Can Expect More Tax Revenue Next Year," September 16, 2015 (www.governing.com/topics/finance/tns-detroit -michigan-income-tax-collection.html).

8. Marco Görlinger, Silvia Stiller, and Isabel Sünner, "Ökonomische Eckdaten und wirtschaftsstrukturelle Entwicklung in der Metropolregion Hamburg" [Economic facts and structural development in metropolitan Hamburg] (Hamburg, Germany: Hamburgisches Weltwirtschaftsinstitut, February 26, 2013) (www.hwwi.org/fileadmin/hwwi/Publikationen/Studien/2013_02_26_Metropolregion_Hamburg.pdf).

9. See, for example, City of Munich, Department of Urban Planning and Building Regulation, "Shaping the Future of Munich," development report (Munich, Germany, 2005).

10. Munich is among the top European cities in the OECD's international comparisons on the basis of the PISA (Program for International Student Assessment) tests that thousands of schoolchildren take in all participating countries.

11. See chapter 7, the section titled "Investing in Social Assets during Childhood."

12. See, for example, Markus Jäntti, Knut Røed, Robin Naylor, Anders Björklund, and others, "American Exceptionalism in a New Light: A Comparison of Intergenerational Earnings: Mobility in the Nordic Countries, the United Kingdom and the United States," IZA Discussion Paper No. 1938 (Bonn, Germany: Institute for the Study of Labor [IZA]), 2006) (http://ftp.iza.org/dp1938.pdf).

13. Raj Chetty and Nathaniel Hendren, "The Impacts of Neighborhoods on Intergenerational Mobility: Childhood Exposure Effects and County-Level Estimates" (Cambridge, Mass.: Harvard University and National Bureau of Economic Research, 2015).

14. Ibid. In this study "neighborhood" means either commuting zone or county.

15. Edward Glaeser, *Triumph of the City: How Our Greatest Invention Makes Us Richer, Smarter, Greener, Healthier and Happier* (New York: Penguin, 2011).

16. For rich kids, geography doesn't really matter. The Chetty and Hendren study found that the chances that children of rich families will grow up to be rich is pretty much the same across metropolitan areas around the country. Of children who grew up as one-percenters, one out of three will be making at least $100,000 annually by the time they turn thirty. See Chetty and Hendren, "Impacts of Neighborhoods on Intergenerational Mobility."

17. Ibid. Regions with larger black populations had lower upward-mobility rates. But the researchers' analysis suggested that this was not primarily because of their race. Both white and black residents of Atlanta have low upward mobility.

18. Pew Research Center, "America's Shrinking Middle Class: A Close Look at Changes within Metropolitan Areas" (Washington: Pew Charitable Trust, 2016). Middle-income Americans are defined by Pew as adults who earn two-thirds to double the national median income, adjusted for household size. In the 229 urban centers that are home to three-quarters of the U.S. population,

median household incomes, adjusted for the cost of living in the area, grew in just 39 out of those metro areas between 1999 and 2014.

19. Janet Currie and Hannes Schwandt, in "Inequality in Mortality between Rich and Poor U.S. Counties Decreased among the Young While Increasing for Older Adults, 1990–2010," *Science*, April 2016, DOI: 10.1126/science.aaf1437, compare the health of people living in poverty in different American cities.

20. Pew Research Center, "America's Shrinking Middle Class."

21. Anne Case and Angus Deaton, "Rising Morbidity and Mortality in Midlife among White Non-Hispanic Americans in the 21st Century," *Proceedings of the National Academy of Sciences* 1, no. 6 (2015): 15078–83.

22. Between 2000 and 2010 the urban cores (the area within a radius of two miles of the city's center) of the fifty-one largest metropolitan areas added a total of 206,000 residents. But the surrounding rings, two to five miles from the core, actually lost 272,000. In contrast to those small gains and losses, the suburban areas—ten to twenty miles from the center—experienced a growth of roughly 15 million people. See Jed Kolko, "Even after the Housing Bust, Americans Still Love the Suburbs," *New Geography*, October 12, 2012 (www.newgeography.com /content/003139-even-after-housing-bust-americans-still-love-suburbs).

23. See the table "Major US Cities Ranked by Neighborhood Diversity," in "The Least Segregated Cities in America," *Priceonomics* (http://priceonomics.com /the-most-and-least-segregated-cities-in-america/). Other indexes that focus on income and other factors arrive at somewhat different rankings. See, for example, Richard Florida, Charlotta Mellander, and Kevin Stolarick, "Inside the Black Box of Regional Development," *Journal of Economic Geography* 8, no. 5 (2008): 615–49.

24. See International Monetary Fund, "The Fiscal Transparency Code" (http://blog-pfm.imf.org/files/ft-code.pdf), and the fiscal transparency evaluations that the International Monetary Fund publishes (www.imf.org/external/np /fad/trans/).

25. American Society of Civil Engineers, "Failure to Act: Closing the Infrastructure Investment Gap for America's Economic Future" (Reston, Va.: American Society of Civil Engineers, 2016).

26. Chris Christie, New Jersey's governor, has had other troubles with bridges. Two of his former top lieutenants were convicted for a scheme to exact political revenge by creating a traffic jam that punished a mayor who declined to endorse Christie's 2013 bid for reelection. See Kate Zernike, "2 Ex-Christie Allies Are Convicted in George Washington Bridge Case," *New York Times*, November 4, 2016.

27. "Street Cars and Urban Renewal: Rolling Blunder," *The Economist*, August 8, 2014 (www.economist.com/news/united-states/21611123-federal-sub sidies-have-inspired-some-silly-transit-projects-rolling-blunder).

28. According to Walter Hook, Stephanie Lotshaw, and Annie Weinstock, "More Development for Your Transit Dollar: An Analysis of 21 North American

Transit Corridors," report (New York: Institute for Transportation and Development Policy, 2013), on some high-volume stretches, light rail or subways can be a better investment than a bus transit system (BRT), but inner-city streetcars rarely are (see p. 21).

29. See Ron Nixon, "$11 Billion Later, High-Speed Rail Is Inching Along," *New York Times*, August 6, 2014.

30. See, for example, Jad Mouawad, "Technology That Could Have Prevented Amtrak Derailment Was Absent," *New York Times*, May 13, 2015.

31. For a general discussion and examples, see International Bank for Reconstruction and Development/World Bank, "Railway Reform: Toolkit for Improving Rail Sector Performance," staff report (Washington: World Bank, June 2011), chapter 5, "Creating the Industry Structure."

32. The Maritime Administration stated this in its Annual Report to Congress in 2006 based on its own analyses. These results have later been confirmed in research such as O. Merk and T. Dang, "Efficiency of World Ports in Container and Bulk Cargo (Oil, Coal, Ores and Grain)," OECD Regional Development Working Paper No. 2012/09 (Paris: OECD Publishing, 2012) (DOI: 10.1787/5k92vgw39zs2-en).

33. Maria Börjesson, "Explaining 'Peak Car' with Economic Variables," *CTS Newsletter*, April 2016 (the newsletter is published by the Royal Institute of Technology, Center for Transport Studies, in Stockholm).

34. Jonas Eliasson, Maria Börjesson, James Odeck, and Morten Welde, "Does Benefit/Cost Efficiency Influence Transport Investment Decisions?," CTS Working Paper (Stockholm: Royal Institute of Technology, Center for Transport Studies, 2014), p. 6.

35. Richard Florida, *The Rise of the Creative Class and How It's Transforming Work, Leisure and Everyday Life* (New York: Basic Books, 2002).

36. Richard Florida, "More Losers than Winners in America's New Economic Geography," *From the Atlantic/CityLab* (blog), January 30, 2013 (www.citylab .com/work/2013/01/more-losers-winners-americas-new-economic-geography /4465/).

37. See Steven Malanga, "The Curse of the Creative Class," *City Journal*, winter 2004 (www.city-journal.org/html/curse-creative-class-12491.html).

CHAPTER 3

Chapter opening image: Skyline of Seattle, Washington, at sunset (Di Brova, Shutterstock).

1. Joel Kotkin, *The City: A Global History* (New York: Modern Library Chronicles, 2006).

2. Chang-Tai Hsieh and Enrico Moretti, "Why Do Cities Matter? Local Growth and Aggregate Growth," NBER Working Paper No. 21154 (Cambridge, Mass.: National Bureau of Economic Research, May 2015).

3. See Jason Furman, "Barriers to Shared Growth: The Case of Land Use Regulation and Economic Rents," remarks to the Council of Economic Advisers, Urban Institute, Washington (November 20, 2015), and Raven Saks, "Job Creation and Housing Construction: Constraints on Metropolitan Area Employment Growth," *Journal of Urban Economics* 64 (2008): 178–95.

4. Statistics Canada, "Population Census of Metropolitan Areas" (www .statcan.gc.ca/tables-tableaux/sum-som/l01/cst01/demo05a-eng.htm).

5. Kenan Fikri and T. Juni Zhu, "City Analytics: Competitive Cities for Jobs and Growth, Companion Paper 1," working paper (Washington: World Bank, December 2015) (https://openknowledge.worldbank.org/handle/10986/23569).

6. A recent study by Sanghoon Lee, "Ability Sorting and Consumer City," *Journal of Urban Economics* 68, no. 1 (2010): 20–33, investigates the sorting of human capital between urban and rural areas. This is in line with the findings of Edward Glaeser, Jed Kolko, and Albert Saiz, "Consumer City," *Journal of Economic Geography* 1, no. 1 (2001): 27–50, that show how consumption opportunities can attract urban clusters of high-skilled workers.

7. Nicolas Bosetti, Sam Sims, and Tony Travers, "Housing and Inequality in London" (London: Centre for London, April 2016).

8. For a map and further discussion, see "Is Developing the Green Belt the Answer to London's Housing Crisis," Citygeographics: Urban Form, Dynamics, and Sustainability (website) (https://citygeographics.org/2014/11/11/is-releasing -the-greenbelt-the-answer-to-londons-housing-crisis/).

9. Paul Cheshire and Christian A. L. Hilber, "Office Space Supply Restrictions in Britain: The Political Economy of Market Revenge," *Economic Journal* 118, no. 529 (2008): 185–221.

10. Raj Chetty and Nathaniel Hendren, "The Impacts of Neighborhoods on Intergenerational Mobility: Childhood Exposure Effects and County-Level Estimates" (Cambridge, Mass.: Harvard University and National Bureau of Economic Research, 2015).

11. This aggregate measure comprises eleven subindexes that summarize information on the different aspects of the regulatory environment. Nine pertain to local characteristics, and two reflect state court and state legislative and executive branch behavior. See Joseph Gyourko, Albert Saiz, and Anita A. Summers, "A New Measure of the Local Regulatory Environment for Housing Markets: The Wharton Residential Land Use Regulatory Index," *Urban Studies* 45, no. 3 (2008): 693–729.

12. For example, Peter Ganong and Daniel Shoag, "Why Has Regional Income Convergence in the U.S. Declined?," unpublished paper, Harvard

University, January 2015 (http://scholar.harvard.edu/files/shoag/files/why_has
_regional_income_convergence_in_the_us_declined_01.pdf), find that states
with a less-constrained supply of housing (including from looser land-use regulations) experienced a more consistent and substantial pace of income convergence
over the last fifty years, closing about 2 percent of the across-state income gap on
average per year. In contrast, states with a more constrained supply of housing
(including from tighter land-use regulations) have experienced a substantial decline in the speed of income convergence.

13. For an evaluation see Peter Steinbrueck, Karen Dyson, Meredith McNair,
and Mathew Patterson, "Seattle 2035 Urban Village Study Final Report," report
prepared for the Seattle Department of Planning and Development (Seattle: City
of Seattle, August 2015) (www.seattle.gov/DPD/cs/groups/pan/@pan/documents
/web_informational/p2357239.pdf).

14. Bruce Katz and Julie Wagner, "The Rise of Innovation Districts: A New
Geography of Innovation in America," report (Washington: Brookings, May 2014).

15. Bruce Katz and Jennifer Bradley, *The Metropolitan Revolution* (Washington: Brookings, 2014).

16. White quoted in Josef Goodman, "Rust Belt Renaissance: The Future
American City," *The Politic*, March 4, 2013 (http://thepolitic.org/rust-belt
-renaissance-pittsburgh-and-the-future-of-the-american-city).

17. Antoine van Agtmael and Fred Bakker, *The Smartest Places on Earth: Why
Rust Belts Are the Emerging Hotspots of Global Innovation* (New York: Public-
Affairs, 2016).

18. Research Triangle Foundation of North Carolina, "Research Triangle
Park: Master Plan," 2011, (http://aws-master.s3.amazonaws.com/wp-content
/uploads/2014/08/CONCISE-MASTER-PLAN.pdf).

19. The strategy places the emphasis on getting the basics right, rather than
focusing on spectacular projects. See "Invest in Columbus 2020: A Regional Growth
Strategy for Central Ohio," The Columbus Region (website) (link to download
strategy document at http://columbusregion.com/Columbus2020/Investors.aspx).

20. Austin Kilroy, Louis Francis, Megha Mukim, and Stefano Negri, "Competitive Cities for Jobs and Growth: What, Who, and How" (Washington: World
Bank Group, 2015).

21. Neil Kleiman and Tom Hillard, "Innovation and the City" (New York:
New York University, Wagner Graduate School of Public Service, Center for
an Urban Future, 2013) (www.citigroup.com/citi/foundation/data/Innovation_
and_the_City_2016.pdf).

22. Several interesting "value capture" examples in Latin America are described
in Martim O. Smolka, "Implementing Value Capture in Latin America: Policies
and Tools for Urban Development" (Cambridge, Mass.: Lincoln Institute of Land
Policy, 2013).

23. Liz Alderman, "Under Chinese, a Greek Port Thrives," *New York Times*, October 10, 2012.

24. See, for example, *Wikipedia*, s.v. "London Congestion Charge" (https://en .wikipedia.org/wiki/London_congestion_charge).

25. On social impact bonds, see, for example, Nonprofit Finance Fund, "'Massachusetts' Juvenile Justice Pay for Success Initiative' Secures $18 Million Investment" (www.payforsuccess.org/resources/massachusetts-juvenile-justice-pay -success-initiative-secures-18-million-investment).

26. Edward L. Glaeser and Joseph Gyourko, *Rethinking Federal Housing Policy— How to Make Housing Plentiful and Affordable* (Washington: AEI Press, 2008).

27. Roderick Hills and David Schleicher, "Planning an Affordable City," *Iowa Law Review*, vol. 101 (2015): 91–136.

28. David Schleicher, "City Unplanning," *Yale Law Journal* 122, no. 7 (May 2013): 1670–1738.

CHAPTER 4

Chapter opening image: Louvre Palace reflecting in the side of the Pyramid both belong to the world's most famous museum (Margarita Povarenkina | Dreamstime .com).

1. A balance sheet is commonly defined as a snapshot of an entity's financial position—its assets and liabilities—at a specific point in time.

2. City of Cleveland, "Comprehensive Financial Report—2014" (www.city .cleveland.oh.us/node/7815).

3. The IFRS requires that financial instruments and realizable noncurrent assets be assessed at market value, but not plant, machinery, and equipment.

4. The figures in figure 4-1 are the most recent available as this goes to press. They are partly based on an IMF assessment, but have been complemented and partly updated in Dag Detter and Stefan Fölster, *The Public Wealth of Nations: How Management of Public Assets Can Boost or Bust Economic Growth* (London: Palgrave Macmillan, 2015), where the exact method is also described (see pp. 50–54). Note that these figures are estimates.

5. International Monetary Fund, "Another Look at Governments' Balance Sheets: The Role of Nonfinancial Assets" (Washington: IMF, 2013).

6. Detter and Fölster, *Public Wealth of Nations*.

7. Jacob Soll, *The Reckoning: Financial Accountability and the Rise and Fall of Nations* (New York: Basic Books, 2014).

8. Denise Schmandt-Besserat, "Oneness, Twoness, Threeness: How Ancient Accountants Invented Numbers," *The Sciences* 27, no. 4 (July–August 1987): 44–48.

9. Soll, *The Reckoning*.

10. Albrecht Heeffer, "On the Curious Historical Coincidence of Algebra and Double-Entry Bookkeeping," *Foundations of the Formal Sciences*, vol. 7 (2009) (www.math.uni-hamburg.de/home/loewe/FotFS/VII/Book/FotFS_VII _Heeffer.pdf).

11. Ibid.

12. Charles Roxburgh, Susan Lund, and John Piotro, "Mapping Global Capital Markets 2011," report (Brussels: McKinsey Global Institute, August 2011) (www.mckinsey.com/industries/private-equity-and-principal-investors/our -insights/mapping-global-capital-markets-2011).

13. Ted Nesi, "Magaziner: RI Leaders Need to Change How They Borrow Money," *Eyewitness News*, December 2, 2015 (http://wpri.com/2015/12/01 /magaziner-ri-leaders-need-to-change-how-they-borrow-money/).

14. Laurence J. Kotlikoff and Scott Burns, *The Clash of Generations: Saving Ourselves, Our Kids, and Our Economy* (MIT Press, 2012).

15. H.M. Treasury (U.K.), "Government Spending—Whole of Government Accounts," May 26, 2016 (www.gov.uk/government/collections/whole-of-govern ment-accounts).

16. National Audit Office (U.K.), "Report of the Comptroller and Auditor General: Whole of Government Accounts 2013–14" (www.nao.org.uk/wp -content/uploads/2015/03/Whole-government-account-2013-14.pdf).

17. See Wellington City Council, "Annual Report 2014/15" (http://ar2014 .publications.wellington.govt.nz/), for an example of how this approach looks when applied to a whole city's financial reporting.

18. Matthew Rees, "Explaining Discount Rates with Mini Case Studies," *Long Finance* (blog), February 15, 2016 (www.longfinance.net/news/long-finance -blogs/967-explaining-discount-rates-with-mini-case-studies.html).

19. Joseph Lowe, "Value for Money and the Valuation of Public Sector Assets," report prepared for H.M. Treasury (U.K.), July 2008 (www.gov.uk /government/uploads/system/uploads/attachment_data/file/191488/Green _book_supplementary_guidance_asset_valuation.pdf).

20. House of Commons Committee of Public Accounts, "The Sale of Eurostar Sixteenth," report of Session 2015–16, January 2016.

21. The New Zealand government has come the furthest in one respect: their financial statements must revalue assets according to the same rules as companies. See "Overview of the Public Sector OBE Standards," December 13, 2013 (www.treasury.govt.nz/publications/guidance/reporting/ipsas/overview).

22. Telereal Trillium/Savills, "New Homes on Public Sector Land: Accelerating Delivery," research report, April 2016 (http://pdf.euro.savills.co.uk/uk /residential—other/new-homes-on-public-sector-land.pdf), pp 8–9.

23. Ibid.

24. City of Cleveland, Ohio, "Comprehensive Annual Financial Report for the Fiscal Year Ended December 31, 2014," May 2016 (www.city.cleveland.oh.us /sites/default/files/forms_publications/2014CAFR.pdf).

25. Stockholm Stadshus AB is the city holding company. It holds mainly real estate assets, but also a handful of operational assets, such as the those for ports, water utility, broadband fiber, and parking. Some information on the functions and holdings of Stockholm Stadshus AB is available at http:// stadshusab.stockholm.se (using Google translate). Landstingshuset i Stockholm AB is the holding company for the all the county hospitals, as well the county-wide mass transport assets, including Waxholmsbolaget, the ferry service that carries 4 million passenger per year to Stockholm's 30,000 islands, and SL (Stor-Stockholm Lokaltrafik), Stockholm County's land-based public transport system, which carries 780,000 passengers per day—two-thirds of the working population.

26. Delphine Moretti, "New Governance Arrangements for the IPSAS Board," *Public Financial Management Blog*, March 3, 2015.

27. IMF, Fiscal Transparency Code (http://blog-pfm.imf.org/files/ft-code .pdf). The IMF produces Fiscal Transparency Evaluations for many countries (www.imf.org/external/np/fad/trans/).

28. New Zealand Treasury, "Specific Fiscal Risks" (www.treasury.govt.nz /budget/forecasts/befu2014/027.htm).

29. Liz Farmer, "Bankrupt Cities? What about Distressed Cities?" *Governing*, March 2014 (www.governing.com/finance101/gov-bankrupt-cities-overshadow -distressed.html).

30. James E. Spiotto, "Is Chapter 9 Bankruptcy the Ultimate Remedy for Financially Distressed Territories and Sovereigns Such as Puerto Rico: Are There Better Resolution Mechanisms?" December 1, 2015 (link to download at www .chapmanstrategicadvisors.com/insights-publications-18.html), written Statement to the U.S. Senate Judiciary Committee, "Hearing on Puerto Rico's Fiscal Problems: Examining the Source and Exploring the Solution," 114th Congress (www .judiciary.senate.gov/meetings/puerto-ricos-fiscal-problems-examining-the -source-and-exploring-the-solution).

31. Pew Charitable Trusts, "The State Role in Local Government Financial Distress," July 2013 (www.pewtrusts.org/en/research-and-analysis/reports/2013 /07/23/the-state-role-in-local-government-financial-distress).

32. Spiotto, "Is Chapter 9 Bankruptcy the Ultimate Remedy?"

33. For a discussion of this issue see Jennifer Burnett, "3 Questions on State Bankruptcy," Council of State Governments, E-Newsletter, January–February 2017 (www.csg.org/pubs/capitolideas/enews/issue65_3.aspx).

34. Gillian Tett, "Building on Sand," *Foreign Policy*, July 2016 (http://foreignpolicy.com/2016/07/11/building-on-sand-debt-crises-bankruptcy-detroit-atlantic-city-puerto-rico/).

35. The announcement of the bond issues is shown in Empire State Development, "New Issue–Book Entry Only" (https://cdn.esd.ny.gov/corporateinformation/Data/Bonds/OS_PIT_2016_A.pdf).

36. For background, see Eliot Brown, "Silverstein Loses Battle over 9/11 Payouts," *Wall Street Journal*, July 18, 2013.

37. Peter J. Galie and Christopher Bopst, *The New York State Constitution* (Oxford University Press, 2011).

38. Joseph F. Zimmerman, *The Government and Politics of New York State*, 2nd ed. (State University of New York Press, 2008).

39. For more detailed information on the Port Authority, see their website (www.panynj.gov/about/) and annual report (http://corpinfo.panynj.gov/documents/2015/).

40. Jameson W. Doig, *Empire on the Hudson* (Columbia University Press, 2001).

41. Rich Bookman, "The Port Authority Is Sitting on All This Prime Real Estate—but What Can It Really Do with It?," *The Real Deal (New York Real Estate News)*, April 26, 2016.

CHAPTER 5

Chapter opening image: Millennium Bridge crossing the Thames and leading up to Saint Paul's Cathedral (David Brossard, Creative Commons, www.flickr.com).

1. Food & Water Watch, "The State of Public Water in the United States," report, February 2016 (www.foodandwaterwatch.org/sites/default/files/report_state_of_public_water.pdf).

2. "U.S. Electricity Utility Industry Statistics, Number of Electricity Providers" (www.publicpower.org/files/PDFs/USElectricUtilityIndustryStatistics.pdf).

3. CDM Smith, "The Economic Impact of Commercial Airports in 2013," report prepared for Airports Council–North America (Cincinnati, 2014) (http://airportsforthefuture.org/files/2014/09/Economic-Impact-of-Commercial-Aviation-2013.pdf).

4. Dag Detter and Stefan Fölster, *The Public Wealth of Nations: How Management of Public Assets Can Boost or Bust Economic Growth* (London: Palgrave Macmillan, 2015), p. 54.

5. Although "cadastral" originally derived from a Greek word for a list or register, such a land registry is still missing in Greece, a lack that is a contributing factor in the country's financial situation.

6. Dag Detter, "NHS Is Sitting on Solution to Its Problems," *The Times*, February 6, 2016 (pay wall). See also Dag Detter, "NHS Is the Largest Real Estate Company in the U.K.," *Linkedin.com* (www.linkedin.com/pulse/nhs-sitting -solution-its-problems-dag-detter).

7. Vito Tanzi and Tej Prakash, "The Cost of Government and the Misuse of Public Funds," Working Paper 00/180 (Washington: International Monetary Fund, 2000).

8. In the absence of a consolidated public sector balance sheet, the sovereign credit rating system is working with an incomplete assessment of public sector assets and liabilities. In most cases this is the result of a lack of full government disclosure. Sovereign analysis would greatly benefit if analysts had a better understanding of the size and nature of the contingent liabilities of the entire public sector, which in a stress scenario could conceivably drain treasury cash and pose an obstacle to continued bond payments. Nevertheless, governments are providing sufficient information for analysts to gauge a central or federal government's willingness and ability to meet its bonded debt payments on time and in full. Since national financial ministries typically issue all or most of a central government's debt, getting a sense of the treasury's capacity to meet its needs is the main objective of the analysis.

9. Organization for Economic Cooperation and Development, "OECD Guidelines on Corporate Governance of State-Owned Enterprises," 2015 (link to download at www.oecd.org/corporate/guidelines-corporate-governance-SOEs .htm), addresses many important aspects, but it does not address the fundamental need for a balance sheet through a ring-fenced vehicle at arm's length from short-term political interference.

10. Li Yaning Tang, Qiping Shen, and Eddie W. L. Cheng, "A Review of Public-Private Partnership Projects in the Construction Industry," *International Journal of Project Management* 28, no. 7 (October 2010): 683–94.

11. See "About Kammarkollegiet" (www.kammarkollegiet.se/en). See also Nils Edén, Erik Schalling, and Lennart Berglöf, *Kammarkollegiets historia* [History of the legal, financial, and administrative services agency in Sweden] (Stockholm: Isaac Marcus, 1941).

12. For more information on Solidium, see "Annual Report 2016" (www.e -julkaisu.fi/solidium/annual_report-2016/mobile.html#pid=1); on Temasek, see "Temasek Review 2016—Generational Investing" (www.temasek.com.sg/documents /download/downloads/20160706235822/TR2016_Singles.pdf); on Industrivärden, see "Annual Report 2015" (www.industrivarden.se/globalassets/arsredovisnin gar/engelska/2015.pdf); on Investor AB see "100 Years of Investor: Building Best-in-Class Companies since 2016" (https://vp053.alertir.com/afw/files/press /investor/201604059657-1.pdf).

13. See "State Ownership Policy 2006," Government of Sweden website (www.government.se/49b759/contentassets/d8b7bc175d434d0991a56cef187208 a5/state-ownership-policy-2006).

14. See Temasek, "Managing Risk," *Temasek Review 2016* (www.temasek review.com.sg/investor/managing-risk.html).

15. The Ontario Teachers' Pension Plan, Canada's largest single-profession pension plan, invests on behalf of its 316,000 retired and working teachers. Among other things it invests in real assets, such as infrastructure and real estate. The rate of return for the total plan was 13 percent in 2015 and 10.3 percent since its inception in 1990. For more detailed information see the plan's website (www.otpp.com/).

16. See, for example, "Annual Review: Lithuanian State-Owned Commercial Assets 2009" (www.euroinvestor.dk/pdf/cse/11176061_17359.pdf).

17. Dag Detter, "Women—A Competitive Advantage," *Huffington Post*, October 31, 2011 (www.huffingtonpost.com/dag-detter/women-a-competitive-advan_b_1068106.html). For a detailed description of the Swedish governance of state-owned enterprises, see Detter and Fölster, *Public Wealth of Nations.*

CHAPTER 6

Chapter opening image: HafenCity Hamburg (Thomas Wolf, www.foto-tw.de).

1. See National Library Board, Singapore, "Public Housing in Singapore," *Singapore Infopedia* (http://eresources.nlb.gov.sg/infopedia/articles/SIP_1585_2009 -10-26.html.

2. The TEU is an inexact unit of cargo capacity often used to describe the capacity of container ships and container terminals. It is based on the volume of a twenty-foot-long intermodal container, a standard-sized metal box that can be easily transferred between different modes of transportation, such as ships, trains and trucks.

3. McKinsey & Company, "The 'Rail Plus Property' Model: Hong Kong's Successful Self-Financing Formula," June 2016 (www.mckinsey.com/industries /capital-projects-and-infrastructure/our-insights/the-rail-plus-property-model).

4. Lee Min Kok, "Dubbed 'the Best in Class': 6 Things about Hong Kong's MTR Rail System," *Straits Times*, October 29, 2015.

5. Land Transport Authority (Singapore), "Comparison of Public Transport Operations," *Journeys*, November 2011 (www.lta.gov.sg/ltaacademy/doc/J11Nov -p71ComparisonofPublicTransportRevised.pdf), p. 75.

6. Locum, *Annual Report 2015* (www.locum.se/Global/4.Om%20Locum/6 .%20Ekonomi/%C3%85rsredovisningar/Locum_A%CC%8Ar2015_A4_web _rev_160415.pdf).

7. Stockholm Stadshus AB, "På väg mot 140 000 nya bostäder: en skrift om bostadsförsörjningen I Stockholm Stad" [On course for 140,000 new homes: a report on housing in Stockholm City] (http://stadshusab.stockholm.se/globalas sets/pa-vag-mot-140-000-nya-bostader.pdf).

8. Robert Emanuelsson, "Supply of Housing in Sweden," *Riksbanken Economic Review* (2015): 2.

9. Kat Hanna, "How Many More Homes Could We Squeeze into London's Housing Estates?," CityMetric (website), September 29, 2016 (www.citymetric .com/fabric/how-many-more-homes-could-we-squeeze-london-s-housing -estates-2472).

10. Andrew Adonis, *City Villages: More Homes, Better Communities* (London: Institute for Public Policy Research, 2015) (http://ippr.org/read/city-villages-more -homes-better-communities#city-villages-more-homes-better-communities).

11. Telereal Trillium and Savills Research, "News Homes on Public Sector Land: Accelerating Delivery," research report, April 2016 (http://pdf.euro.savills .co.uk/uk/residential—other/new-homes-on-public-sector-land.pdf).

12. Adonis, *City Villages*.

13. Hanna, "How Many More Homes Could We Squeeze into London's Housing Estates?"

14. "Business and Infrastructure: A Conversation with Lord Adonis," Legatum Institute (website), October 2015 (www.li.com/events/business-and-infrastructure -a-conversation-with-lord-adonis).

15. London Legacy Development Corporation, "Ten Year Plan, 2015/16– 2024/25" (www.queenelizabetholympicpark.co.uk/~/media/lldc/ten%20year% 20plan.pdf).

16. PwC, "Crossrail 2: Funding and Financing Study, 2014," study prepared for Transport of London, March 14, 2014 (http://1267lm2nzpvy44li8s48uorode .wpengine.netdna-cdn.com/wp-content/uploads/2014/04/Crossrail-2-Funding -and-Financing-Study.pdf).

CHAPTER 7

Chapter opening image: City kids (iStock/Image Source).

1. Lester is an actual person whom one of the authors interviewed in Chicago in the summer of 2015.

2. M. Lori Thomas, Jeffery K. Shears, Melanie Clapsadl Pate, and Mary Ann Priester, "Moore Place Permanent Supportive Housing Evaluation Study: Year 1 Report, Executive Summary" (Charlotte, N.C.: University of North Carolina, College of Health and Human Services and Urban Ministry Center,

February 14, 2014) (www.urbanministrycenter.org/wp-content/uploads/2014/06/moore-place-executive-summary-eval-study.pdf).

3. Another study is Dennis P. Culhane, Stephen Metraux, and Trevor Hadley, "Public Service Reductions Associated with Placement of Homeless Persons with Severe Mental Illness in Supportive Housing," *Housing Policy Debates* 13, no. 1 (2002): 107–63.

4. The government of New Zealand describes its stance and social investment activities on its home page (www.treasury.govt.nz/statesector/socialinvestment).

5. Uppsala University and Skandia, "Public Health Calculator" (www.hälsokalkylatorn.se). The university launched this tool in 2011, but continuously improves it. It is now being extended to include the likely effects of various types of interventions for which evidence is sufficiently robust.

6. The city of Uppsala has commissioned Stefan Fölster to do this calculation; the study is under way but not yet published.

7. At the Public Health Calculator page (www.hälsokalkylatorn.se) are shown 2014, 2015, and 2016 versions of the calculator.

8. New Zealand Treasury, "Cost-Benefit Analysis Primer," 2015 (www.treasury.govt.nz/publications/guidance/planning/ costbenefitanalysis/primer), and New Zealand Treasury, "Tool for Social Cost-Benefit analysis," 2015 (www.treasury.govt.nz/publications/guidance/planning/costbenefitanalysis/cbax).

9. New Zealand Treasury, "Social Investment," October 27, 2016 (www.treasury.govt.nz/statesector/socialinvestment).

10. For more detailed analysis of this group of children, see Sarah Crichton, Robert Templeton, and Sarah Tumen, "Using Integrated Data to Understand Children at Risk of Poor Outcomes as Young Adults," Analytical Paper 15-1 (Auckland: New Zealand Treasury, September 2015).

11. The American economist Gary Becker, of the University of Chicago, winner of the 1992 Nobel Prize in Economics, argues in "Crime and Punishment: An Economic Approach," *Journal of Political Economy* 76, no. 2 (1968): 169–217 (doi:10.1086/259394. JSTOR 1830482), that improved schooling attainment and labor market prospects reduce crime by increasing the "opportunity costs" of illegal activity.

12. See L. J. Schweinhart, J. Montie, Z. Xiang, W. S. Barnett, C. R. Belfield, and M. Nores, "Lifetime Effects: The HighScope Perry Preschool Study through Age 40," Monographs of the HighScope Educational Research Foundation, No. 14 (Ypsilanti, Mich.: HighScope Press, 2005). Another study found that more schooling that increased the chance of high school graduation significantly reduced crime rates and yielded considerable social value. See Lance Lochner and Enrico Moretti, "The Effect of Education on Crime: Evidence from Prison Inmates, Arrests, and Self-Reports," *American Economic Review* 94, no. 1 (2004): 155–89.

13. According to Raj Chetty and Nathaniel Hendren, in "The Impacts of Neighborhoods on Intergenerational Mobility: Childhood Exposure Effects and County-Level Estimates" (Cambridge, Mass.: Harvard University and National Bureau for Economic Research, 2015), for children in U.S. families in the 25th percentile of the income distribution, growing up from birth in a county that is one standard deviation better than another increases the child's income by approximately 10 percent compared to the other county.

14. *Wikipedia*, s.v. "Crime in New York City" (https://en.wikipedia.org/wiki/Crime_in_New_York_City).

15. John Donohue and Steven Levitt, "The Impact of Legalized Abortion on Crime," *Quarterly Journal of Economics* 116, no. 2 (2001): 379–420.

16. See Sara B. Heller, Anuj K. Shah, Jonathan Guryan, Jens Ludwig, Sendhil Mullainathan, and Harold A. Pollack, "Thinking, Fast and Slow? Some Field Experiments to Reduce Crime and Dropout in Chicago," NBER Working Paper No. 21178 (Cambridge, Mass.: National Bureau of Economic Research, May 2015).

17. Franklin E. Zimring, *The City That Became Safe: New York's Lessons for Urban Crime and Its Control* (Oxford University Press, 2011).

18. New York spends more than $2,000 per inhabitant on public safety, compared to LA's more typical $700, according to Derek Prall, "Govalytics Data Highlights Public Safety Spending," *American City & County*, January 13, 2014.

19. Zeeshan Alelem, "14 Years after Decriminalizing All Drugs, Here's What Portugal Looks Like," *Policy.Mic*, February 11, 2015 (https://mic.com/articles/110344/14-years-after-portugal-decriminalized-all-drugs-here-s-what-s-happening#.yIrZM7CUT).

20. David McDaid, A-La Park, Valentina Iemmi, Bayo Adelaja, and Martin Knapp, "Growth in the Use of Early Intervention for Psychosis Services" (London: London School of Economics, Personal Social Services Research Unit, January 2016).

21. Thomas and others, "Moore Place Permanent Supportive Housing Evaluation Study: Year 1 Report." The Moore Place facility is run by Charlotte's Urban Ministry Center in partnership with local government.

22. Jonathan Ingram, "The Power of Work—How Kansas' Welfare Reform Is Lifting Americans Out of Poverty" (Naples, Fla.: Foundation for Government Accountability, 2016). Previously, Kansas had been spending $5.5 million per month on food stamp benefits for able-bodied adults; it now spends $1.2 million. The experience was similar in Maine. The caseload of able-bodied adults receiving food stamps plunged by 80 percent from December 2014 to March 2015 after workfare was introduced.

23. Kenneth Hanson and Karen S. Hamrick, "Moving Public Assistance Recipients into the Labor Force, 1996–2000," Food Assistance and Nutrition

Research Report No. FANRR-40 (U.S. Department of Agriculture, May 2004) (http://webarchives.cdlib.org/sw1vh5dg3r/http://ers.usda.gov/publications /fanrr40/ fanrr40.pdf).

24. Bo Xilai became a rival to President Xi Jinping and was imprisoned in 2012. For more on Bo Xilai and his dramatic career and downfall, see *Wikipedia*, s.v. "Bo Xilai" (https://en.wikipedia.org/wiki/Bo_Xilai).

25. Wu Guangqiang, "Why Chongqing Has No Property Bubble," *Shenzhen Daily*, October 24, 2016 (www.szdaily.com/content/2016-10/24/content_14046427 .htm).

26. George L. Kelling, "How New York Became Safe: The Full Story," *City Journal*, 2009 (www.city-journal.org/contributor/george-l-kelling_100).

27. See also European Commission, "Guide to Social Innovation" (Brussels: February 2013) (http://s3platform.jrc.ec.europa.eu/documents/20182/84453/Guide _to_Social_Innovation.pdf/88aac14c-bb15-4232-88f1-24b844900a66), which emphasizes the investment perspective. They suggest formulating innovation investments similarly to risk capital projects in the private sector, establishing criteria for investment selection based on evidence, social costs and benefits, risk analysis, and distributive analysis. They also propose systems for ex-post evaluation and distribution of good results.

28. See Lars Hultkrantz, "Sociala investeringsfonder i Sverige" [Social investment funds in Sweden], research report (Stockholm: SNS, 2015); see also "Social Investment Funds in Sweden—Facts and Lessons," SNS website (www .sns.se/en/archive/social-investment-funds-in-sweden-facts-and-lessons-2/).

CHAPTER 8

Chapter opening image: Students studying (Rawpixel.com, Shutterstock).

1. Christopher R. Berry and Edward L. Glaeser, "The Divergence of Human Capital Levels across Cities," NBER Working Paper No. 11617 (Cambridge, Mass.: National Bureau of Economic Research, September 2005), document the growing divergence of human capital levels across cities, finding that the distribution of human capital has gone from relatively even among U.S. metropolitan areas to increasingly divergent.

2. Jesse M. Shapiro, "Smart Cities: Quality of Life, Productivity, and the Growth Effects of Human Capital," NBER Working Paper No. 11615 (Cambridge, Mass.: National Bureau of Economic Research, September 2005), finds that nearly half of this causal effect was not generated by enhanced productivity growth, but by growth in the quality of life, which helped to attract business and employers.

3. One of the most recent studies is Martin Obschonka and others, "Entrepreneurial Regions: Do Macro-Psychological Cultural Characteristics of Regions

Help Solve the 'Knowledge Paradox' of Economics?" *PLoS ONE* 10, no. 6 (2015) (DOI: 10.1371/journal.pone.0129332).

4. Research confirms the relation between human capital and growth on the national level. See Robert J. Barro, "Economic Growth in a Cross Section of Countries," *Quarterly Journal of Economics* 106, no. 2 (1991): 407–43; James Rauch, "Productivity Gains from Geographic Concentration of Human Capital: Evidence from the Cities," *Journal of Urban Economics* 34, no. 3 (1993): 380–400; Curtis Simon, "Human Capital and Metropolitan Employment Growth," *Journal of Urban Economics* 43, no. 2 (1998): 223–43; Edward L. Glaeser, "The New Economics of Urban and Regional Growth," in *The Oxford Handbook of Economic Geography*, edited by Gordon L. Clark, Maryann P. Feldman, and Meric S. Gertler, pp. 83–98 (Oxford University Press, 2000). Firms locate in areas of high human capital concentration to gain competitive advantages, rather than letting suppliers' and customers' locations dictate their own location. See Edward L. Glaeser and A. Saiz, "The Rise of the Skilled City," NBER Working Paper No. 10191 (Cambridge, Mass.: National Bureau of Economic Research, 2003), who find that skilled cities grow through increases in productivity. Relatively less-skilled cities miss out on this growth factor.

5. In some cases, it may be worthwhile to make special allowances in how the value of the human asset is calculated. For example, in towns with an unusually high number of self-employed, their earnings can be integrated into a measure of the return to human assets. Similarly, in a town with an unusually high number of students, these might be excluded from the number of persons of working age.

6. Joel Kotkin, *The New Geography: How the Digital Revolution Is Reshaping the American Landscape* (New York: Random House, 2001).

7. Eric Hanushek, "Why Standard Measures of Human Capital Are Misleading," *KDI Journal of Economic Policy* 37, no. 2 (2015): 22–39.

8. Edward Glaeser, *Triumph of the City: How Our Greatest Invention Makes Us Richer, Smarter, Greener, Healthier and Happier* (New York: Penguin, 2011), p. 27.

9. See Z. Joe Kulenovic and Alexandra Cech, "Six Case Studies of Economically Successful Cities" (Washington: World Bank Group, 2015).

10. Fredrik Erixon and Björn Weigel, *The Innovation Illusion: How So Little Is Created by So Many Working So Hard* (Yale University Press, 2016); Michael Storper, Thomas Kemeny, Naji Makarem, and Taner Osman, *The Rise and Fall of Urban Economies: Lessons from San Francisco and Los Angeles* (Stanford University Press, 2015).

11. Jorge Guzman and Scott Stern, "The State of American Entrepreneurship? New Estimates of the Quantity and Quality of Entrepreneurship for 15 US States, 1988–2014," NBER Working Paper No. 22095 (Cambridge, Mass.: National Bureau of Economic Research, 2016), find that entrepreneurial potential

leading to start-ups is far greater in some cities, such as San Francisco and its hinterland, than in others, such as Detroit.

12. Stefan Fölster, Li Jansson, and Anton Nyrenström Gidehag, "The Effect of Local Business Climate on Employment," *Journal of Entrepreneurship and Public Policy* 5, no. 1 (2016): 2–24.

13. At the national level a number of studies have in recent years correlated measures of business climate with employment or employment growth. Some use an index such as the World Bank "Ease of Doing Business" index and relate these measures to employment. Another strand of the research literature examines the predictive power of regional or local business climate measures. See Jed Kolko, David Neumark, and Mejia Cuellar, "What Do Business Climate Indexes Teach Us about State Policy and Economic Growth?," *Journal of Regional Science* 53, no. 2 (2013): 220–55.

14. A number of studies have found a significant effect of self-employment on overall employment in panels of countries and regions. Some of these have also succeeded in separating the genuine effect of self-employment on employment from the so-called "refugee effect," which is that the unemployed become self-employed more frequently than the employed. A common result is that both effects are significant. See, for example, Arthur Roy Thurik, Martin A. Carree, André V. Stelb, and David B. Audretsch, "Does Self-Employment Reduce Unemployment?," *Journal of Business Venturing* 23, no. 6 (2008): 673–86; Stefan Fölster, "Do Entrepreneurs Create Jobs?," *Small Business Economics* 14, no. 2 (2000): 137–48.

15. Fölster, Jansson, and Gidehag, "The Effect of Local Business Climate on Employment."

16. Our measure of the local business climate is based on an extensive survey undertaken annually by the Confederation of Swedish Enterprise, which results in municipality rankings. The rankings take into account eighteen different factors, and are partly based on a survey of 66,000 entrepreneurs and partly on variables from Statistics Sweden, the government statistics agency. For the rankings and the statistics underlying them see Confederation of Swedish Enterprise, "Ranking 2016" (www.foretagsklimat.se/ranking).

CHAPTER 9

Chapter opening image: Diversity in the workplace (BikeRiderLondon, Shutterstock).

1. Laura Bacon and Rushda Majeed, "Palermo Renaissance Part 1: Rebuilding Civic Identity and Reclaiming a City from the Mafia in Italy, 1993–2000," paper in the series Innovations for Successful Societies (Princeton, N.J.: Princeton

University, Woodrow Wilson School of Public and International Affairs and the Bobst Center for Peace and Justice, 2012).

2. Stefan Fölster and Nima Sanandaji, *Renaissance for Reforms* (London and Stockholm: Institute of Economic Affairs and Timbro, 2014).

3. Daron Acemoglu and James Robinson, *Why Nations Fail: The Origins of Power, Prosperity, and Poverty* (New York: Crown, 2012).

4. Albert Hirschman, *The Rhetoric of Reaction: Perversity, Futility, Jeopardy* (Harvard University Press/Belknap Press, 1991).

5. Described in more detail in Dag Detter and Stefan Fölster, *The Public Wealth of Nations: How Management of Public Assets Can Boost or Bust Economic Growth* (London: Palgrave Macmillan, 2015).

Index

accounting. *See* balance sheet management

Adonis, Andrew, 174, 175

agglomeration, 3, 12

Akron, Ohio, as turnaround city, 70

Albany, New York, investment in, 10

alcohol use/abuse, 184–85

Amtrak, 46–47, 139

Argent, 164

Army Corps of Engineers, U.S., 28–29

arts and culture: failing cities' investment in, 50–53; turnaround cities' investment in, 72

asset management: added value determination in, 75–81; balance sheet management in, 20, 89–120, 126–27, 130–31, 132–34, 137–38; clear objectives of, 136, 138–39, 155, 163, 166; of commercial assets, 16, 20, 22, 83, 92, 95, 105–06, 109–13, 117–20, 123–46, 149–77; democracy strengthened by, 5, 22, 81, 83, 213–21; of economic assets, 15–16, 20 (*see also* commercial assets; policy assets); fact- and evidence-based decision making in, 74–75; failing cities' lack of, 27, 29–30, 31–32, 34–42; of human assets, 16–18, 21, 27, 32, 33, 35, 36–42, 65–67, 72–73, 196, 201–09; independent governance of, 81–83, 84, 137, 139–41, 154–55, 163, 166, 169–70, 173, 221 (*see also* urban wealth funds); investment and, 5, 6–9, 15–18, 20–22; knowledge of assets for, 20–21; of noneconomic assets, 16–18, 21, 27, 36–42, 92, 94 (*see also* human assets; social assets); of policy assets, 15–16, 109, 112,

asset management (cont.)
139; professional management of, 21–22, 81–83, 84, 123–24, 128–31, 136–41, 144–46, 171, 221 (*see also* urban wealth funds); rich *vs.* poor city approaches to, 5, 6–9; of social assets, 16, 17, 21, 36–42, 65–67, 79, 181–98 (*see also* social investment); in turbo cities, 15, 72–73, 74–85; in turnaround cities, 72–73, 84; urban wealth funds for, 22, 83, 123–46, 149–77

Associated British Ports, 49

Athens, Greece, as failing city, 27

Atlanta, Georgia: as extensive city, 64; upward mobility in, 37, 40

Austin, Texas: as extensive city, 64; "knowledge economy" in, 36

Australia: balance sheet management by, 103, 107; infrastructure investment in, 47; transportation systems in, 162; urban wealth funds in, 149

Australian-Super, 164

balance sheet management: accountability for, 95–96, 102, 117; accounting practices for, 95–105 (*see also international standards subentry*); accrual accounting for, 99, 100, 106, 107, 108, 113; antiquated debt and asset control *vs.*, 102–04, 109; asset and account consolidation in, 117–20; asset-debt comparison in, 92, 93; in Cleveland, 91–92, 110; commercial asset valuation in, 92, 95, 105–06, 109–13, 117–20, 126–27, 130–31, 132–34; debt structure in, 90, 115–17; double-entry bookkeeping for, 96, 97–100, 106; economic growth promotion

via, 114–20; GAAP standards for, 110–11; international standards for, 91, 104, 106–08, 111, 112, 137–38; market value assessment in, 91, 110–13; municipal bond market development and, 100–02; net debt in, 92, 94; net worth change in, 95; nonfinancial asset valuation in, 92, 94; overview of, 89–91; policy asset distinction in, 109, 112; public balance sheet importance, 104–05; risk-based approach to, 112–14, 133; single-entry bookkeeping for, 96–97; transparency of, 20, 90, 92, 103–04, 111, 112, 114, 126–27, 137–38; turbo city *vs.* treadmill town approach to, 105–14; underestimating market value in, 110–13; urban wealth fund prerequisite of, 126–27, 130–31, 132–34, 137–38; WGA approach to, 107–08; yield or return assessment in, 91–92

Baltimore, failures in, 38

Berlin, Germany, failures in, 32–33

Blakely, Edward, 32

block-chain technology, 126

Bloomberg, Michael, 196

Bloomberg Philanthropies, 81

BMW, 35

Bogotá, Colombia, reform and change in, 215–17

Boston: as exclusive city, 58, 64, 68; fact- and evidence-based decision making in, 75; "innovation district" in, 68; land use in, 71–72; upward mobility in, 38

bridges, 44

buses, 45–46, 48

business climate, 18, 32, 33, 35,
72–73, 208–09
By og Havn I/S, 162–63

cadastral maps, 126
Cali, Colombia, reform and change in,
218–19
canals and waterways, 44
CapitaLand, 154
Capital Beltway, 76
Carmel, Indiana, as turbo city, 74–75
Castro, Jaime, 216–17
Central Falls, Rhode Island, balance
sheet management by, 103
Changsha, China, land use in, 77
Charlotte, North Carolina: as extensive
city, 64; social investment in, 190–91
Chicago: Chicago Infrastructure Trust,
79; income inequality in, 39; land
use in, 67; reforms and transitions in,
19; social investment in, 181–82,
188; upward mobility in, 67; value
creation programs in, 78–79
China: infrastructure investment in,
45; social investment in, 194–95;
as "soft state," 219–20;
transportation systems in, 161.
See also specific cities
China Construction Bank, 152
Chongqing, China, social investment
in, 194–95
Christie, Chris, 44
Citi, 79
cities: asset management by (*see* asset
management); balance sheet
management by, 20, 89–120,
126–27, 130–31, 132–34, 137–38;
"creative class" cities, 50–51 (*see also*
arts and culture); democracy in, 5,
12, 22, 81, 83, 95–96, 213–21;
emerging-market cities, 194–95;

exclusive cities, 57–64, 65–68,
83–84; extensive cities, 57–58,
64–68, 83–84; failure of, 27–53;
investment by (*see* investment);
national government relationships
with (*see* national governments and
policies); population of (*see*
population, urban); smart cities, 4;
social investment by (*see* social
investment); "soft cities," 219–21;
state government relationships with,
44, 115–16; treadmill towns (*see*
treadmill towns); turbo cities (*see*
turbo cities); turnaround cities,
68–73, 84–85; urban wealth funds
of (*see* urban wealth funds). *See also*
specific cities
City of London Corporation, 21–22,
130–31
civic engagement, 40
Cleveland, Ohio: balance sheet
management by, 91–92, 110;
infrastructure investment in, 48
Coimbatore, India: human assets in,
206–07; national growth impacted
by, 12
Columbus, Indiana, as turnaround
city, 72
Columbus, Ohio, upward mobility
in, 37
commercial assets: asset management
of, 16, 20, 22, 123–46, 149–77;
balance sheet management of, 92,
95, 105–06, 109–13, 117–20,
126–27, 130–31, 132–34; publicly
owned, 125–26; urban wealth funds
of, 22, 83, 123–46, 149–77; yield
or return on, 92, 124, 125, 126,
127–28, 149, 161, 166, 167, 173.
See also real estate; transportation
systems; utilities

Copenhagen, Denmark, urban wealth funds in, 162–63

Cosco, 76

"creative class" cities, 50–51. *See also* arts and culture

crime rates: failing cities' struggles with, 34; reforms and reduction in, 19; social investment impacting, 14, 41, 79, 80–81, 187–88, 195, 196, 219; in treadmill towns, 14; in turbo cities, 14, 80–81

Crossrail, 76, 161, 176–77

crowdfunding, 79, 80

Cuidad Juárez, Mexico, social investment in, 195

culture. *See* arts and culture

Daley, Richard M., 67

Dallas, Texas, as extensive city, 64

DBS Group/DBS Bank, 152, 154

democracy: accounting and accountability links to, 95–96; asset management strengthening, 5, 22, 81, 83, 213–21; Bogotá, improvements in, 215–17; national governments and policies impacting, 218; reinventing city democracy, 213–21; "soft cities" improvements toward, 219–21; state government authority in, 12

Denver: "knowledge economy" in, 36; Peak Academy of, 214–15

Detroit: arts and culture investment in, 50–51; asset management lack in, 8, 22, 34–36, 82, 221; balance sheet management by, 89; bankruptcy of, 115, 221; Detroit Institute of the Arts, 50–51; failures in, 10, 27, 34–36, 42, 45, 50–51; human assets in, 203; infrastructure investment in, 45; "innovation

district" in, 68; investment failures in, 10; land use in, 67

digital technologies: exclusive cities' promotion of, 62–63; investment in, 5, 11, 62–63; in turnaround cities, 69–70

drug use/abuse, 189–90. *See also* alcohol use/abuse

Dulles Greenway, 76

DuPage County, Illinois, upward mobility in, 38

economic assets: asset management of, 15–16, 20; commercial assets as, 16, 20, 22, 92, 95, 105–06, 109–13, 117–20, 123–46, 149–77; policy assets as, 15–16, 109, 112, 139

Edsbyn, Sweden, human assets in, 206

education: asset management approach to, 7, 17, 18, 35; employment ties to, 7, 201, 205–07; failing cities' struggles with, 34; "knowledge economy" ties to, 36; lifelong learning and, 204–05; national policy impacts on, 9; school real estate for, 129; social and human asset impacts of, 40, 196, 201, 202, 204–07; social investment in, 7, 14, 17, 18, 40, 196; treadmill towns' cuts to, 15; turbo cities' investment in, 14, 70; in turnaround cities, 70

Emanuel, Rahm, 78

emerging-market cities, social investment in, 194–95

Empire State Development (ESD), 118–19

employment: asset management of, 6, 7; business climate impacting, 18, 32, 33, 35, 72–73, 208–09;

education ties to, 7, 201, 205–07; in exclusive cities, 58, 59, 61, 62–63; in extensive cities, 64; in failing cities, 34, 35, 38, 40, 41, 43, 51; human asset investment impacting, 201, 202, 203, 205–09; income from (*see* income); infrastructure impacting, 43; national policy impacts on, 9; social investment impacting, 10, 17–18, 21, 191–94; in turnaround cities, 68–70; work programs for, 191–94. *See also* unemployment

exclusive cities: employment in, 58, 59, 61, 62–63; false promises of, 57–64, 65–68, 83–84; income in, 58, 60–62; land use and housing in, 58, 59, 60, 61–62, 63–64, 65–68; national growth impacted by, 58, 60–61; quality of life in, 58, 59–60; "regulatory taxes" in, 62, 63; segregation in, 64, 67

extensive cities: employment in, 64; false promises of, 57–58, 64–68, 83–84; income in, 65–67; land use and housing in, 64–68; segregation in, 64

failing cities: arts and culture investments by, 50–53; asset management lack in, 27, 29–30, 31–32, 34–42; bad advice adherence in, 49–53; Berlin as, 32–33; Detroit as, 27, 34–36, 42, 45, 50–51; gentrification in, 41–42, 53; income changes and, 37–42; infrastructure choices in, 34, 42–50; Manchester, UK as, 51–53; national government and policy impacts on, 28–29, 35, 43–44; New Orleans as, 28–30, 31–32; population decline in, 28, 30, 33–34; segregation in, 35, 42,

43; social and human asset disregard in, 27, 36–42; state government and policy impacts on, 44; successful cities *vs.*, 30–31, 34–36, 45; treadmill town characteristics of, 28–36. *See also* treadmill towns

Fannie Mae, 138

Federal Accounting Standards Advisory Board, 111

Federal Highway Administration, U.S., 74

Fibonacci (Leonardo of Pisa), 97–98

Financial Accounting Standards Board, 111

Finland, urban wealth funds in, 138

Five Star Movement (M5S), 218

flood protection, failing cities' lack of, 28–30, 32

Florida, Richard, 50, 51

Fluor-Transurban, 76–77

Fore Systems, 69

Fort Worth, Texas, as extensive city, 64

Freddie Mac, 138

Gaziantep, Turkey, as turnaround city, 72–73, 84

generally accepted accounting principles (GAAP), 110–11

gentrification, in failing cities, 41–42, 53

Germany: cities impacting national growth in, 4; education in, 204–05; failing cities in, 32–33; infrastructure investment in, 44, 47. *See also specific cities*

GIC Private Ltd., 155

Giuliani, Rudolph, 196

Glasgow, Scotland, national growth impacted by, 12

Goldman Sachs, 80–81

Google, 69–70
Gothenburg, Sweden: investment in, 11; urban wealth fund development in, 166, 168
Governmental Accounting Standards Board, 111
Greater London Authority (GLA), 162, 175
Greece, asset management in, 81–82, 221
Greenwich, Connecticut, as exclusive city, 58
Guerrero, Rodrigo, 218–19

HafenCity Hamburg GmbH, 163–64
Hamburg, Germany: HafenCity UWF in, 163–64; national growth driven by, 4
Harrisburg, Pennsylvania, bankruptcy of, 115
health care: national policy impacts on, 9; Public Health Calculator, 183–85, 197; social investment in, 41, 183–85, 189–90, 196, 197; urban wealth fund real estate management for, 168–71
highway systems, 43–44, 45, 76–77
Ho Chin, 155
homelessness, social investment impacting, 17, 38, 39, 79, 181–82, 190–91
Hong Kong: asset management by, 21, 84; infrastructure investment in, 45, 48; MTR Corporation in, 159–62; urban wealth funds in, 159–62
housing options: asset management of, 9, 35–36; in exclusive cities, 58, 60, 61–62, 63–64; in extensive cities, 64–65; failing cities', 51, 52; for homeless people, 190–91; national issues of, 9, 11; Singapore's public

housing, 150–51; social investment in, 190–91, 194, 196; transportation impacting, 159–60; in turnaround cities, 69, 70–71, 84–85; urban wealth fund involvement with, 150–51, 159–60, 162–64, 165, 171–77. *See also* real estate
Houston, Texas: as extensive city, 64, 68; "innovation district" in, 68
human assets: asset management of, 16–18, 21; business climate impacting, 18, 32, 33, 35, 72–73, 208–09; education of, 40, 196, 201, 202, 204–07 (*see also* education); employment value of, 201, 202, 203, 205–09 (*see also* employment); failing cities' disregard for, 27, 36–42; income changes among, 37–42 (*see also* income); increasing value of, 201–09; lifelong learning of, 204–05; political barriers impacting, 209; turnaround cities' focus on, 73; upward mobility of, 37–40, 65–67

IKEA, 6, 125
income: antipoverty programs impacting, 75; in exclusive cities, 58, 60–62; in extensive cities, 65–67; failing cities and changes in, 37–42; human asset valuation based on, 202, 203; inequality of, 39; middle class decline of, 41–42; social investment impacting, 10; in turnaround cities, 72; upward mobility of, 37–40, 65–67
India: asset management in, 82; cities impacting national growth in, 12. *See also specific cities*
Indianapolis, Indiana: jurisdiction of entities in, 219; upward mobility in, 37

Industrivârden and Investor AB, 138
infrastructure: bad advice about
investment in, 49–50; balance sheet
management of investment in,
114–20; as commercial asset, 16;
crowdfunding for, 79, 80; failing
cities' struggles with, 34, 42–50;
infrastructure trusts to fund, 79;
investment in, 3, 5, 9, 22, 42–50,
75–78, 79, 80, 114–20, 124, 125,
159–62, 163, 166; urban wealth
funds supporting investment in,
124, 125, 159–62, 163, 166; "white
elephants" in, 45–47
"innovation districts," 68
International Accounting Standards
Board (IASB), 106
International Federation of
Accountants, 106
International Financial Reporting
Standards (IFRS), 91, 106–07, 111,
112, 137–38
International Public Sector
Accounting Standards (IPSAS),
104, 106–07, 111, 112
investment: asset management and, 5,
6–9, 15–18, 20–22; balance
sheet management of, 114–20;
consumption expenditure shift to,
22–23; contrasts in, 3–5; in digital
technologies, 5, 11, 62–63; in
infrastructure, 3, 5, 9, 22, 42–50,
75–78, 79, 80, 114–20, 124, 125,
159–62, 163, 166; national growth
driven by cities', 4, 9–13; overview
of, 3–5; professional management
of, 21–22; rich *vs.* poor city
approaches to, 5–9; social (*see* social
investment); of treadmill towns,
4, 14–15, 18–23, 42–49; of turbo
cities, 4–5, 12, 13–14, 15, 18–23,

75–78, 79; in urban wealth funds,
22, 83, 123–46, 149–77
Italy, cities impacting national growth
in, 11–12. *See also specific cities*

Jacksonville, Florida, jurisdiction of
entities in, 219
Jamaica, Singapore comparison to, 8,
155–56
Japan: failing cities in, 33;
infrastructure investment in, 47–48
Jefferson County, Alabama,
bankruptcy of, 115
Jernhusen, 158, 162, 166–68
Johnson, Boris, 192, 197
JPMorgan Chase, 79

Kammarkollegiet, 135
Katrina, Hurricane, 28, 31–32
Kee Kwan Yew, 78
Kiel Canal, 44
Kigali, Rwanda, national growth
impacted by, 12
Klarna, 63
"knowledge economy," 36
Kresge Foundation, 22, 221

LandstingsfastigheterAB (LFS), 169
Landstingshuset i Stockholm AB
(LIS), 168
land use: asset management of,
8, 35–36, 77; balance sheet
management of, 109–10; in
exclusive cities, 58, 59, 61–62, 63,
65–68; in extensive cities, 65–68;
failing cities', 45, 52; in turnaround
cities, 69–72, 84; waterfront, 71 (*see
also* seaports). *See also* housing
options; real estate
Las Vegas, as extensive city, 64
Lendlease, 165

Leonardo of Pisa (Fibonacci), 97–98
limited liability companies,
101, 133
Locum AB, 168–71
London: asset management by, 21–22,
76, 78, 130–31; balance sheet
management by, 110, 130–31; City
of London Corporation, 21–22,
130–31; as exclusive city, 59, 61–62;
fact- and evidence-based decision
making in, 75; Greater London
Authority, 162, 175; infrastructure
investment in, 76; national growth
driven by, 4; Project Oracle in,
192–93, 197; real estate assets in,
110, 127, 130; social impact bonds
in, 80; toll/congestion charges in,
78; transportation systems in, 76,
78, 158, 161, 162, 164–65, 176–77;
urban wealth fund development in,
130–31, 158, 161, 162, 164–65,
174–77
London Continental Railways, 158,
162, 164–65
London Overground, 161
Los Angeles: as exclusive city, 64, 67;
human assets in, 208; jurisdiction
of entities in, 219; land use in, 67;
reform and change in, 218–19
Lower Manhattan Development
Corporation (LMDC), 118

Malmö, Sweden: investment in, 11;
urban wealth fund development in,
166, 167–68
Manchester, United Kingdom: arts
and culture investment in, 51–53;
urban wealth fund development
projects in, 165
Manpower Demonstration Research
Corporation (MDRC), 80–81

Medellín, Colombia: social investment
in, 195; turnaround in, 84
Meknes, Morocco, national growth
impacted by, 12
Memphis, Tennessee, upward
mobility in, 37
Microsoft, 63
middle class: income decline among,
41–42; social investment in, 189–90
Minneapolis-St. Paul: investment in,
10; land use in, 68; upward mobility
in, 67
MND Holdings, 151
Mockus, Antanas, 217
Mojang, 63
mortality rates, social investment
impacting, 41
Mt. Isa, Australia, national growth
impacted by, 12
MTR Corporation, 159–62
Mumbai, India, infrastructure
investment in, 45
Munich, Germany: asset management
by, 34–36; investment in, 10;
"Perspektive Munich" process
in, 35

national governments and policies:
cities as locomotives for, 4, 9–13;
democratic reform impacted by,
218; exclusive cities impacting, 58,
60–61; failing cities impacted by,
28–29, 35, 43–44; infrastructure
investment by, 43–44
Neptune Orient Lines, 151
New Orleans, failures in, 28–30,
31–32
New York: balance sheet management
by, 118–19; Center for Economic
Opportunity in, 75; CompStat
system in, 188; crime rates in, 19,

187–88; as exclusive city, 64, 67;
fact- and evidence-based decision
making in, 75; income inequality
in, 39; investment in, 4, 11, 14–15;
jurisdiction of entities in, 219;
land use in, 67, 71; national growth
driven by, 4, 11; reforms and
transitions in, 15, 19; social impact
bonds in, 80–81; social investment
in, 80–81, 187–88, 196; treadmill
town challenges for, 14–15, 19;
upward mobility in, 38–39
New Zealand: balance sheet
management by, 103, 107, 108, 114;
infrastructure investment in, 47;
social investment in, 183, 185–86,
187; urban wealth funds in, 149
noneconomic assets: asset
management of, 16–18, 21, 36–42;
balance sheet management of, 92,
94; failing cities' disregard for, 27,
36–42; human assets as, 16–18, 21,
27, 32, 33, 35, 36–42, 65–67, 72–73,
196, 201–09; social assets as, 16, 17,
21, 36–42, 65–67, 79, 181–98
Norrköping, Sweden, social
investment fund in, 197
Norway, infrastructure investment
in, 50

Obama administration, infrastructure
investments under, 46–47
"Occupy" movement, 213
Olympic Park Legacy Corporation,
177
Orlando, Florida, as extensive city, 64
Orlando, Leoluca, 196
Orr, Kevyn, 51

Paris, France, real estate assets in, 130
Peak Academy, 214–15

Penalosa, Enrique, 217
Perry Preschool, 186–87, 205
Petris Social Capital Index (PSCI),
182
Philadelphia, failures in, 42
Phoenix, Arizona, as extensive city, 64
Piraeus, Greece, privatization of
infrastructure in, 76
PISA (Program for International
Student Assessment), 204
Pittsburgh, Pennsylvania: "innovation
district" in, 68; as turbo city, 36; as
turnaround city, 68–70, 84; upward
mobility in, 38
policy assets: asset management of,
15–16, 139; balance sheet
management of, 109, 112
population, urban: agglomeration
increasing, 3, 12; exclusive cities'
limited growth of, 58, 60; extensive
cities' growth of, 58; failing cities'
decline of, 28, 30, 33–34; growth
of, generally, 3–4; turnaround cities'
changes in, 72, 73
Port Authority of New York and New
Jersey: balance sheet management
with, 118, 119–20; infrastructure
funds from, 44; urban wealth fund
of, 22
Portland, Oregon: as exclusive city,
57–58; investment in, 10
Portugal, social investment in, 190
privatlzation: of infrastructure
investment, 76, 79, 80; public-
private partnerships with, 134–35,
162, 164, 165, 169–71; of social
investment, 79–81; of
transportation systems, 47–49,
76–77. *See also* urban wealth funds
Project Oracle, 192–93, 197
PSA International, 152, 154

Public Health Calculator, 183–85, 197
public-private partnerships (PPPs),
134–35, 162, 164, 165, 169–71
Puerto Rico, balance sheet
management by, 116
Pulaski Skyway, 44, 117

QuickenLoans, 22, 221

Raggi, Virginia, 218
railroads, 45, 46–48, 76, 82, 84, 158,
159–62, 164–68, 176–77
Raleigh-Durham: as extensive city,
64; investment in, 10; "knowledge
economy" in, 36; Research Triangle
Park in, 70
real estate: asset management of, 6–7,
8–9, 123–24, 125, 126–32; balance
sheet management of, 95, 108,
109–10, 111, 118–20, 126–27,
130–31; block-chain technology for,
126; cadastral maps of, 126; as
commercial asset, 16; in exclusive
cities, 58; health-care-related,
168–71; market valuation of,
127–28; portfolio development for,
131–32, 157–59, 166–67; social
investment impacted by, 40;
transportation impacting value of,
75–76, 159–62, 164–68; turbo
cities', 14, 58, 75–76, 85; urban
wealth funds managing, 123–24,
125, 126–32, 154, 157–77; value
maximization of, 132. *See also*
housing options; land use
"regulatory taxes," 62, 63
Rhode Island, balance sheet
management by, 103
Rio de Janeiro, Brazil: real estate
assets in, 129; social investment
in, 195

Rita, Hurricane, 28
Riverside, California, as extensive
city, 64
Rome, Italy: reform and change in,
218; treadmill town challenges
for, 15

Saltillo, Mexico, national growth
impacted by, 12
Salt Lake City: land use in, 68;
upward mobility in, 38, 67
San Bernadino, California,
bankruptcy of, 115
San Francisco: arts and culture
investment in, 50; as exclusive city,
58, 59, 64; fact- and evidence-based
decision making in, 75; human
assets in, 208; income inequality
in, 39; investment in, 11; land use
and housing in, 85; quality of life
in, 59
San Jose, California: bankruptcy of,
115; investment in, 11
São Paulo, Brazil, social investment
in, 195
Scranton, Pennsylvania, bankruptcy
of, 115
seaports, 48–49, 76, 123, 154, 162–63
Seattle: arts and culture investment in,
50; land use and housing in, 67–68,
71, 85; upward mobility in, 38, 67
segregation: in exclusive cities, 64, 67;
in extensive cities, 64; failing cities'
issues of, 35, 42, 43
self-driving vehicles, 5, 130
Sheng-Li Holdings, 151
Shenzhen, China, as turnaround
city, 72
Silicon Valley: human assets in, 203;
national growth impacted by, 12
Silverstein, Larry, 118

Singapore: asset management by, 7–8, 21, 30–31, 76, 78, 83, 84; infrastructure investment in, 45, 48; Jamaica comparison to, 8, 155–56; Marina Barrage investment by, 30–31; public housing in, 150–51; toll charges in, 78; urban wealth funds in, 138, 149–56 (*see also* Temasek)

Singapore Airlines, 154

Singapore Technologies, 151, 154

Singtel, 152, 154

Skandia, 183, 184, 185

Skype, 63

smart cities, investment policies of, 4

social assets: asset management of, 16, 17, 21; during childhood, 185–87; crime-reducing, 187–88, 195, 196; emerging-market city development of, 194–95; failing cities' disregard for, 36–42; freeing from entrenched interests, 196–98; homeless people benefiting from, 17, 38, 39, 79, 181–82, 190–91; income changes among, 37–42; middle class-focused, 189–90; social investment in (*see* social investment); upward mobility of, 37–40, 65–67; work programs creating, 191–94. *See also* human assets

social investment: asset management of, 16–18, 21; childhood-based, 185–87; crime rates impacted by, 14, 41, 79, 80–81, 187–88, 195, 196, 219; in emerging-market cities, 194–95; failing cities' lack of, 27, 36–42; freeing from entrenched interests, 196–98; homelessness impacted by, 17, 38, 39, 79, 181–82, 190–91; in human assets, 16–18, 21, 27, 32, 33, 35, 36–42, 65–67, 72–73,

196, 201–09; in middle class, 189–90; mortality rates impacted by, 41; national impacts of, 10; overview of, 181–85; Public Health Calculator for, 183–85, 197; rich *vs.* poor city approaches to, 7; in social assets, 16, 17, 21, 36–42, 65–67, 79, 181–98; social capital defined for, 182–83; social impact bonds funding, 79–81; social investment funds for, 197–98; of turbo cities, 14, 79–81; work programs as, 191–94. *See also* human assets; social assets

"soft cities," 219–21

Solidium, 138

South Korea, failing cities in, 33

sovereign wealth funds, 155

Spacehive, 80

Spain, infrastructure investment in, 45. *See also specific cities*

Spotify, 62

state governments and policies: balance sheet management importance to, 115–16; democratic authority of, 12; failing cities impacted by, 44; infrastructure investment by, 44

Stockholm, Sweden: balance sheet management in, 111; as exclusive city, 62–64; infrastructure investment in, 49–50; land use and housing in, 11, 63, 85, 171–74; national growth driven by, 11; social investment in, 183, 184; Stockholm Stadshus in, 171–74; toll charges in, 77; transportation systems in, 77, 161, 166–68; urban wealth fund development in, 158, 166–74

Stockton, California, bankruptcy of, 115

treadmill towns: balance sheet management by, 105–14; failing cities with characteristics of, 28–36; infrastructure investment of, 42–49; investment of, 4, 14–15, 18–23, 42–49; transition to turbo cities, 18–23. *See also* failing cities

turbo cities: added value determination in, 75–81; asset management by, 15, 72–73, 74–85; balance sheet management by, 105–14; education in, 14, 70; employment in, 58, 59, 61, 62–63, 64, 68–70; exclusive cities ranked as, 57–64, 65–68, 83–84; extensive cities ranked as, 57–58, 64–68, 83–84; fact- and evidence-based decision making in, 74–75; false promises of alleged, 57–68, 83–84; income in, 58, 60–62, 65–67, 72; independent and professional asset governance in, 81–83, 84; infrastructure investment in, 75–78, 79; "innovation districts" in, 68; investment of, 4–5, 12, 13–14, 15, 18–23, 75–78, 79; land use and housing in, 58, 59, 60, 61–62, 63–68, 69, 70–72, 77, 84–85; national growth impacted by, 12, 58, 60–61; overview of, 57, 83–85; quality of life in, 59–60; "regulatory taxes" in, 62, 63; segregation in, 64, 67; social impact bonds in, 79–81; treadmill towns' transition to, 18–23; turnaround cities as, 68–73, 84–85

turnaround cities: asset management in, 72–73, 84; education in, 70; employment in, 68–70; land use and housing in, 69, 70–72, 84–85

unemployment: in failed cities, 34, 38; national policy impacts on, 9; social investment reducing, 7; in treadmill towns, 14

United Kingdom: arts and culture investment in, 51–53; Associated British Ports in, 49; balance sheet management by, 103, 107–08, 109–10, 127; cities impacting national growth in, 4; infrastructure investment in, 47, 49, 79, 80; London Continental Railways in, 158, 162, 164–65; real estate assets in, 109–10, 127, 168–69; social investment in, 189–90; transportation systems in, 158, 161, 162, 164–65; urban wealth funds in, 149, 162, 164–65, 174–77; WGA approach in, 107–08. *See also specific cities*

United States: balance sheet management in, 92, 110–11, 115–20; cities impacting national growth in, 4, 9–11; crime rates in, 187; failing cities in, 27, 28–30, 31–32, 34–36, 37–42, 50–51; GDP of, 8, 92; infrastructure investment in, 43, 44, 45–47; urban wealth funds in, 123–24; work programs in, 191–93. *See also specific cities*

University of Pittsburgh Medical Center, 69

Uppsala, Sweden: social investment in, 184–85; as turnaround city, 71

Uppsala University, 183, 184

urban wealth funds: asset management via, 22, 83, 123–46, 149–77; balance sheet management as prerequisite for, 126–27, 130–31, 132–34, 137–38; board appointment

urban wealth funds (cont.)
and evaluation for, 142–44; case
studies of, 149–77 (*see* urban wealth
funds, case studies *for details*); clear
objectives of, 136, 138–39, 155, 163,
166; creation of, 141–46; definition
of, 135; fundamentals of, 135–41;
governance structure of, 140–41,
142–46, 154–55, 164, 166, 169–70,
173; health-care real estate in,
168–71; infrastructure investment
support via, 124, 125, 159–62, 163,
166; political independence of, 137,
139–41, 154–55, 163, 166, 169–70,
173; professional asset management
via, 22, 83, 123–24, 128–31,
136–41, 144–46, 171; professional
management of, 144–46, 171;
publicly owned commercial assets
in, 125–26; public-private
partnerships and, 134–35, 162, 164,
165, 169–71; real estate in, 123–24,
125, 126–32, 154, 157–77;
transparency of, 135–36, 137–38,
155, 163, 164, 166, 169–70;
transportation systems in/impacted
by, 123, 125, 154, 157–63,
164–68, 176–77; utilities in, 123,
157–59, 173; value maximization
via, 132, 166; yield or return on,
124, 125, 126, 127–28, 149, 162,
166, 167, 173
urban wealth funds, case studies:
Copenhagen, city and port UWF,
162–63; Hamburg, HafenCity,
163–64; Hong Kong, MTR Corp.,
159–62; Jernhusen, property
developer, 158, 162, 166–68;
Locum, health-care real estate,
168–71; London, Continental

Railways, 158, 162, 164–65;
London, potential for UWF,
174–77; overview of, 149; portfolio
management of real estate *vs.*
operational assets, 157–59;
Singapore, Temasek, 149–56;
Stockholm Stadshus, residential
property, 171–74
utilities: asset management of, 7, 8,
123; balance sheet management of,
108; as commercial assets, 16;
investment in, 3; turbo cities', 14,
75; urban wealth funds managing,
123, 157–59, 173

value: commercial asset valuation, 92,
95, 105–06, 109–13, 117–20,
126–27, 130–31, 132–34 (*see also*
real estate valuation subentry);
increasing value of human assets,
201–09; market value assessment,
91, 110–13, 127–28; nonfinancial
asset valuation, 92, 94; real estate
valuation, 75–76, 127–28, 132,
159–62, 164–68; UWF value
maximization, 132, 166; value
creation or added value programs,
75–81
Vancouver, Canada, as exclusive city, 60
Vancouver, Washington, as extensive
city, 57–58
Vasterås, Sweden, as turnaround
city, 71
Vickrey, William, 77
Villaraigosa, Antonio, 218–19

Walmart, 6, 125
Washington, D.C.: income inequality
in, 39; infrastructure investment
in, 45

Wellington, New Zealand, balance sheet management by, 108

Wharton Residential Land Use Regulatory Index (WRLURI), 65–67

Whole of Government Accounts (WGA) approach, 107–08

work programs, social investment in, 191–94

Wowereit, Klaus, 32, 33

Young Men's Initiative, 80

Ypsilanti, Michigan, social investment in, 186–87, 205

Zurich, Switzerland, as exclusive city, 60